the
Celtic Spirit

the
Celtic Spirit

Daily Meditations for the Turning Year

CAITLÍN MATTHEWS

HarperSanFrancisco
A Division of HarperCollins*Publishers*

FIRST EDITION

Design by Helene Wald Berinsky

Library of Congress Cataloging-in-Publication Data
Matthews, Caitlín.
The Celtic spirit : daily meditations for the turning year /
Caitlín Matthews. — 1st ed.
p.   cm.
Includes bibliographical references and index.
ISBN 0–06–251538–1 (pbk.)
1. Celts—Religion—Miscellanea. 2. Calendar, Celtic—Miscellanea.
3. Devotional calendars. I. Title
BL900.M4654 1998   98–27087
299.16—dc21

99 00 01 02 03 RRD(H) 10 9 8 7 6 5 4 3 2

For Philip & Stephanie Carr-Gomm and
Cairistíona & Bill Worthington
with love and respect for the peace they have mediated,
and for all—past, present, and future—who tread the druid path

CONTENTS

I would like to thank the people of the gift and the keepers of the lore for their inspiration in preparing this book. Special thanks to Philip Carr-Gomm, John Matthews, Kathleen Raine, Robin Williamson, and Jay Ramsay, editor of Earth Ascending, *for permission to quote from their work. Unascribed quotations are drawn from my own translations of Gaelic and Welsh sources and are indicated by my initials.*

INTRODUCTION

The limbs of science are equal to the limbs of man; for there
are 365 joints in the body, 365 days in the year, and 365 herbs
through the earth.

—*Auraicept na nEces*, anon. Irish text

A Sunwise Circuit

Increasingly today, ancient wisdom is seen as something archaic and forgotten, of use only to learned exponents of arcane lore. But, truly, the wisdom of the ancients is no different from the wisdom that springs from our own life experience. I hope that you will find a deep connection between what is written in this book and your own daily life.

As season succeeds season and one year cascades into another, so our lives spiral into new constellations of understanding. If we look over the years, we will see the unique spiral of our life-course interweaving its dance with that of the planet's own revolutions within the solar system.

The cycles of day and night are ruled by the sun, the cycle of months by the moon, the cycle of the year by the wheeling stars. In every age, human beings have looked to the heavens and been astonished and inspired. The course of a year is but a small compass for change in one human life, but it nevertheless provides a useful chart on which to plot our spiritual voyage.

The nature of each season brings its own wisdom and insight, testing the practical grasp of our understanding from winter's cold grip through spring's unfolding and summer's heat to autumn's bounty— and on again. Through each season's eye we see the earth and its inhabitants. The changes in animals, plants, trees, and landscape reflect back to us the changes to which we ourselves are subject.

In the apparent world—the realm that we perceive and know with our physical senses—the year turns its circuit of seasons, providing us with much wisdom. But the apparent world is not the only world with which we interact. Just as real, though perceivable only by our subtle senses, is the otherworld, the world of Spirit which all of us experience through the receptor of our soul.

Throughout the year, our comprehension of the unseen changes in the country of our soul fluctuates. Sometimes we clearly hear the music of the otherworld leading us on; sometimes we have to strain to hear it; at other times it seems to be absent. The changing seasons in the apparent world teach us to trust that, though the skies be cloudy, the stars still shine in the dark or the day; that though there are no blossoms, leaves, or fruit upon the tree, the cycle of growth will turn again. So too in the country of the soul, we trust that silence will be replaced by singing and that inspiration will flow once more.

As we make our own pilgrimage round the seasons of the year, we simultaneously make what is called in Irish a *turas* (TU'ras)—a word that means "journey," "pilgrimage," and "time" all at once. A *turas* usually refers to the circular, spiraling prayer and meditation form used by people in the Celtic countries as they walk sunwise around a sacred site.

As our planet spins around the circling year, we too simultaneously experience the turning of our soul toward the source of greatest spiritual light. Each season is a mystical gateway of opportunity and understanding, a sacred time of wisdom. If we live with awareness of the year's cycles, we will achieve a direct alignment with those sacred opportunities.

The Druidic Inheritance

Before the Roman eagles spread their colonizing wings over the ancient world, the druids and their precursors—the native shamans, healers, and diviners—were walking between the worlds of the apparent and unseen realms. The druids are our own ancestral mystics and teachers, maintaining the balance and harmony of the land and its inhabitants with the spiritual presences of the unseen realms of the otherworld.

They put their special skills and talents to the service of the universal truth as prophets, diviners, counselors, healers, philosophers, geometricists, musicians, historians, and so on, each respecting the interconnectedness of all life and honoring the immortal soul in all its aspects. Such insights involved druidic students in long periods of stillness, observation of nature, meditation, prayer, and repetition of lore. Before any student was reckoned mature and wise enough to practice or serve in the community, periods of often painful self-clarification, leading to better self-knowledge and imperturbable equilibrium, were undergone.

When new ways of perceiving and mediating the sacred replaced the older ways, the druidic way did not come to an end. The elder ways were not forgotten but percolated through the traditions and customs of the land, through bardic memory and storytelling, through the lore of country people, seers, poets, and lovers of the ancestral wisdom. Druidry transmigrated for a season, taking other shapes and forms. This was perfectly natural, since the druids believed that the soul was still the soul, whatever shape it took. Thus in every generation, the wisdom passed down.

Wisdom is not found in human beings alone; it is found in all places and beings. It is etched upon the fabric of the land itself, where it speaks from groves, hills, and springs. It is found in the tracks of the animals, birds, and beasts of the natural world—shapes that the druidic soul did not despise to take, as we hear told in Celtic myth. The traditions of stone, sea, and star that were the triple guardians of the druidic otherworld are still available to us—by the same stone, sea, and star that shine in the earth, waters, and sky of our living planet.

The sacred circling of the sun, symbol of the life that courses through all beings, still encircles us as we prepare to enter another millennium. Its warmth, light, and brightness give us cycles of growth; its setting, darkness, and cold give us the necessary periods of rest and reflection. Through many cycles of the sun, the druids, like the mystics of every age, have recognized and respected wisdom where they found it, incorporating the riches of successive cultures, stressing the connections rather than the divisions, not insisting upon separate or exclusive ways of belief.

Today the druidic dedication to the interconnectedness of all life continues among those who follow the Celtic wisdom as, all over the world, people of spiritual commitment are being drawn to examine their lives in relationship both to their ancestry and to their current way of living, and with concern for their children's future.

The Celtic stream of wisdom is a living river that flows on. An enduring Celtic philosophy or life-view is recognizably present in Britain, Ireland, Cornwall, Scotland, and Wales, as well as in the Celtic diaspora worldwide. Although some meditations in this book dip into the ancestral traditions, into historical and mythological lore of the ancient Celts, they also bring us very much into the practical present.

The Celtic tradition offers great hospitality of spirit, welcoming the seeker as a sacred guest, honoring each personal quest without regard for spiritual background. Similarly, the sunwise circuit of meditations included in this book is suitable for people of all backgrounds. It can be used to enhance and strengthen existing spiritual practice or it can help the reader explore a more authentic and personal practice that arises from his or her own depths. The reclamation of our spiritual authority from the alienation of institutionalization begins with our reclamation of the world of Spirit *as we experience it,* in the daily, seasonal, and annual cycles of our lives.

Without giving away your authority to others, take permission now to begin your own spiritual quest in the course of the year that lies ahead. Allow this year to be the beginning of your own path, leading you ultimately to your own spiritual home. I do not ask that you make the Celtic path your own; I only invite you to walk the path of this coming year with an open heart. With insight into your own experience, allow the wisdom of the days and seasons to inform and guide your own year of discovery. May there be peace upon your path!

Caitlín Matthews
Oxford
Epona's Day
18 December 1997

HOW TO USE THIS BOOK

This book contains 365 short meditations, one for each day of the year, to enable you to walk along and learn something of the sacred wisdom of the Celtic path. Each page is headed by a short quotation from a Celtic source or from another inspirational source that acknowledges the ancestral wisdom of our culture. These quotations draw on a wide variety of eras, from ancient to modern times. They were chosen because they reflect some aspect of the sacred path.

Each accompanying meditation was drawn from my druidic and shamanic experience of walking between the worlds. You are invited to reflect upon each entry, to meditate upon the deep sources of the natural world, upon personal approaches to living as well as upon universal concepts that are relevant to us all. You may follow the sun's circuit and read a portion as set for each day, or you may choose to dip into the book, using the thematic index to draw upon those passages most relevant to your condition.

Each month of this book provides interrelated themes for meditation within the framework of the four seasons and the Celtic festivals, which stand like sentinels to mark each part of the year's turning: Samhain (SOW'en) or Hallowe'en in November, which marks the beginning of winter; Imbolc (IMM'bolk) in February, which sees the season of spring; Beltane (BEL'tenn-a) in May-time, which marks the summer; and Lughnasa (LOO'nas-ah) in August, which guards the three months of autumn. The arrangement of the meditations in this book, from November to October, follows the old Celtic and agricultural cycle of the year from barrenness to plenty, rather than the more conventional calendrical year.

Each meditation can be seen as a tree in the sacred grove of the year, a place of reflection under which the reader can seek sanctuary, peace, and restoration of spirit. Meditation is simply making a space of time wherein our souls can be purposefully engaged and focused. It *deepens* us, giving us *soul-capacity*.

Finding a daily space in which to be still and receptive is a discipline in our busy world. Your place of meditation can be inside or outside, as long as it is free from disturbance.

As you read each day's meditation, actively enable the words to go beyond the page by interacting with the subject. Regard each meditation as an extension of your own meditation space, so that it can become your own sacred grove. From that grove, you may discover pathways that gradually lead you from personal space in the apparent world into the universal space of the unseen world. As you contemplate, let the words and meanings become like sparks that leap from idea to idea, strongly connecting with your own understanding and allowing your own memory-resident realizations to join up in new conflagrations of inspiration.

Many people have forgotten how to understand the soul; they do not recognize its signals any longer, mistaking deep soul-urgings for paranoia, creative inspiration for psychic disturbance. In such ways are the deep sendings of the soul dismissed and many wonderful opportunities lost! To be responsive to the messages the soul sends us, we need a deep listening ability to pick up the frequencies beyond the surface-level transmission of daily anxiety and business. These subtle messages are easily ignored as irrelevant or too difficult to deal with; sometimes they are mistakenly dismissed as self-delusions. The daily practice of meditation can help us retune to the soul's frequency again and gain a sense of proportion.

On the days when you are ill, emotionally disturbed, or burdened by worry, do not be meditationally ambitious. Look after yourself, get some help, and temporarily reduce your commitments. Make your meditation time one of refreshment, concentrate upon your breathing, and commune with the inspirers and helpers of your spiritual tradition.

At the end of each meditation there is an invitation for you to make your own contribution. Sometimes this involves considering an aspect of your own life experience; at other times you will be invited to meditate upon or visualize something. Some meditations invite you to visit a place by soul-flight: this means sending part of your soul out to that place and, with your own vision, being aware of whatever happens there. Some meditations conclude with an invitation to put a concept into practice in your daily life, for spiritual wisdom evolves not in solitary meditation but when it is implemented in ordinary life. Such implementation helps us avoid the imbalances and delusions that may arise from a purely theoretical approach to spirituality.

Some meditations end with a question. Questioning was a method of oral teaching given by the druids. Questions are like keys for opening doors. When we ask ourselves the right questions, the resulting synaptic leaps take us into profound areas of realization.

It is easy to read a portion of this book every day; it is less easy to become involved in your own spiritual path. Some days you will not have the time, of course; but it is only by your own practice that the spiritual path opens. As you make your own sunwise *turas* round the year, you will make many interesting discoveries about yourself, your own natural mode of spiritual practice, and you will learn from traveling the spiral path of the year.

Many meditations suggest consulting your spiritual allies: this means consciously contacting the spiritual beings whom you hold as sacred guardians and guides on your path. Spiritual allies can include the manifest aspects of the Divine with whom you have close relationship, as well as saints and heroes, and the spirits of animals, trees, and places with which you are strongly aligned.

As a unique human being with an immortal soul, you have the capacity for discrimination, imagination, and spiritual adventure. Learn to commune with your soul, giving it space to speak to you. Cherish your dreams. Allow the inspiration of your soul to pave the way to creative endeavors that have haunted your unfulfilled desires for many years.

As you meditate around the year, be aware of others who have walked this path before you. Their inspiration, endeavor, and hope have kept open the track. Remember too that the way you walk the path matters—it clears the way for those who come after you.

I have alternated male and female pronouns throughout the text. Rough pronunciation of Celtic words is given in parentheses after the word in question—for example, Fionn mac Cumhail (FINN mak KOOL) or Rhiannon (Hree-ANN'on). Stress is given on the capitalized syllables. This book offers only approximate pronunciation, as Welsh and Gaelic have their own subtle consonantal and vowel qualities, which are apparent in the spoken rather than the written languages.

If you are reading this book in the southern hemisphere, please reverse the reading sequence to take into account your own seasons:

Seasons in this Book	Seasons in the Southern Hemisphere
January	July
February	August
March	September
April	October
May	November
June	December
July	January
August	February
September	March
October	April
November	May
December	June

Samhain

Season of Winter

NOVEMBER

Month of November—very fat are the swine;
Let the shepherd go; let the minstrel come;
Bloody the blade, full the barn.

—anon. Welsh poem

The season of winter begins at Samhain, the Celtic New Year, on the eve of November. The meditation themes this month include destiny and fate, cycles and ages, fullness and emptiness, enduring traditions, overcoming difficulty by finding deep resources, the nature of action, and directions and spaces.

The Assembly of Peace

It was their custom at the Feis of Tara to pass six days in feasting
together before the sitting of the assembly: three days before
Samhain and three days after it, making peace and entering into
friendly alliances with each other.

—Geoffrey Keating, *Forus Feasa ar Eirinn*

The Festival Assembly of Tara, at which the nobles and learned people of Ireland ratified and renewed laws, took place every three years. During the festival it was strictly forbidden for any robbery, assault, or legal wrangles to take place. Anyone so engaged was summarily sentenced to death, and not even the king himself had power to pardon the one who had disrespected the assembly of peace. Samhain (SOW'en) marked the beginning of winter and the cessation of hostilities between warring factions. The poets and their retinues quartered with the rich households of Ireland until Beltane (BEL'tenn-a; May) so that the winter months might pass more quickly by their entertainment.

Samhain means "the summer's end." In early days, this festival heralded a period when the gates of *síd* (SHEE), the faery gates of the otherworld, were open and when the ancestors were nearer to the otherworld than at any other time.

After a preliminary evening of half-fearful, half-mischievous activities, the daytime temper of Samhain was one of gravity, wherein all the changes could be acknowledged and assimilated. Of all the Celtic festivals, this is the one at which we best experience the overlap of one world with the other. It is time to assemble peacefully and be conscious of the ordering of our affairs, bringing ourselves into alignment with the blessings, work, and opportunities of the darker half of the year.

Spend part of this day in assessing your place in life: look at unfinished
Assess your current spiritual position, scrutinize your motives, clarify
your commitments; recognize and discard inappropriate patterns that
no longer serve you.

Making Peace with the Ancestors

Dear ones in the house of the dead,
Can you forgive
An old woman who was your proud
Daughter, who now too late
Returns your love?

—Kathleen Raine, *The Oracle in the Heart*

We often do not understand those who are closest to us until it is too late. This is especially true of our parents, upon whom we heap the faults of our upbringing. Parents struggle to do the best thing for their children, but these efforts are seldom appreciated until the children themselves become parents and enter into the war of attrition that we call growing up. When we are adults, our activities take us far from our parents' domain. The death of parents is perhaps the last part of growing up, usually happening when we are raising our own children, so that we stand midway between youth and age. Those who now find themselves in the eldest generation of a family discover new responsibilities: as they become grandparents, they look to the new generation to solve old, long-standing problems. This ancestral bequest tends to gather weight and momentum as it rolls from generation to generation, sometimes becoming too heavy for any one person to carry.

Making peace between ourselves and our ancestors requires two things: the ability to speak the truth lovingly, and the ability to forgive and let go of issues that have muddied the way between us and the dead. We need to offer a word of love, a sign of admiration or praise, a visit, a gift, even a phone call—some direct communication while there is opportunity, before the time for regret is all that is left.

Make a soul-flight to a place where you and a relative who is now dead used to meet together. Speak the words that you would have liked to say before death intervened. Listen to the words that your relative speaks to you. Thank and bless your relative.

The Ancestral God

The Gauls all claim to be descended from Dis Pater, claiming that this is the tradition preserved by the Druids.

—JULIUS CAESAR, *The Conquest of Gaul*

On his Gaulish campaign, Julius Caesar studied the nature of the people he intended to conquer, learning that they believed themselves to be descended from Dis Pater, or the Father God of the Underworld. Caesar noted that it is on account of this fact that they celebrated all their festivals and holy days from the eve of the previous day, when darkness falls, rather than from the morning of the day itself. The primacy given to the night over the day by the Celts is a respectful remembrance of their beginnings and of their divine ancestor.

One Irish figure who fills the role of Dis Pater is Cú Rói (KOO roy) with his otherworldly revolving tower in the West of Ireland. He wields a long-handled beheading axe and oversees the awarding of the champion's portion at Bricriu's Feast by coming, in the guise of a dark giant, to offer the contenders a sportive game: he will kneel for them to behead him in return for being beheaded themselves! Only Cuchulainn (Koo-HULL'en) is brave enough to take up his challenge: he kneels willingly, is spared by Cú Rói, and so is proved the worthiest champion.

Cú Rói's partner is Blathnad (BLAN'id), the Goddess of Flowers. Theirs is a partnership that reminds us of the relationship between the Greek Goddess of Returning Spring, Persephone, and Plutos, the Underworld God of the Dead. Life and death are a partnership like day and night: after growth, decay; after death, new growth. The message of Dis Pater to all his descendants is, "All of you shall come to me, to my house, when you die." The secret of his consort is that we too shall grow again, emerging from the darkness of night.

Meditate upon the cycles of life and death, night and day.

The Habit of Familiarity

We are every day betrayed by the blank state of custom. The com-
monplace accessories . . . weigh us down.

—Llewelyn Powys, *Earth Memories*

As the dark November days draw in, our working lives begin similarly to draw close about us. The daily round begins to grind: the very position of a desk or a table, the same blank faces on the street, the systematic regularity become like the beat of a hammer, emphasizing how very dull and ordinary every day seems.

How do we keep our lives fresh and sparkling with energy when we hit the doldrums of the habitual and the familiar? If our daily surroundings and routine are beating out a rhythm so regular and unchanging that we are going to shoot the conductor soon, then it is time to introduce a new melody, a counterpoint to the rhythm. That does not mean that we stop our daily tasks, only that we begin to dance through them in a more conscious way.

When personal focus becomes one-eyed, it is always good to get another perspective, to invite a friend over, spring a change on our partner. If we are the routine-holders in our family, we have a special responsibility to ring the changes; without help, we can get into "corporate" ruts so deep that we cannot leave them. If we live alone, we need to go out with our friends, practice our special skills, find the deep nurture of the things we enjoy.

In nature, all life is stripping off its finery to reveal its essential bare self. If the surface of our life seems dull and unmoving, we have only to look deeper and find where our energy is tending. In what secret place is it biding to wake refreshed?

What are your strategies for coping with the habitual? How can your
own routines be enlivened?

Gifts of the Directions

Star of the East, give us kindly birth,
Star of the South, give us great love,
Star of the West, give us quiet age,
Star of the North, give us death.

—Fiona MacLeod, *Iona*

Throughout the world, every traditional society has its own local understanding about the gifts of the different directions. These are seldom written down, remaining firmly embedded in consciousness and folklore.

In Britain, the gifts of the directions above are commonly accepted in many locations. The east—the place of beginnings, where the sun rises—guards the time of birth and development; the south—the place of growing, where the sun is at its warmest—is where our love is most strongly engaged; the west—the place of maturity, where the sun sets—is the place of vision; the north—the place of endings, where only the midnight sun shines—is commonly thought of as the place of death and still abiding.

The gifts of the directions depend upon the location of a land mass on the globe and are affected by the prevailing winds, the nature of topographical features, the position of the sea, and many other factors. Many books attempt to assign fixed definitions to the gifts of the directions, but these cannot hold in every place on the earth. The only way to learn more about these gifts is to seek them out in the place where *you* live—from your own experience, not from a book. Then you will truly be in a position to receive and experience those gifts for yourself and to give thanks for their guiding qualities.

Standing or sitting outside, face each of the directions in turn. With eyes closed, meditate upon each direction, feeling for its particular gift and opportunity. Try repeating this at different times of day and night. How do these qualities intermesh with your life?

The Lay of History

Were poetry to be suppressed, my friends, with no history, no ancient lays, save that each had a father, nothing of any man would be heard hereafter.

—GIOLLA BRIGHDE MHAC CON MIDHE,
in Osborn Bergin, *Irish Bardic Poetry*

Celtic poets not only sang praises and songs to their patrons, but they were also the repositories of history and genealogy. These were passed down to poets from generation to generation, until the era when the church wrote them down.

Before the coming of St. Patrick to Ireland, it is said that only three classes of people were permitted to speak in public with any authority: the chronicler to relate events and tell stories, the poet to eulogize and satirize, and the *brehon,* or judge, to pass sentences from precedents and commentaries.

We may wonder at the way that poetry and history are conjoined. In order that historical, poetic, and legal traditions could be recalled accurately, memory was aided and strengthened by the "thread of poetry" that bound together the teachings. The memory of these teachings can be likened to a preserving shrine or storehouse of knowledge, or to a bright candle of knowledge conveyed from one person to another. The memory of wise traditions is called "the old road to knowledge"—the road by which people can walk to their ancestral wisdom.

Our own chronicles normally record events, trends, and times, and are rarely seen as the preservers of wisdom. The poetry of the living knowledge of a skill is of more benefit than a bald recital of events: it becomes a road upon which we too can walk all the way down to the depths of time and find the ageless knowledge. Without its mythic levels, history is shorn of glory and usefulness.

Meditate upon the history of your people. What parts of it come alive for you? Down which "old roads of knowledge" can you walk?

Constancy

They'll turn me in arms, lady,
Into a deer so wild;
But hold me fast, let me not go,
The father o' your child.

—"The Ballad of Tam Lin," anon. Scots ballad

The Scottish ballad of Tam Lin describes how a young heroine, Janet, becomes pregnant by a man whom she meets in the woods. But Tam Lin is a mortal who has become stuck in the realms of faery, in bondage to the faery queen. The only way for Janet to win her lover home is for her to come to the crossroads at Hallowe'en, when the faeries ride by, and pull him from his horse. Then she must hold him fast while he changes into a variety of shapes. No matter what monstrous shape he assumes under the enchantment of the jealous faery queen, she must hold on tight, remembering that he is the father of her child. Janet does so, and Tam Lin is restored to her again.

No relationship is proof against change, whether it be through illness, unhappiness, new ambitions, discontent, or overfamiliarity. In such circumstances, constancy and patience are required, as well as support.

But when we experience a time of neglect or a failure to communicate changing needs, rather more than constancy is required. A clear challenge to re-engage in the mutual contract of relationship needs to be issued, giving a strong signal that neglectful behavior will not be tolerated.

Sometimes we just need the patience to endure a period in which our partner is undergoing changes in her physical, emotional, or spiritual life. Such changes cannot be rushed; they can only be accompanied with sensitivity. When we ourselves undergo such changes, we need to ask for a period of patience, to express our need for support so that, like Tam Lin, we can eventually re-emerge into our daily lives.

What changes are you and your partner undergoing now?

Ethics

Ethics teach us the mysteries of morality, and the nature of affections, virtues and manners, as by them we may be guided to our highest happiness.

—Thomas Traherne, *Centuries*

It is no longer customary for men to take off their opponents' heads, to boast of their own achievements after dinner, or to buy less fortunate people into slavery—all aspects of the ancient Celtic world that are not missed.

Manners and moral codes may alter, but not the structures that underlie. Ethics are the invisible scaffolding upon which our actions are built and without which life would be insupportable. Ethical conduct follows an unwritten law that runs in every part of the world, forming a path for all action. Becoming sensitive to its dictates is like acquiring taste, poise, or insight. Its invisible lines run laser-straight from our soul to the object of our consideration. Sensing the dynamic of that tug is like sailing a ship and having to be attentive to the winds and currents that move our vessel.

Ethics uphold the rights, privileges, and identity of every living soul: a maintenance that stretches to include the soul of what we may previously have considered inanimate or lifeless—the land, growing things, animals. Our subtle interrelatedness to all life walks these ethical lines, and when we are insensitive to the lines—when we forget that interrelatedness—we sever them. If any action that we undertake warps or threatens to sever the soul-lines of ethical connection, we may be sure that there is something intrinsically wrong with our idea or our approach.

Meditate upon a future plan. Visualize the line that stretches between you and it. Is there any discomfort or tug on the line? What is causing it? Does your plan uphold the dignity and rights of all who are involved in or affected by it?

Creative Destiny

Welcome, oh life! I go to encounter for the millionth time the reality of experience, to forge in the smithy of my soul the uncreated conscience of my race. . . .

—JAMES JOYCE, *Portrait of the Artist as a Young Man*

These words of Stephen Dedalus are the ecstatic greeting of a young man on the verge of exile and adventure, creative destiny and the fulfillment of his heritage. "Creative destiny" sounds a very grand proposition, the kind of thing that poets and artists might get themselves excited about. That we each have a creative destiny to fulfill is often conveniently forgotten, especially if we have carved out our niche in the world of work or have put the aspirations of our youth far behind us.

We think of creativity as the production of professional and beautiful artwork or music or other achievements, but the whole course of our lives is one creative endeavor: not only the work of our hands, but the way we weave our relationships, the way we make our homes, the way we raise children, cook food, dream, garden, shop—all these and more are our creative fields. Our creative destiny is not fated by distant galaxies or proscriptive deities; it is nothing other than the mindful growth, development, and manifestation of the gifts that lie *in potentia,* the talents, aptitudes, and heritage with which we were born.

Every year, millions of young people begin their active, determined, and intentioned lives as adults. Like salmon returning to their source, they set their faces toward the fulfillment of their creative destiny. It is a great adventure that few pursue unswervingly to the source; but for all who undertake it, there is no greater joy than to enter "the smithy of the soul" and bring into manifestation something that was not possible before we brought our creative destiny to play there.

What is your creative destiny? If it seems far off or unknown, consider the shape of your life to this point. Where has your life been wanting to flow?

The Wisdom Within

The faery queen of wisdom lived
Within the sun-room of a tree;
From there she saw the wide, wide world,
But no fool could her beauty see.

—Scots Gaelic folk story (trans. CM)

This story tells of a faery queen who invited all the women of the world to visit her so that she might give them wisdom. Some declined, thinking themselves wise enough already, while others came in order to be seen and admired. When the guests had assembled, the faery queen went among them with a blue limpet shell containing the essence of wisdom. Those guests who were there for the wrong reasons refused to drink, but those women who sought the wisdom within their own hearts drank gladly, each receiving a portion of wisdom until there was nothing left in the shell.

The wisdom that is already within each of us often needs only a small catalyst to develop, as long as we are open and receptive to wisdom when we meet it elsewhere. The unwritten wisdom of the heart abides within us as our motherwit, the wisdom of the body that we inherit from our ancestors. That wisdom is in the process of developing all the time as new information and experiences are brought into contact with it. We often mistakenly assume that wisdom must come from without, but external wisdom cannot develop within ourselves until our own wisdom meets and assimilates it in a practical way.

Valuing our own wisdom is hard in a world that offers so many expert opinions wherever we turn. It is often easier to defer to professionals than to regard our own views on a subject. Only when we have been to the limits of our own wisdom can we find the humility and receptivity to increase it.

Where are the limits of your knowledge? How many of your opinions are really your own, rather than adopted from others?

13

Tearing the Cloak in Two

Happy and young and gallant,
They saw their first-born go,
But not the strong limbs broken
And the beautiful men brought low.

—Ewart Alan Mackintosh,
"In Memoriam, Private D. Sutherland"

Within the last five generations, there has probably not been a family living that did not have some remembrance of war and conflict, some dead to mourn as a result of warfare. This day, November 11, has commemorated dead warriors, throughout the Western world, since the armistice of the First World War.

Those who serve in the defense of their families and countries—like the Gaulish soldier St. Martin of Tours, who tore his fine cloak in two to cloth the needy—tear the cloak of their lives in two, severing themselves from accustomed comfort and habitual kindness to enter a zone of pain and confrontation.

In our own age, where much of the warfare is against ignorance, heartlessness, and environmental devastation, new kinds of warriors learn the art of sacrifice with a different set of weapons. They seek to tear their lives in two to make a greater mantle in the defense of the poor, the innocent, the needy.

We no longer glorify war as our ancestors did; the loss, grief, and bewilderment of families for their fallen have been too great in this century for such assuaging. We count the cost and bless the sacrifice of those who have had the courage to tear the cloak in two, knowing that *they* did not glory in the pain and bloodshed any more than we ourselves now do.

Make your own prayer of remembrance for those who have died in war and for those who are on the battlefield of conflict throughout the world today.

Three Rocks of Judgment

The three immovable and perfect rocks on which the judgments of the world are sustained: the poet, the written word, and nature.

—Irish triad from *Senchus Mor*

This triad speaks of the three kinds of authority by which judgments can be made: authority from the divinatory composition of poets, from the letter of the law, and from the law of nature. These are the three traditional "courts of appeal" that sustain the law.

The first court of appeal is the oral word, and its exponent is the poet. The divinatory prowess of the ancient poets was considered to be both wise and authoritative. The spoken word is still a lively defender and prosecutor in modern courts of law, able to sway juries and reveal discrepancies in evidence.

The second court of appeal is the written word, which now has precedent over the spoken word in our society. The written word is not so flexible as its spoken counterpart and has tended, over the centuries, to become the "dead letter of the law" rather than a perfect rock upon which judgments may be based. The written word is indeed a strong rock if it is administered and maintained by people of probity and good guardianship, but it can also be interpreted in narrow and unhelpful ways. Many traditional legal frameworks stand in need of redrafting to encompass the changes that have overtaken our world.

The third court of appeal is nature itself, which has its own immutable laws to which both word and writing must bow. The natural laws cannot be overset by human judgments. They govern the whole round of life. As we seek to manipulate nature, to bypass its natural processes, we find out just how enduring and implacable its laws are. Beyond human memory and written judgment stands nature, the final court of appeal, reflecting the truth of our actions and desires.

What are the three rocks that sustain your world?

Pilgrimage Routes

Though the long tracks know no glad step,
And the circle goes unblessed.
From their long homes may the old ones
Welcome travellers upon their quest

—CAITLÍN MATTHEWS, "Pilgrims' Blessing"

Pilgrimage is a step beyond tourism, which merely comes to look at places and enjoy them; pilgrimage involves a deeper engagement with the land, with the sacred nature of the experience that is had not only at the destination but along the route as well. Those who travel with spiritual purpose find pleasure and enjoyment no less than the tourist, but their experience is colored by the reality of their contact with the unseen world—not only with the apparent landscape about them, but with its inhabitants and guardians.

When we re-engage with the sacred places of our spiritual heritage, the ability to be a pilgrim affects our experience of the places we visit: the ability to see beyond the desacralization, the skill to travel the road with expectant and prayerful hearts, the greeting we send out—before we even begin to travel—to the ancestral guardians and spiritual presences who have awaited our coming this long time.

In pilgrimage, it is the ability to give blessing upon the places we visit, rather than seek blessing for ourselves in our travel, that is most appreciated. In offering our blessing, we are able to resacralize both the way and the site: for if we become alive to the generous and sacred nature of each place, so may many others; and we will have become guardians and pilgrims of a new generation for all the generations to come.

Make your own pilgrimage to a special or sacred place during the wintertime, drawing upon some of the ideas above.

Misunderstandings

The last thing I intended
Was for a deed to come between us.

—"The Song of Liadan," early Irish text (trans. CM)

Liadan (LEE'dun) and Curithir (KOO'reer) were poets who met while on their poetic circuit of noble houses and fell in love. Curithir suggested that they marry immediately, adding that any child of theirs would be famous. Perhaps piqued by his words and by the suggestion that Curithir thought more of any future child than of their very real love, Liadan took religious vows of chastity. When Curithir came to claim her as his wife, he was too late: she would not sleep with him, preferring to honor her poetry above her sexuality. The muddle was not helped when the lovers put themselves under the direction of the severe St. Cummine, who gave Curithir the choice of seeing Liadan and not talking to her, or of speaking to her without seeing her. Since he was a poet, he chose speech. In due time, the suspicious St. Cummine banished Curithir from his monastic settlement, accusing him of sinful lust; Curithir then became a pilgrim and renounced Liadan's love. Liadan's subsequent poetry is a heart-rending self-condemnation of her action. She eventually died while clutching the stone on which the exiled Curithir used to sit.

When misunderstandings arise, they usually germinate in small and insignificant ways: a slighting glance, a failure to greet, a thoughtless word, a sense of exclusion or neglect—and so grow into substantial disasters. A phone call or letter or small token of apology can quickly bring reconciliation.

Consider a situation in which you were misunderstood or were the agent of misunderstanding. What factors exacerbated the situation? How could the misunderstanding have been prevented? Is there a go-between who could have brought about reconciliation? Apply your realizations to a situation in which you are currently involved.

Guardians of Power

Who has seen the Cup flame in the West,
who has not also seen the breath of Nine
smoke on the air above the Cauldron's rim?

—John Matthews, "The King's Moon-Rite"

In British folklore, the Lord of the Underworld has a cauldron whose brew is available only to those who are courageous and worthy. In one of the earliest written texts to mention Arthur, the hero himself goes in quest of this cauldron as proof of his sovereignty. It is tended by nine women who heat and empower the broth by their exhalation: these are nothing less than the guardians of the powers of life.

The nine sisters of the cauldron are the forerunners of the two Grail guardians of medieval Arthurian tradition: the beautiful Grail maiden who carries the blessed vessel and the ugly Grail messenger who stimulates the knights to quest for the vessel. Whether Grail or cauldron, the vessel in question bestows special qualities upon those who imbibe its contents, conferring immortality, healing, or specific virtues that manifest the quester's intrinsic life-purpose.

These nine sisters are the ones who guard the vessel of life and grant every living soul special gifts. Each breath that they breathe across the cauldron of our life's essence imbues each of us with our particular vocational gifts and tendencies. If we ignore the blessings of the guardians of life, we do not flourish easily: life is an uphill grind, and we have to reinvent the wheel at every turn. If, however, we examine the nature of our particular brew and discover with what blessings and potentialities we are each imbued, we can find a wonderful unfolding richness in all we attempt.

List up to nine qualities that are blended in your unique brew of life.
Speak to the Gifting Mothers and ask how their blessings may be used.

Scandal

Fionn, Prince of the Fianna,
Shall deliver me from the lie,
The son of Cumhail of the sharp blades,
And Goll of the strokes shall be my shield.

—Scots Gaelic charm against ill-report (trans. CM)

In this Scots Gaelic charm, the speaker invokes the help of Fionn mac Cumhail (FINN mak KOOL), the great champion of the Gael, and one of his heroes, the hard-hitting Goll. When our own good name is brought into disrepute through the spiteful words of others, we need strong heroes to champion us against a world of back-stabbing gossips.

Ill-report and scandal are like forest fires, sweeping through a circle of acquaintance faster than the wind. For anyone, regardless of prominence or anonymity in the world, the assault of scandal is the most difficult to parry or refute. When the rights of livelihood or marriage or parenthood are stripped away as a result of false report, the injustice rankles to the core.

Every person alive has a responsibility to those in his shared circle of life. If by one unregarded word of ours we cause pain or hurt unjustly, if we endanger the public esteem of someone without warrant, we are no better than the armed assailant who mugs people on the streets. To steal someone's good name is theft, however we wrap it up. Scandal flourishes only because there are willing ears to receive it. If we close our ears to unjust gossip and restrain our tongues from passing it on, its muddy outpourings will cease to foul our lives.

How have you entertained gossip? How can you cease to be the exponent of ill-report?

～ 17 November ～

The Clan Bond

The bonds of affection that unite the present chief and her clans-
men in all the arts of the world is indeed a living tie that neither
mountains nor a waste of seas can divide.

—Sir Iain Moncrieffe, *The Highland Clans*

Sir Iain Moncrieffe, the late Albany herald of arms, speaks warmly here of the late Dame Flora MacLeod, clan chief of the Clan MacLeod. The special bonds that bring the clan and its chief together are very different from those of president and citizen or of monarch and subject. The clan chief is responsible to the clan as the head of a family is responsible for her children; the clan's responsibilities toward the chief are likewise familial and intimate. Despite the decline of the clan system, the clans and their chiefs still gather in familial assemblies from all parts of the world to rejoice in each other's company.

With the breakdown of extended families into nuclear units, few families can enjoy a similar intimacy and recognition. The strongest sense of clan affection is now experienced among those families that are members of the vast diaspora of immigrants who have left their homeland for a new country. The sense of clan may remain in the new land, with those from a particular area who have settled in a given region, or it may extend back over the water to the people of the old homeland.

The sense of wanting to belong is part of our human identity, but even this special bond is shifting as human consciousness seeks a more personalized identity, as it reaches for a wider connection. We are all moving toward a greater clan bond that is planetary and universal. We are not altogether happy or convinced about this belonging: it lacks intimacy and could so easily come to nothing very much. Whether we can be part of this larger clan is yet to be seen.

Which clan bonds include you in their embrace? Which do you admit
to?

Living in the World

Were All the World a Paradise of Ease,
'Twere Easy Then to Live in Peace.

—THOMAS TRAHERNE, *Centuries*

When we first plunge into the full flood of response to our spiritual path, the world seems a wonderful place. Our ecstasy is often so persuasive that we enter a period of convert fervor and rapidly become bores, singing the delights of our chosen way for the benefit of any friends (or total strangers) unfortunate enough to meet us.

For anyone descending from the spiritual high-ground, the next phase is the most challenging to our chosen way. All the delights, joys, and insights that we enjoyed at the peak suddenly run up against all the lethargies, doldrums, and seemingly meaningless interludes of daily life. If our prayer life has been connective, it becomes prone to a strange interference in this phase; if our meditations have been colorful, they suddenly start receiving black-and-white transmission; if our spiritual allies have favored us with intimate interviews, they suddenly become amazingly elusive. No one and nothing seems to be on the same wavelength anymore.

The individual who finds himself in such a predicament needs to look at each new challenge to his newfound spiritual peace as a practical opportunity to manifest some of his theoretical notions.

It is not solely in the otherworld or in paradise that spirituality is to be implemented, but in the world in which we live. If our spirituality cannot supply us with resourceful encouragement, then it is very shallowly rooted in us. It is in the challenges to our spiritual peace that we find the strongest solutions. Like a parched tree that has to send out deeper roots to sources of water, we also have to send our spiritual roots deeper in search of help. To live our sacred text, to implement our holy philosophy, there is no better place than here and now.

Apply your spiritual wisdom to the most challenging daily trial.

Deferred Decisions

Do not go Monday, be still on Tuesday,
Wednesday's a bad day, Thursday is slow,
Friday's unlucky, Saturday's grudging,
So give up your troublesome travel tomorrow!

—Scots Gaelic song (trans. CM)

This song is sung to beguile the welcome guest, to delay her departure and cause her to stay longer. Sometimes, though, we cannot be so self-indulgent; we need to take incisive action rather than defer it.

Procrastination is subtle and invasive self-persuasion that second-guesses all avenues of possibility as they present themselves. It is always easier to leave a difficult decision to the next day, to put off reading and signing a complex document until a later date, to ignore a request until the time is more convenient and our mood more amenable. The prince of procrastination is Shakespeare's Hamlet, who virtually worries himself into mental illness. When deferred actions are deferred too long, the fear around their performance becomes horrifically amplified.

When we are stuck in procrastination, we need "a rabbit-bolter"—something that flushes realizations out of their deep hiding places up to the surface of our attention. This bolter may involve taking a day off work and away from the family, going into nature or to a place of some peacefulness, without stimulus and interference from any outside source, so that our minds can cease their squirrel-cage contortions and come to rest in focused attention upon how we must act. In our prayers and in the companionship of our spiritual allies, we can ask for help, clarity, and strength to make the right decisions and to defer them no longer.

Choose one current predicament and meditate upon possible solutions.

The Voice of the Soul

*Who is this Singer that sends his voice through the dark forest, and
inhabits us with ageless and immortal music, and sets the long
echoes rolling for evermore?*

—MARY WEBB, *Gone to Earth*

In all people there is a potent voice sounding from the very depths of
their being. When we stand at the timeless intersections of our lives,
when danger threatens, when beauty awakens us to deeper levels of
being, we hear its clear call. It speaks words of urgent survival, of
potent arousal, of immediate and uncontrollable response. It may not
speak with words that we hear with our physical ears, but its vibrations
permeate our very body. Many people who have been aware of this
voice fear it with an almost superstitious terror: they fear its strength, its
persuasion, and especially its passion. They believe that this voice is
from some dark malevolence, rather than from the very heart of love.

It is the voice of the soul itself, which has its wavelength tuned
exactly to our personal pitch. In our society, which validates only that
which is seen, "hearing voices" is associated with serious mental disturbance. Our society's inability to recognize the unseen as real in turn
causes us to distrust our deepest beliefs and instincts. Instead of listening to the voice that surges passionately into every aspect of our understanding, we attempt to blot it out, expunge its presence, substituting
our rational explanations as being more authoritative.

Beginning to make sense of the soul's voice often requires us to "tune
out" the interference that our suspicions and conditioning have created.
The voice of the soul speaks from the heart of love. True love does not
injure; rather, it upholds the good of the beloved before itself. By the
fruits of our experience, our trust in that voice will grow until we can
progress to a stage wherein we will be borne up in love and trust.

*Listen to the deep voice of your own soul. Feel what it is saying. Do not
be distracted by the voice of your mind.*

Daring

He either fears his fate too much,
Or his deserts are small,
That dares not put it to the touch,
To gain or lose it all.

—James Graham, Marquis of Montrose,
"My Dear and Only Love"

When the young Setanta was being taught by the druid Cathbad, the students asked their teacher, "What deeds are favorable for this day of all days?" Cathbad replied, "This day is one on which any young stripling who claims the arms and armor of a man shall become the hero who surpasses all the youth of Ireland. His name will be glorious, but his life will be fleetingly short." On hearing that, Setanta—who would become the hero Cuchulainn—immediately decided that the day had come for him to take valor and claim his status as a man.

When we are young, we are fearless, heedless of both hidden and obvious perils. We have the brash arrogance and ignorance of youth, a combination that is oddly endearing and chillingly frightening at the same time. Age and experience bring us to greater circumspection.

Whence do we draw the daring to perform the deeds of adult life? There is no time to dither when we stand in danger of losing our livelihood or well-being. To take up the gage of daring is dangerous, but to have never dared is to have never won. Is it good to spend our lives in risk-free circumstances, never challenged or stretched beyond our personal comfort factor? Sometimes we have to become vulnerable, and suffer risk to protect and defend that which we love beyond our personal lives. When our response is absolute, we seize our fate with urgent hands, fly out on the spiral loop of our soul's thread, without a parachute: only by the truth and integrity of our actions are we protected.

What feels risky in your life? How are you endangered? Where are you being stretched to dare?

The Kindling of Love

There are three sparks that kindle love: the face, the demeanor, and the way of speaking.

—ancient Irish triad

These sparks are like three lights that shine from the beloved, beacons that shine upon our dark and lonely landscape and illumine it in a way that no other person can achieve. The first light strikes us from the eyes: there is a liquid light within the eyes of the beloved that illumines her face. Because the soul can be seen in the eyes, the glance of the beloved warms and welcomes us, while the glance of the enemy chills, repels, or withers us like a laser beam.

The whole nature of the soul is seen in the demeanor of the beloved: the way the person moves, his body language, his way of guarding and shielding his soul with respect. The demeanor of the beloved is like an aurora of dawning that permeates the surrounding area with a gentle light and picks out features that are important and noteworthy in our own soul.

Most wonderful is the light shed by the voice of the beloved. It is tuned to our own cadence, becoming a pathway of welcome, a resonant and gently penetrating music. Of all the sparks that we value about our beloved, the voice is probably the one we remember longest. Even those lovers whose beloved is dead and who can now scarcely remember every loved feature, who become impatient with the false memory of a photograph, say that the voice of the beloved is the most beautiful thing they still remember. The beloved speaks of things beneath the spoken words, like a ray of light that carries the shape and the shadow in its wake. To that shape we cleave while others linger in the shadow.

Consider your own beloved, whether alive or dead. Which of his or her qualities spark love within you? How are loving qualities present within yourself?

Axes of Contest and Contention

In the northern martial arts, the opponents in serious struggles faced each other along the north-south line. . . . When the fighting was for recreation or practice, such as in tournaments, the combatants fought east-west.

—Nigel Pennick, *Celtic Sacred Landscapes*

The subtle lore of the directions as studied by Nigel Pennick reveals some interesting considerations. In the northern hemisphere, the two poles represent the solstices of midwinter and midsummer. When north faces south it is winter against summer, where serious opponents stand in their relative places of strength, prepared for the onslaught of strife.

The east and the west, respectively, represent the spring and autumn equinoxes. When we face east-west, we align to the daily passage of the sun and the promise of its return, and our conflict is tinged with hope. The combat of north and south, on the other hand, is a more serious and lasting contention. In ancient times, divorces were enacted by couples standing north-south, back-to-back, and then walking away from each other as a symbolic and final demonstration of their parting.

We each have our own subtle geomantic way of aligning our friends, enemies, rivals, and opponents and keeping them in separate areas.

Take a piece of paper and divide it into four quarters by drawing an X from top left to opposite bottom right, from top right to opposite bottom left. In the northern (top) quarter, write down those things and people who cause you difficulty or contention. In the southern (bottom) quarter, write down those things and people whom you enjoy. In the right-hand quarter, write down your strengths. In the left-hand quarter, write down your weaknesses. Now meditate upon how the northern and southern quarters, the eastern and western quarters are related. Where do they exchange understanding? What does one side teach the other?

The Initiations of Youth

Youth's native sadness
dramatizes itself ever against time
in experimental mime
against the immensities.

—ROSS NICHOLS, *The Cosmic Shape*

There are no formal rites of passage (see February 23) in our society to help children become adults: young people graduate, take their driving test, become sexually active, try intoxicants, get tattooed or pierced. Forever testing the limits of their powers, they seem to know no restraint. This applies to girls just as it does to boys. In societies where rites of passage are customary, physical ordeals push participants to their limits of endurance, courage, and dedication; sometimes failure means actual death. While we may view such rites of passage as barbarous and unnecessary, we should note that our own children create their initiatory rites in the same daring spirit: running across the freeway, climbing up tall buildings, and driving at top speed down winding coastal roads are just a few of these initiations. Yes, youth dramatizes itself all right!

We have made our choice not to initiate our children into adulthood with formal ceremonies that bring them to the edge of their powers. Having done so, we cannot blame them for making their own rites. Young people need to claim a name for themselves. In Celtic society, adolescence was often the time when a nickname became attached to the childhood name, or when the original name was changed to one that reflected a more adult commitment—a name "discovered" in someone's chance remark, perhaps. How can our children make their own name in our society unless they are given the initiations that bring them to opportunity?

Make your own initiatory blessing for adolescents about to launch themselves on the world.

Integrity of Action

We of the Fianna never told a lie. Falsehood was never attributed to them. But by truth and the strength of our hands, we came safe out of every combat.

—*Ladoidh Chunaic an Air,* anon. Irish poem

The Fianna (FEE'enn-a) was the prestigious war band of the hero Fionn mac Cumhail, whose honor was bound up in their maintenance of truth, as their motto says: "Truth in our hearts, strength in our hands, consistency upon our tongues."

If we divert the truth in pursuit of our ambitions, however marginal the lie, we also divert the course of our honor; we weaken our soul's thread. It is often easier to lie than to admit the truth. To state our honest objections, to cut across the dishonesty of those with whom we associate, to challenge falsehood in the workplace or in high places may seem a kind of foolhardiness today.

The practice of honesty is a daily exercise that hones our integrity. In both trivial and important actions, the experienced truth-bearer is like a hero who has practiced her sword strokes so many times that she can cleave through thistledown with accuracy and perception.

The integrity of truth offers a clean way of dealing in our lives—a way of dealing that sets down better and more honorable patterns upon which our society can be reformed.

Try to tell the truth for twenty-four hours. Feel in your body how living honestly changes your life's experience. If your life is wholly or partially built on lies, begin to examine the scaffolding on which it is based: ask help of your spiritual allies to discover how the scaffolding can be dismantled and how you can become true to your soul's thread.

Generosity

As long as sun and moon shall last
The generous one shall never be empty.

—Scots Gaelic saying (trans. CM)

True generosity flows from the one who is full to the one who is empty. With whatever gift we are full—whether it be a skill, a resource, even time and space themselves—we have the ability to dispense from our own fullness. The truly generous one gives without stint, like Fionn mac Cumhail, of whom it was said:

If only the brown leaf were gold the tree sheds when the year is old!
Silver, the foam upon the bay, Fionn would give it all away.

Where, then, are the limits of generosity? Generosity is limited by a patronizing attitude that condescends to another's need. It is curtailed by a miserly spirit that gives only to "the deserving"—a category that few seem to fit when it comes right down to it. Generosity can also be abused by recipients who do not reciprocate any kind of thanks. It does not matter if the reciprocated gift is of a different kind only that thankfulness is expressed in some measure. The law of hospitality is the law of return—a law that makes sense only when we regard all beings, all strangers, as potentially our family.

This is the curious paradox about giving from the depths of our gift: if we give, the giving wells up in us more strongly than ever like an ever-renewing fund of hospitable welcome from the source of life itself. As the planets light our world with unbegrudging light, illumining the good and the bad, the poor and the rich, the sick and the healthy, so the impetus of generosity is a well that does not discern to whom the draft is to be given: all may drink freely.

With what are you full? How does generosity irrigate your life?

Grace Before Food

Be with me, O God, at the breaking of bread,
Be with me, O God, at the end of my meal.
May no morsel of my body's partaking
Add to my soul's freight!

—Scots Gaelic grace (trans. CM)

The blessing of food or the saying of "grace" before eating is regarded as old-fashioned behavior in most households these days, except perhaps on Thanksgiving, when it plays a traditional role.

The blessing upon our food is itself a thanksgiving to all who have participated in the preparation of our meal: the grains, the earth, the elements, the animals, the ones who have processed our food and sold it to us—everyone is involved. If we contemplate only one item of food on our table and trace back through the steps that brought it there, the scale of our thanksgiving becomes very real—a network of cooperation that is one strand of our life.

The Gaelic blessing above seems very relevant today. With the addition of chemicals and pesticides and the genetic manipulation of the cellular structure of our food, many people are very worried about swallowing anything these days. The need to return to organic food-production methods where only the usual growing agents—air, sunlight, water, and root nurture—are allowed to influence the food we eat is now widely recognized.

Very few people wish to harm their bodies or souls by participating in immoral and disrespectful food-production methods. The same goes for foodstuffs whose gathering and production endanger other species of animals or plants or further exploit already exploited people. Our choice of food is determined by the staple items of our region and our culture, many of which are in short supply. Can we change our eating habits in order to be able to breathe a true blessing upon our table?

Write your own grace or meditate upon silently before you eat.

Spiraling P

People visited groves and springs at the sacre
the Turas, circling these holy places and wells. ᵢ *made ···*
prayer, spiralling inwards. ₙcentric

—from a speech by Nuala Ahern,
Irish Member of the European P.

The word *turas* (TU'ras), which means "journey," "pilg, " and
"time," refers especially to the circular, spiraling prayer and , tation
form used by people in the Celtic countries as they walked wise
around a sacred site. Making the *turas*, or circling around a sacre ite,
well, tree, or stone, is still a living part of Celtic spirituality today.

The motion of this walking prayer is always *deiseal*, or sunwise—
that is, from left to right. The clockwise method of making the *turas* is
customary in the northern hemisphere; it is considered to be the fortunate and appropriate way of moving, while *tuathal*, or counterclockwise, is considered to be less fortunate. (Note: In the southern hemisphere, sacred motion is counterclockwise.)

We need to circle, spiraling around the sacred site with our body, in
tune with our intentions and with the presence of the site. The process
of spiraling around builds power, strengthens intention, and brings us
into attunement with our soul's thread. It also attunes us in another
way: as our planet spins around the circling year, we too simultaneously
experience the turning of our soul toward the source of greatest spiritual light. Each season is a mystical gateway of opportunity and
understanding, a sacred time of wisdom. If we live with awareness of
the year's cycles, we will achieve a direct alignment with those sacred
opportunities.

Visit a tree, rock, well, or other place in nature to which you feel par-
ticularly drawn. Make your own turas *about it. If you live in an urban*
environment, find a stone that can represent a sacred site within your
own home.

31

Renewal

> concrete megaCity chokes the globe from pole to
> When ready have, bedded in some hidden crack, the sacred
> pole in disintegration and collapse.
> see
>
> —David Rudkin, *Penda's Fen*

What ve paved over feels safe, secure, permanent, habitable, civilized ady a majority of people feel uneasy in the countryside or in
ope d, without sight of buildings, shops, and the full panoply of
urb living.

hen a civilized place is abandoned by people, the green world takes it back again. The first tough weeds quickly force their way through the concrete, splitting the man-made amalgam of civilization, and soon the wild seeds of life celebrate their return by germinating unchecked until that stone is covered with green.

The prospect of ending or decay is greatly dismaying to people who feel that it means the end of life as they know it. And they are rightfully fearful, for the enemy of life is stasis. The seeds of renewal are always mysteriously buried within the thick of decay and corruption, ready to spring up when all seems lost.

At this time of the year, when the trees look disheveled, when growth stops, we may feel the loss as a personal thing and cross the threshold to depression. Yet the roots of renewal lie in the contemplation of the way in which this year's leaf mold on the forest floor will become the rich earth for next year's glorious growth.

The urbanization of the soul has become in many ways like a "great concrete megaCity" that petrifies the living impulses of our natural heart. The lesson of this season is to welcome the elements that free our soul into wider ways of living, to burst out of the urban soul into the great expanses where renewal can clear away all that impedes our way.

What is static or decaying in your current life? Commune with the fruits of this season and find out how you can welcome change in.

~ 30 November ~

Spiritual Space

We see only the loving hollow
Of a tomb which is always a womb:
A perfect, wondering O of beginnings.

—CAITLÍN MATTHEWS,
"Conference of the Trees"

Spiritual space, silence, the emptiness from which things can be born—these spaces worry us. We are fretful to fill them. As Christmas approaches, we can be pulled into cycles of gift-buying, into hectic socializing, and so abandon the empty spaces that our soul needs so badly. From the empty spaces, from the tasklessness of a spare afternoon, we can find the place wherein we actually fit. This gap is like a tunnel that joins our world with the otherworld, a tunnel wherein our own sequential time meets the timelessness of the otherworld. In these moments of blankness or emptiness comes the invitation to be ourselves, to bury the old busy self, to give birth to a new self that is sensitive to these precious moments.

This is especially so when we have received a great revelation, or encountered an immense thought, or experienced a world-changing situation: instead of rushing off to complete the next task, we benefit from stopping and allowing the precious, wondering O to envelop us in a circle of calm contemplation. Within this circle, we can re-experience and ponder all that has befallen us, allowing it to connect with the wisdom that is already ours.

Creating spiritual space is an art. Consider the forbearance of the artist who stops when the picture is finished rather than painting in yet more, inessential detail. Our own spiritual space needs the same kind of forbearance, needs patience and deep listening for revelation to be made manifest: a wondering O in which profound realizations can dance and sing.

Be attentive to, and give allowance for, spiritual space to encompass you.

DECEMBER

Month of December—the shoe is covered with dirt:
Heavy the land, flagging the sun;
Bare are the trees, still is the muscle.

—anon. Welsh poem

December sees the winter solstice and the return of gradually longer days. The themes of this month include the nature of work, revenge and forgiveness, gifts and blessings, belief and disbelief, and practicing being human.

Integrity in Work

He should be constitutionally and habitually devotional, so that blessing of God may be upon him, and what he does, and that he may be conscientious to do what is right and beneficial in the practice of his art.

—The Herbal Remedies of the Physicians of Myddfai

Whether we work for an employer or are self-employed, whether we have retired or are taking a sabbatical from work, the integrity of our actions contributes to the universal web of life. If an employer begins to bend the rules for his own benefit, then his staff may be tempted to follow his example. One person's actions may affect the company in such a way that certain positions or products are canceled—for who robs one, robs all. Occupations that strip the earth of its resources or leave it polluted are easy to target as culpable of gross theft and planetary vandalism, yet the actions of everyone living enable such results to some degree.

To be in right relationship to our universe, a certain integrity and code of practice in our work and actions is necessary. Most of us have no explicit code by which to steer, but what we value is revealed when we consider why and for whom we are conscientious in our work and actions. Surely it is not only our employer or fellow workers who inspire us to do well but those who consume or use what we make, or our families who are supported by our work.

Hands that work are the partners in manifestation of the unseen world wherein Spirit (by whatever form or forms we recognize it) is the keeper, maker, and inspirer of all that is. Any code of practice must first apply to the sacred source of spiritual inspiration to keep its actions pure, to operate from the highest of motives, to irrigate all work from the wellspring of integrity.

Draw up a short, realistic personal code of practice both for your occupation and for your actions in general.

Defending the Country

They are passionately devoted to their freedom and to the defense of their country; for these they fight, for these they suffer hardships.

—GERALD OF WALES, *Journey Through Wales*

Love of freedom and the rights of free speech and free congregation are at the heart of the British character, and the response today is just as mutinous as in medieval times, when these words were written, if anyone attempts to overturn these ancient, druidic freedoms.

The defense of one's country has become an issue of uneasy contemplation these days. Our minds stray to nuclear armaments and the unpleasant ironmongery that wreaks so much pain and destruction. We shy away from the consideration of national service, conscription, and other military preparations for defensive war. Yet if we look deeply at the defense of country, we discover that it requires something more worthy of us than naive back-stabbing of other nations, cultures, and religions. The essential freedoms and privileges that we enjoy are enshrined in our laws and statutes for all to read, but there are also more profound and subtle freedoms that we are all called upon to defend.

The enemy to these freedoms is not always so obvious as a foreign power but is all about us, within our own society. It is our own disregard for the authentic loyalties of life that is the enemy attacking our country. We who live in our land are its defenders by our very way of life, by our attitudes, by our actions, by our intentions, by the integrity, joy, and engagement we bring to our country's life. To become a defender rather than an enemy, we must be in tune with our country in a deeply spiritual way.

Commune with the spirit of the country in which you live. Ask it what are the freedoms and privileges that it guards. Ask how these freedoms are to be defended, and what is the greatest threat to them at this time.

Intellectual Stimulus

Too many men and women spend their time between an office and a home in a state of intellectual stupor.

—LLEWELYN POWYS, *Earth Memories*

Among the bards and druids, the training of the mind and memory was of paramount importance; the continual use of memory kept open the neural pathways, making response quick and incisive. Speed of mind meant speed of tongue: the swifter-than-thought pronouncement of judgment or pithy and apposite verse was expected of bards and druids. While there are many professions today that use training methods to sharpen the intellect, most of us do not exercise our minds to any great degree. Instead of thinking deeply about a thing, we often summon up our sensations, emotions, and instincts and create an opinion woven of these strands. Although the intellect needs stimulus and training, it still has its place in the scheme of things.

In the wintertime, the air is clearer and crisper, the brain seems to work just that little bit more quickly than it does in the summer. Those of us who are intellectually flabby may find that now is a good time to exercise our intellect, to stretch it further than it is accustomed to. The process of learning something is one way to engage the intellect; if there is no time for that, however, engaging in deep discussion about a topic important to you with friends or reading something that stretches your conceptual apparatus is also beneficial. There are no set boundaries on the limits of human intellect: see how far we each can go!

Exercise your mind in a new or different way: a new language, a different way of looking at the universe. Choose something that intrigues you and see how it connects with what you know.

Marriage Blessing

*Length of life and sunny days, and may your souls not go
homewards till your own child falls in love!*

—traditional Irish blessing (trans. CM)

For most people entering marriage today, such thoughts are far from their heads. Indeed, many disillusioned wedding guests sit and discuss—even as they toast the happy couple—how long this marriage will last. Though the statistics show that many marriages now end in divorce, there are still a number of long-term relationships that continue—especially if the partners are supported by well-wishing and encouraging friends.

When we celebrate a marriage, we are essentially celebrating the continuance of life: a factor that is now often subsumed in the mutual satisfaction of the couple, who may indeed have chosen to have no children. Yet the heart of the marriage blessing enshrines the possibility of life's continuance: the birth of children and the perpetuation of humankind. The best-laid plans to defer a family until a more convenient time are often overturned by nature, which finds a way for life to flourish. In the eyes of new parents, the marriage blessing often seems to be a rather dubious or double-edged one, cutting short personal pleasures and dampening mutual delights.

But the privilege of parenthood, the feeling of blessedness, is also experienced as children grow, change, and surprise us. The true fruit of our partnership, they will grow up to marry and have children of their own, so that when our souls go homeward, our offspring will have the happiness, love, and initiation into parenthood in their turn.

*Make your own marriage blessing for those celebrating the beginning
of their partnership today. Draw upon the fortunate elements of your
own relationships.*

Tasks of a Bard

*The three chief endeavors of a bard: to learn and collect knowl-
edge; to teach; to make peace and put an end to all injury. To act
contrary to these things is not usual or fitting to a bard.*

—ancient British triad

How can these bardic tasks become part of our own spiritual path
today? How can they be integrated into our culture? Each society
needs knowledge that informs and is appropriate for its members: it
does not want to hear about bygone lore. This means that every
would-be bard should indeed research to the very roots of knowledge
the thing that she wishes to convey, but she must also seek out the relevance and practical wisdom of that topic.

The ancient bards could inspire, encourage, enchant their listeners.
The modern bard must learn the old art of oral performance rather
than of written exposition. These skills may be learned from our spiritual allies, who are the true teachers of the bardic knowledge, as well
as from situations in which the solution to difficulty is imparted by
spontaneous, synaptic inspiration: where knowledge, problem, and
answer line up.

This leads to the making of peace and the cessation of injury—skills
that we need very badly in our own time. The bardic performance can
bring the end to hostility, especially if music is part of the picture. In
the presence of music, all people are brought into harmony and understanding as its universal language speaks to the soul. We may bring an
end to injury and offense through the offices of a modern bard in times
not so far distant from our own.

*Meditate upon the bardic teachers of your ancestry. Make a soul-flight
to one of their schools and ask to meet with a bard who will teach you
the skills necessary for bringing peace to our world.*

Traveling Slowly

By increasing the speed at which we pass through the landscape,
we may greatly alter the time-sequences which are an integral part
of our perceptive experience of it.

—JAY APPLETON, *The Experience of Landscape*

We notice and remember features about walking journeys that are not apparent to us when we drive. The spirit of the land cannot speak to us directly when we speed through it; it cannot catch our eyes through the outstretched branches of trees, or in the gleam of hidden water, or in the deer-brown bracken of the hillside under the glancing winter sunlight.

The time-sequencing of our landscape perception changes radically when we speed by unaware of what we are passing, or when we use a journey to work or read. We can pass through areas and have no recollection of having traveled through them.

Our subtle perceptions are never engaged when we are car-bound because our senses themselves are not engaged; these outer and inner senses are connected. The sense of our own velocity when we move under our own steam, rather than with the help of wheels, imparts the message of the wind; the feeling of our feet upon the ground brings us into relationship with the presence of the land; our ears, unshielded by carriage walls, are able to tune into the subtle sounds of the earth; our noses can smell the distinctive scents of the landscape, most potent messengers of memory. Infused into all these experiences, but predominating over them all, is the sense of the land itself and its own story into which we are straying.

Wherever we walk, we enter the story of the land, becoming part of it. But only the one who travels slowly can perceive that story and learn from it.

Take a walking journey along a route you would normally drive along.
What is different? How did you relate to the land you journeyed through?

Perseverance

An eident drap will pierce a stane. [A steady drop will pierce a stone.]

—Scottish proverb

One of the prime figures of perseverance within the Scottish tradition is King Robert the Bruce. The apocryphal story of his hiding in a cave and watching a spider attempt to make its web again and again tells us that this was how the Scottish hero mustered his own perseverance to struggle on. When life seems stacked against us, whence do *we* find the perseverance to continue?

When is perseverance not enough? When we have tried to the limits of our ability, when we have tried all avenues of pursuit, when there is no more help to be sought, it is reasonable to consider whether this project is the right one or if it is being approached in the right way. Sometimes a reappraisal of method can bring about a fresh change. If you are still pushing a rock up the mountain after a reasonable period of perseverance, it might be time to stop and reassess.

Perseverance is not a common virtue these days, especially among those who expect quick or instant results. The ability to carry on with a project and see it through is often a painful, painstaking, incremental task that does not yield results in an obviously satisfactory way. It is a task scorned by many as a waste of time and effort. Yet many wonderful achievements have come to birth as the result of daily, incremental, crablike progress.

We must have the patience of water itself, which cleaves the stone over many centuries.

Are your plans on target; are they realistic and achievable? What changes would their manifestation bring to your life? Are you approaching your goals by the best possible route? Is other help available? What factors are still lacking?

Revenge

Three incitements to revenge: screaming of female relatives, and seeing the bier of their relation, and seeing the grave of their relation without compensation.

—triad from *Laws of Hywel Dda*

Both the Welsh laws of King Hywel Dda (HOO'wel THA) and the Irish *brehon* laws understood the deep-seated nature of revenge upon people who receive neither compensation nor apology for their wrongs.

When wrongs fester without justice, revenge raises up its own host to deal with things. When we are pondering the causes of terrorism or vendetta, we should remember that these abuses arise among a people when appropriate compensation or justice is denied. The causes of revenge lie deep in the human heart: a need for revenge is evoked by loss, grief, anger, the inability to gain compensation or redress, the bold-faced behavior of the guilty, the desire to cause a like injury to the guilty "so that they can see what it feels like."

Revenge can be maintained beyond the grave and cascade from generation to generation down the bloodline until all descendants are likewise infected by the disease. When revenge enters the bloodstream of a whole nation, then we face a situation that has defied boardrooms of arbitrators and peace-brokers. Proponents of terrorism seek redress on behalf of countries and nationalist sensibilities that they perceive have been abused or neglected. Terrorists are fueled by ancestral appeasement: they are no longer individuals with ordinary concerns, but the living incarnation of ancestral revenge feuds.

If peace and reconciliation are to be brought about, the wronged party must be listened to seriously and the source of the injury must be investigated by impartial witnesses. Whatever the rights and wrongs of the matter, the release of forgiveness is the only sure balm to revenge.

How has revenge been a factor in your own life and that of your ancestors? What solutions have been found to be acceptable?

Prophecy

O hear the voice of the Bard
Who present, past and future sees,
Whose ears have heard the holy Word
That walked among the ancient trees.

—WILLIAM BLAKE, "Songs of Experience"

Celtic tradition has abounded in prophets: King Arthur's Merlin, the uncanny Brahan Seer, Thomas the Rhymer, the Welsh *awenyddion* (ah-wen-ITH'ion) or "inspired ones," and the many unnamed seers and seeresses of history. The ability to see through the veil from the temporal world into the world where time is always *now* is one that runs in the blood and surfaces in certain family lines and in lone individuals alike.

Moments of true seeing and true utterance happen to everyone. They occur when we see clearly through the veil between the worlds, all unbidden, and observe what will be. Then we experience the slowing down of time, the growing sense of communion with precise coordinates of knowledge that click in our brain into startling patterns of revelation. Because our society tends to ignore such revelation, we usually shrug off what we have experienced as something of little importance, ignoring these subtle messages.

These moments sometimes happen when we are on the brink of decisions, meetings, or agreements: we suddenly have a sense that we are present at something momentously charged and potent, maybe having a flash vision of a future event when the fruits of the decision have matured. We may experience a sense of warning, a flash of insight that tells us clearly that the person we are meeting does not mean us well. We sometimes even remember past insights and visions that we indeed predicted and are now actually living through. At those times the same sense of timelessness and encompassment rises within us.

Use your prophetic soul to look between the worlds to understand a recent action's consequences.

Forgiveness

Pardon's the word to all.

—William Shakespeare, *Cymbeline*

The call to forgiveness—whether it be the laying aside of vengeance, the releasing of people from obligation, the canceling of debts—sounds a general amnesty between ourselves and those who have wronged us. If they are not dealt with, wrongs and claims against others can become like ropes that tie the souls of victims to the souls of perpetrators.

The true meaning of forgiveness is releasing ourselves and others from the bonds of blame. If we remain in situations where we suffer wrong continually, we must face the priorities and strive to remove ourselves from this danger as soon as possible, or else we must forbear to condemn. Situations where our love and care are greeted with indifference, violence, and abuse are situations in which we endanger our very soul. We must get help or get out. To forgive does not mean to condone, but it does mean the end of condemnation.

No person living is free of condemnation: we have all wronged someone at some time. Yet to set aside condemnation and release someone from the obligation of restitution takes great resolution and courage. To forgive is to detach the bond that keeps us locked in mortal combat with our enemy. The obligation to forgiveness grows stronger as time wears on, before we weave too strong a bond, before the anger, strife, or wrong pollutes our very soul.

Meditate upon a situation that requires your forgiveness. Who or what do you release?

Respect

The three most ill-mannered sons of the earth: a boy mocking an old man, a strong man swaggering in front of a sick one, a wise man jesting at the expense of a foolish one.

—ancient Irish triad

Good manners are nothing less than the respect that we owe a fellow being, an acknowledgment of another's presence and space wherein we restrain our own normal or unthinking behavior.

The respect that is due to age has virtually evaporated in our society, which favors a fast-track youth culture. In the job market, on the streets, in the media, we see a growing disrespect for age. In this era when personal power and ability are paramount, to be sick is held to be the worst of misfortunes. Despite the wonderful technological discoveries that have banished so many diseases, fewer people are able to afford the health care that they need. People with mental disabilities and poor reading skills suffer a marginalization against which little headway is being made; the physically handicapped are little better understood than they, although at least society no longer mocks the unfortunate as a form of low-grade entertainment.

The kinds of respect that we offer to other people are so often formulated from prejudged factors. The social status of an individual, along with affluence, fame, or professional status; the relative age and importance of that person in society; his or her gender or religious background—all these factors color how we respond. Yet the respect owed to another human being bypasses all these designations. Respect is a currency that must be paid soul to soul, regardless of the externals.

Monitor your own levels of respect today. Notice how they change according to the changing characteristics of those you meet. What factors change your behavior? In what ways can you exercise common courtesy to all equally?

~ 12 December ~
Reality and Belief

Nothing here is real without belief.

—AIDAN ANDREW DUN, *Vale Royal*

Belief continually changes the way we perceive reality. When a group of people speak of "reality," they are not actually understanding the same thing, since each individual invests reality with different sets of characteristics. Spiritual belief invests reality with many different qualities: simultaneously, a fundamentalist believer will see the world as a place of fear, a mystical believer will see it as a place of peace, a creative believer will see it as a place of potentiality, a pragmatic believer will see it as just a place to live. It is the same for ideological beliefs, which define reality by different criteria.

Reality and belief simply cannot be disentangled from each other.

Beliefs evolve their own mythology and symbolism, methods of encoding meaning into the perceived and observed correlative of life. It is only when our views are challenged that reality shakes. True belief brings trust with it, a trust that things will not change, that we will be supported. Belief can both support and enclose us, so that the nature of reality seems to become unchanging.

The changing views of reality during this century have shaken many, causing fear and consternation. It is at this point of panic that fundamentalist beliefs become strangely attractive, for their dogmatic character ensures an unchanging stability for the fearful. For the rest, our own beliefs walk beside reality, giving it color, meaning, and purpose. Its subtle messages are the signposts of a greater reality that embraces both the seen and the unseen.

How do your own beliefs color reality? Compare your views with someone else's.

Our True North

There's one white star, of all the rounds
That wheels high overhead,
And it is hung on heaven's pole
And will not rise nor bed.

—John Morris-Jones, "The North Star"

If we could set up a stop-frame film of the solar year and point it up toward the northern heavens, we would see revealed the dance of the circumpolar stars about the polestar in a fantastic circle dance. Among the peoples of the north, the polestar is called "the nail of heaven" because of its unchanging position in the sky: an unfailing and welcome guide to travelers and sailors in the darkest night. Discovering our own true north as the compass point of our soul's direction is a worthwhile enterprise on our spiritual path. Our true north may not be an actual belief system or ideology, not a religious figure or archetype, if we are still searching. It may be something that is nearer to an instinct or feeling of traveling in the right direction, something that we sniff in the wintry air or intuit from the glancing rays of the sun through the leafless trees. Our true north is a homing instinct innate to each us, privileged information that defines the nature of our goal—even though we may have no clear idea of that goal or of an otherworldly locus.

In the middle of a darkened room, or in nature at night, with sufficient space about you for you to revolve with outstretched hands on the spot, close your eyes and, asking to be shown your true north—your spiritual home—slowly turn until you find the direction that feels right for you. Facing that direction, sit down and make a soul-flight toward it, asking for spiritual allies to aid your search. What kind of landscape do you pass through; what encounters do you have; who accompanies you? If you have any difficulties, consult the spiritual allies in your company, asking them for help. Repeat this journey later to clarify your findings.

Rediscovering the Sacred Places

Through the medium of revelation, forgotten sacred places can re-manifest themselves.

—Nigel Pennick, *Celtic Sacred Landscapes*

What makes a place sacred? Is it some hallowed action? Is it the siting of a shrine or temple? Is it the occupation by people who have honored the spirit of that place? Although there is no part of the earth that is not intrinsically sacred in its own right, our recognition of a place's sacredness tends to rest upon what other human beings have done at that spot, what they have erected by way of memorial, what holy actions and rites they have conducted to hallow it.

Certain spots draw us to them, there is no doubt. Even if they harbor no ancient monument, if there is no story associated with their borders, we feel somehow at peace or exalted when there. It must be through just that intangible process that our ancestors discovered their own sacred places—places of natural beauty whose potency drew them again and again to spiritual exploration. Some places act as natural thresholds, junctions between this world and the other where we feel in communion with the unseen world and its inhabitants.

Some sacred places can be lost through neglect and forgetfulness; others are lost by a gross act of desacralization. But a place can be rediscovered and resacralized if we attend to the spirit of the place and learn what it is that makes that place sacred. The prospect of the resacralization of the earth is just a lofty idea for many people, but it is one that all of us can foster, in cooperation with the spirits of the earth itself.

Call to mind a place—it need not be recognized by others as a sacred place—where you have felt empowered and uplifted. Dwell upon the qualities and gifts that you associate with that site and how they make connection with your own spiritual path. Take the first opportunity you can to verify your meditation by visiting this place in person. Sense again the spirit of the place.

Pride

The proud man's arrows swiftly bring pain.

—LLYWARCH HEN, "Gorwynion"

Pride is a defensive and self-boosting current that can hard-wire our whole life. It keeps us in and everyone else out. We can hide behind it, as in a fortress, firing our poison-tipped arrows of pain against all who come against us. It elevates us above our natural stature in life, giving us a false and lofty frontage that is both illusory and dishonest. Having pride does not actually enhance any gifts that we have or make us better people; it merely enables us to look down upon other people and demean their actions.

How do we break down the fence of pride surrounding our own lives? Once we have erected defenses, they can prove hard to shift, for pride soon becomes habitual, like an addiction. Climbing down and over that fence is a humiliating capitulation that brings no applause, as we have seen when famous public figures have attempted to pick themselves up after notable humiliations. How do we deal with pride when we find it beginning to create a shell about our lives?

A little self-effacement and commitment to the welfare of others is good medicine against the creeping ivy of self-regard. Anything that forces us out from our defensive castle into the arena of the world, where we meet and interact with people, is good for our pride. Pride cannot be cured once and for all time, however. It is persistently perennial, like grass, springing up a few blades at a time. Only constant vigilance and endless patience will keep it back.

How does pride manifest itself in your life? Meditate upon ways in which it can be checked.

The Tasks of a Druid

The three tasks of a Druid: to live fully in the present; to honour
tradition and the ancestors; to hear the voice of tomorrow.

—Philip Carr-Gomm, *The Druid Renaissance*

The most difficult task is to live fully in the present. We are nearly always ahead or behind ourselves, planning the future or reminiscing and reliving the past.

For the druid, the past is a potent place, redolent of past glories and triumphs. Nostalgic for authority and respect, the druid, along with other spiritual seekers who follow an ancient path, is tempted to bathe indulgently in the rosy glow of myth and history. Yet the druid has to find ways of honoring tradition and the ancestors that truly respect them rather than enshrining and fossilizing them. And that can be done only in the *now*.

The future is such an unknown quantity that it is easier to project scenarios of doom or bliss than to hear its echoes. It is peopled by our descendants and by the sacred lore of tradition that we will have surrendered into their hands for practical use. The only way to access that future voice is to listen now.

As we meditate upon the conundrum of these druidic tasks, we find ourselves rebounding from invisible walls. The sixteenth-century German mystic Jakob Böehme knew the secret of this riddle: "He to whom time is the same as eternity, and eternity the same as time, is free of all adversity."

Those who walk the druid path and regularly walk between the worlds learn that time does not run in the otherworld: past, present, and future are all accessible in an eternal *now*. The traditions and ancestors live now; the future is seeded in the now. There can be no disrespect or sentimentality forward or backward in time without severe imbalance to the now of this present moment.

In the silence of your own grove, your own sacred space, consider your
own tasks upon the path and what they entail.

Aids to Healing

Three things bring healing at Myddfai: water, honey, and work.
—ancient Welsh triad

The healing arts of the Physicians of Myddfai (MUTH'vay) in North Wales were renowned throughout Britain. This famous family was descended from the alliance between a human man and a faery woman who came out of a lake and taught her healing skills to her children.

The source of illness lies not with physical symptoms but with some spiritual cause, and that cause must be treated if healing is to come about. Many things cause illness to constellate: not only physical predispositions such as infection, lowered resistance, bad hygiene, and physical weakness, but also messy relationships, fear, anger, neglect of vocational or emotional needs, and so on. Any good healer knows that these factors must be understood and included within any diagnosis. This means working to establish a basis of trust with the client.

The work of the client is also important. The minimum requirement of the client is that some benefit should come, and the minimum obligation is a readiness to make radical change in order to facilitate healing: we may have to leave a situation or relationship or reform beliefs, attitudes, or ways of life before healing can have its effect.

Our society embraces the concept of "self-healing." In its truest sense, self-healing is not about taking credit for health. It is about our willingness to change, our ability to receive; about taking steps by which healing can happen. Healers know that healing comes with the help of many things: plants, chemicals, human support and attention, and spiritual guidance of allies, as well as the client's predisposition to be healed. The miracle of healing lies in treating the cause of illness, not merely quelling its symptoms.

Consider a current or past illness. What factors caused the illness to constellate? Which healing agents were helpful? What changes in situation or attitude had to take place before healing could come about?

Practice

The three pillars of achievement: a daring aim, frequent practice, and plenty of failures.

—ancient Welsh triad (trans. CM)

Whatever our art or skill, achievement certainly starts with our focus upon the direction of our work. It comprises researching for whom we are working and why, discovering what effect we are trying to achieve, and having the dynamism and courage to aim high. As in archery, it is better to aim higher than you imagine your target is sited. Modest ambitions aside, the one who aims too low often never gets off the ground.

But it is by virtue of practice that we oil the wheels of our achievement. Practice is hard, unending, and often dull. Those who practice an instrument or any skill know that it means daily effort and time. However, the very nature of our habitual custom comes to our aid if we persist in practice. Very soon a new kinesthetic curve begins to be described as practice itself becomes habitual. We begin to feel that we have cracked the secret of success.

The ability to assess our failures is a precious achievement in itself. If we are very fortunate, we have tutors and coaches who point neutrally to the source of the problem. Like surgeons excising a troublesome tumor, our teachers can anatomize our failures in ways that are scarcely less painful than an operation. Failure is not the end of the line: if we can think of it as merely the tryout for the next stage of our work, we can stand on its shoulders next time we try.

What are you attempting to achieve right now? Meditate upon the trajectory of your aims; discover and implement the right amount of practice; assess past failures and what you have learned from them.

Suspension of Disbelief

People must believe what they can, and those who believe more must not be hard upon those who believe less. I doubt if you would have believed it all yourself if you hadn't seen some of it.

—GEORGE MACDONALD, *The Princess and the Goblin*

Our long-standing beliefs—whether they be about the scientific nature of reality and temporal time or about our spirituality—have a tendency to become hidebound and static, comfortable and unchallenging. When we encounter situations and things that push at the boundaries of our comfortable enclave of belief, we have two options: we can totally ignore the challenge, safe in the belief that we are right, or we can enter into a temporary suspension of disbelief while we entertain the possibility that things are other than we have believed them to be. The suspension of disbelief is something that happens every time we attend a play or a movie: we lose all sense of separation between audience and performer as we see the story unfold before us, as we become immersed in events and protagonists. At the end of a moving performance, movie, or novel, we leave the world of that story and return to our own reality again.

The strongest challenges to belief are the things that we experience: experience is a great changer and shaper of belief because it gives us pragmatic knowledge that offers tangible and physical proof, even though its workings are often mysterious to us—we know what we experienced even though it may be "unbelievable." This tells us that our perceptions are informing and changing belief. Sometimes the facts that we experience in our very body are so overwhelming that we have to enter into a suspension of disbelief, behaving "as if" they were true in order to accommodate the experience.

What is challenging your beliefs right now? Analyze the challenge using both sets of senses—physical and spiritual—to understand the experience.

The Gifts We Really Want

Be sensible of your wants, that you may be sensible of your treasures.

—Thomas Traherne, *Centuries*

At this time of year, when the commerciality of Christmas swamps sacred and seasonal considerations, we ask and are asked, "What do you want this year?" True wants are not easily satisfied by prettily wrapped parcels; they are immensities of space within us that we often block up by needs and yearnings. To consider our real wants is often too frightening.

Our wants are sharper than multibladed razors with super-wrist action, more pungent than the lemon and ylang-ylang highlights of *Excess*—"the perfume that women will seduce for"—more gripping than the latest blockbuster video with scintillating SFX. Our real wants eat holes in us: never resting, never loving, never greeting, never finding, never seeking, never ever being satisfied deep down.

Those ravenous wants define our treasures so truly. They create a Christmas list that no department store could supply: time to stop and enjoy, in a space of quietness and contentment, all the things we were put on earth to do; space to give and receive love reciprocally; grace to seek and find our spiritual joy; freedom from the tyranny of others' expectations and judgments; acceptance of ourselves as we truly are. But we can discover our true treasures and how near we actually stand to them. When we really listen to ourselves say, "I haven't time to . . . ; I never get to . . . ; I'm sick of . . . ," we come within sight of our treasury—that wealth that goes on being unvisited year after miserable year.

The miracle of self-permission and allowance, the willingness to receive, the gift of truth—these are the keys to unlock the treasury that has been open to us this long time.

Make your own list of real wants in order to find your true treasures. Make a present to yourself of one of these by turning one of the keys above.

The Prayer of Midwinter

Who is it who declaims the sun's arising?
Who is it who tells where the sun sets?

—Amergin, *Lebor Gabála Erenn*

On the shortest day of the year, at dawn, a thin finger of dawn light passes into the aperture of Brugh na Boinne (BROOG na BOIN), otherwise known as Newgrange in Ireland. This megalithic enclosure was erected long before the Celtic peoples arrived in Ireland. We can all experience the wonder of this day if we rise before dawn to trace the track of the sun's *turas* on this, the shortest day of the year.

Midwinter day gives the least period of light followed by the greatest period of darkness. For those who watched the heavens in ancient times, it must have seemed as if the sun were standing still or diminishing entirely. Nearly every culture has its own special celebrations to encourage the light on this day. Here is one that we can perform.

Stand in the sunlight at midday, facing the sun, and tune your heart to the season of winter. If a song of thanksgiving rises in you, utter it. Now turn and face your shadow: this is the longest it can be at midday, far longer than it was at the autumn equinox. Consider the deeds of your life, the extent to which the shadow of your own influence has fallen upon the earth. Upon whom has it fallen? How has your own *turas* affected the world in which you live? Turn once more to the sun and draw the sunlight deeply and thankfully into your body; feel it permeating your being. Be aware of the partnership between yourself and the vitality of life itself.

Spend some time silently meditating upon the light in darkness: be aware of the potentialities of light that lie within the darkness; pray to become aware of the potentialities within your own soul, which are vaster and more mysterious than your manifest life.

Commune with the shortest day and longest night, making your own prayer as suggested above.

Waiting for a Birth

The world has tilted far
from the sun, from colour and juice. . . .
I am waiting for a birth that will change everything.

—HILARY LLEWELLYN-WILLIAMS, *The Tree Calendar*

The rebirth of the sun begins on this day, though it seems as short and dark as the previous ones. Although we prepare for the holiday season, there is another urgency in us—to consciously experience the mysterious change that comes over the world at this time, affecting all creatures.

We do indeed wait for "a birth that will change everything" and give us joy and fresh hope. For Christians this sense of waiting has its own special manifestation in the person of Jesus Christ and his Christmas birthday. But many earlier societies have also celebrated the birth of their special Revealer at this time, tuning into the implicit urgency for change and rebirth. Festivals of lights and stories of the triumph of light over darkness are celebrated and told. Our current bustle to conclude midwinter holiday preparations is like the mother's last-minute bustle to make things ready for the baby's birth.

But what waits to be born in us at this time of year? It is a glorious, heroic light that blazes forth with the fierce directness of an innocence that we need now. It is a deep renewal in our lives that we crave; it is the rebirth of innate qualities that will not fail or become slothful or be deterred by obstacles, that will be responsive and true, honest and enduring, bright and shining.

In the busy, celebratory days to come, take time to acknowledge this very necessary rebirth that is happening within ourselves: time to draw apart and be still, to clear a space wherein we can be attentive to the change that is happening within us at the fulcrum of the year.

Meditate upon what needs to be reborn in your own life. Which qualities, skills, and talents bring light and hope into your life?

House Blessing

May God bless the dwelling,
Each stone and beam and stave,
All food and drink and coverings,
May health to you be always here.

—traditional Scots Gaelic blessing at Hogmanay

The heart of winter is a time of homecoming and cessation of travel. We return home, ostensibly to celebrate the holiday with our family, but actually to attend to the domestic shrine that is our family home. Western spiritual culture has tended to emphasize the importance of the temple, church, or place of spiritual gathering over the domestic shrine, but in truth the home is the primary abode of Spirit; if Spirit dwells not there, there is certainly no use seeking for it in other places.

The householder is a true priest or priestess who maintains the holiness of the hearth and gives all guests the welcome of the home's indwelling spiritual presence. As guests gather or are expected, the householder can ritually acknowledge the house as a shrine of blessing by spiritually cleaning it in preparation for holy days ("holidays"). This may entail going about the house with a bowl of burning aromatic herbs or a flame-warmed dish of sweet oils to cleanse the house-space of any worries, arguments, sorrows, or hidden fears. With intentioned prayer, the householder can make all clean and clear again.

After the cleaning comes the hallowing or blessing of the house. Kindle your hearth, if you have a fireplace (see 5 October), or light your heater or a candle if you have not. Be aware of the heart of the house as a beating, living, spiritual presence. Now, leaving the candle or flame at the hearth, kindle a fresh candle and take it throughout your house. Sing a wordless song of blessing. Now the spirit of your home can welcome all guests who come within its walls, that they might share in the blessing that is yours.

Bless your own house as suggested.

Sacred Life

Everything that lives is holy.

—WILLIAM BLAKE,
"The Marriage of Heaven and Hell"

For many hundreds of years, the false tale that whatever is alive is evil has been told: this tale has been told from fear and denial, from pain and rejection, as a way of explaining why things go wrong and why perfection cannot be expected. Many people regard the living world as a predominantly evil place, full of beings of whom we should be suspicious. For such people, the only good place, the only good beings are in heaven. Living defensively in the eye of evil is not a happy way to live. Fear and suspicion darken everything with a sad pall.

The opposite view sees all life as worthy of respect, as potentially able to achieve its fullest stature. Of course, not every being alive reaches its potential; but then neither does it sink into irredeemable iniquity. Entertaining the possibility of all things living being able to achieve their potential of holiness is a powerful and supportive way to live. But, like all life-ways, even this view can be abused: when we live as though no harm could come, we are foolish rather than innocent.

Life is a sacred gift that all beings receive. It is the *manner* of our living that makes all the difference. The way in which we relate to other living beings encourages them to change the world for good or violate the world for ill; the way in which we spend our lives illuminates or darkens those around us. But if we are not aware of the sacred potential in each living being, if we do not acknowledge it and respect it, we may become active agents of the soul's darkening. Everything that lives is holy because it is an abiding place of Spirit; every body is a home where the sacred gifts of Spirit may be born anew.

Contemplate the living beings with whom you are in contact—not just human beings but other living beings of nature as well. Hold each of them in your heart and acknowledge their sacred gift.

The Soul's Beloved

The only beloved is the living mystery itself.

—KATHLEEN RAINE, *The Lion's Mouth*

The incarnation of love in our lives is a special miracle. Our capacity to recognize and receive love is closely associated with the soul's beloved—the spiritual being whom our soul recognizes as supreme. The soul's beloved is not an earthly or human lover that we may have—although we may look for the features of the spiritual form in the human person; it is a spirit. For followers of defined religious paths, this figure will be the lord, lady, or spirit from whom spiritual revelation flows; and this figure will be central to their prayers and practices. Religious iconography may provide specific, traditional images of this figure, or the practitioner may have his own special insight into the appearance of his soul's beloved.

There are now many among us without any formalized spiritual path, people who are still traveling between the rejected images of childhood faith and the unknown potentialities of their soul's country. They may be unaware of any living mystery. This is nothing less than the inapprehensible glory and splendor of spirit that is both formless and has many forms, that is immanent and transcendent, known and unknown to our experience.

The conscious awareness of the soul's beloved is not a continuous awareness for the majority of people: it is fleeting, glancing, glorious, exciting, rapturous. The metaphors we draw upon to describe the feelings and perceptions that we have of this beloved are not always human: sometimes a beautiful animal, a shining lamp, a great tree, a planet, a complex pattern, or a subtle music in the soul is a true reflection of the mystery that we each experience.

Contemplate your soul's beloved. Even though you may have no form or name for that beloved, be still and ask your soul to help you share this living mystery.

The King of All Birds

The wren, the wren, the king of all birds
On St. Stephen's Day was caught in the furze,
Although he is little, his family is great
So rise up, good people, and give us a treat.

—"The Wren Song," traditional Irish lay

The old Celtic custom of hunting for the wren, killing it, and passing it around the village in a holly-bush cage in return for money, food, or drink continues in Ireland on this December day, although a wren is no longer killed. Instead, wren-boys take an empty decorated wren-cage around their neighborhood and beg for treats. The origins of this custom are lost to us, but we may conjecture. A folk story common across Europe tells how the birds had a battle to see who would be their king. The contest required all the birds to fly into the sky and see how near they could get to the sun. As all the birds climbed higher, only the eagle could be seen soaring above the others on its powerful wings. It loudly claimed the kingship, asserting that it had risen higher than the rest. Then a little voice cried out from its back, "But I am higher even than you!" It was the tiny wren, who was then made king of all birds.

The wren, or *dreolan,* is the druid's bird, and its utterances and cries were once the subject of augury and divination by the ovates (or druidic seers). The oracular bird was clearly important to them and was protected throughout the year. Indeed, it is still thought to be unlucky to harm a wren. The sacrifice of living beings is very distasteful to us now, but our ancestors made offerings of precious life to create bridges between this world and the otherworld at certain times. The death and honoring of the wren seems to be inextricably associated with the returning of the sun: a rite of propitiation and celebration at once, a case of "the king is dead, long live the king!"

Set aside, from your winter riches, your own charitable offering.

Being Human

"What is the thing the Creator never saw, that kings see but seldom, and that I see every day?" The Creator never saw another the same as his self, kings are scarce and see each other seldom, but I see my own kind every day—other folk like myself.

—Scots Gaelic riddle (trans. CM)

During the twelve days of Christmas, a Lord of Misrule was appointed to create games, riddles, and forfeits to amuse the company. (See 6 January.) The riddle above, with its witty answer, is a typical brain-teaser. This holiday time of gathering offers us the opportunity to consider what it is to be human. Being human does not keep us from kinship with other animals: the same life passes through our veins, we share the same ability to perceive with the senses, and our bodies die and decay in the same way. What makes us different from animals is our self-awareness and our ability to use our minds in complex and sophisticated ways; our application of language; our ability to record information outside our memories.

There are many stories of deities who have aspired to the human condition, gods and goddesses who have purposely chosen the gifts of mortality in order to share and experientially understand what it is to be human. Within this extraordinary interchange, the divine becomes briefly human, just as through our spiritual striving we attempt to understand the gifts of immortality.

This wonderful reciprocation of the earthly and otherworldly realms seems to be part of the mystery that underlies the depths of midwinter, a season that was understood in the ancient world to be the time when sacred beings incarnated, to be numbered among the peoples of the earth, to understand the gifts of being human. If our human state is so much sought after, how much more precious seems our mortality and its many gifts!

What, for you, are the gifts of being human?

The Chalice of Remembrance

And when the circling year comes round,
And Christmas snows have wrapt the ground. . .
Take the cup, and drink the wine,
"Drinc heil!"—as I to thee and thine.

—John Sobieski Stuart,
"With an Antique Crystal Cup and Ring"

When death or accident befalls us at times of holiday, it is very difficult to re-engage with the general celebration. Some people choose to go away at this season rather than to relive difficult memories that accompany this time. Even the angle of the light or the weather, the carols and songs, the smell of rich foods can enhance the memory of loss. It seems altogether easier to go away somewhere without memories than force a cheerful countenance or dampen the celebrations of others.

This process of anniversarial grieving is not widely understood: family and friends may attempt to draw the bereaved out of her grieving solitude into the heart of the jollification, baffled and perhaps angry at the lack of response to their generosity. Grief and loss are not processes that can be hurried, however; the grieving one cannot "pull herself together" or to order.

A bridge of hope and connection can be erected on the anniversary by a simple ritual known as the chalice of remembrance. A liquid-filled glass that all present can drink from is set in front of a photograph or emblem that represents the dead person. Then all present speak simply and directly to the dead person, drinking to him but leaving a little of the liquid so that the last drink belongs to him. The remaining liquid is left overnight with a candle burning and then poured out upon the earth the next morning. In this way, the anniversary is marked, the mourning shared, and the circle of love reunited.

Meditate upon other ritual acts that might be used to help mark grief and loss in ways that bring integration to the bereaved.

Heart's Desire

You shall receive whatever gift you may name, as far as wind
dries, rain wets, sun revolves; as far as sea encircles and earth
extends.

—Culhwch and Olwen, from *The Mabinogian* (trans. CM)

How many times since childhood have we pondered our heart's desire? When we were young, we grasped the notion of bountiful giving and the granting of wishes very easily from the folk and faery stories that we read. In our growing up, we began to struggle against the denial of heart's desire. As adults, most of us have given over even contemplating it.

The heart's desire is not an illusory or unachievable ambition if we can suspend our adult disbelief. (See 19 December.) The true heart's desire is an integral potentiality, a germinated seed waiting to manifest. So what prevents us from achieving it? Our lives may be littered with unresolved and undeveloped wishes, all of which block the way to our true heart's desire. If we are to achieve the core of our wish, we must first rescind and cancel our immature wishes—unless, of course, we still wish to grow a monkey's tail, obtain a rocking horse, drive a steam engine, or marry Elvis Presley! We must cancel our old and immature wishes by calling them back and revoking them, along with any other idle wishes we may have uttered and since forgotten. Then the way stands clear.

If we can commune deeply upon our true heart's desire, rather than upon our fantasies, if we can envision it with every cell of our body and call to it, then we send a true song to make the pathway between ourselves and our heart's desire.

What is your heart's desire? Which former wishes are preventing you
from attaining it? Cancel them, as suggested above.

~ 30 December ~

Gathering in the Year

It is at the year's end that the fisherman tells of his fishing.

—Scots Gaelic proverb

The end of the calendar year is the time when we traditionally look forward and make good resolutions for the coming year. But before we can do that, we need also to make a summation of the past year's achievements and mistakes so that we have a sense of the year's shape. It may be helpful to wind the year backward, retracing our steps from November back to January. As we go backward, month by month, we can consider the following questions: What was the major theme of this month? Which events made the greatest impression on my life? What did I achieve? What mistakes do I regret? The point is not to indulge in blame and guilt but to neutrally survey our findings.

Now look back over the year as a whole and make a summation of its overall pattern and effect upon you. What has this year meant in real terms to you? How has it changed the world? Which new figures and influences have come into your life?

Now for the third part of this review. Looking at the year just past, move forward from January to December, asking these questions about each month: What seeds were sown in this month that affect me now? What wisdom have I learned? Which patterns and connections are poised to continue unfolding in the year ahead? Which obstructing or unhelpful aspects of my own behavior need to change? Having made our review, we can now consider the year ahead and lay down pathways of resolution and intention that will help guide our steps.

Make your review of the year as suggested above.

Hogmanay

I am now come to your country,
Renewing the duty of Hogmanay;
Of its mysteries, what need I tell?
It began in the time of our ancestors.

—Scots Gaelic song of Hogmanay (trans. CM)

The festival of Hogmanay—a word whose origins are lost—is celebrated in Scotland every New Year's Eve. A festival that outshines Christmas even today, Hogmanay is celebrated with vigor by every Scot. Rich food and strong drink are abundant; shining music and lively dancing are enjoyed. The custom of first-footing—of receiving with celebration the first guest across the threshold after the stroke of midnight—is still practiced. According to tradition, the first-footer should be a dark-haired person from outside the household who is able to bring good fortune to the house: healthy, young, and vigorous people are particularly welcomed. The first-footer brings a "handsel" (or a token of good fortune) to the household. This is usually fuel, food, or a bottle of whisky. The first-footer is then hospitably welcomed and given a gift, usually joining in the party that runs until the small hours of the morning.

The magical turning of the old used-up year into a fresh new one has little to do with chronology and much to do with the hope of new beginnings and all that they bring. The old year can bring no more opportunities to us, but we can give it a good send-off with a party that simultaneously welcomes the new possibilities ahead. If the celebrations of this evening become sometimes riotous or rowdy, it is worth remembering that the mysterious crack between one year and another is best leaped rather than crawled over! In this time between worlds and times, nothing is as orderly as normal. It is a time to celebrate life and the return of the sun from its darkest, deepest depths.

Welcome the new year over your threshold and see the old year out with some fancy footwork and good cheer!

JANUARY

Month of January—smoky is the vale;
Weary the wine-bearer; strolling the minstrel;
Lean the cow; seldom the hum of the bee.
                                        —anon. Welsh poem

January sees the growing of the cold. This month's meditation themes include the soul's circuit, beginnings and approaches, the gifts of youth, mediators, mutual care and separateness, and clarity.

The New Year

Wind from the West, fish and bread;
Wind from the North, cold and flaying;
Wind from the East, snow on the hills;
Wind from the South, fruit on trees.

—Scots new year weather omen

New Year's Day is a time of reading the omens for a fresh beginning. It is widely held that the first twelve days of the year will reveal the disposition of the weather for the year ahead. This is a good day to go for a long walk, to divine the possibilities of the year ahead in a very simple way.

Before you set off on your walk, stop and tune your intentions to the unfolding year ahead; sense the pathway of the year that stands ready before you. Now begin your walk, attentive to everything that is about you, including the mythscape, story, folklore, and feeling of the land. Keeping the year ahead in your consciousness, allow your attention to widen to include everything about you. If you come across something that draws your attention with urgent filaments of greeting—it might be the sudden movement of a bird, the beauty of a patch of moss, the intensity of the light through trees—stop and be attentive to what caught your attention.

Listen and attend to the greeting and intuitively reach out for and feel its meaning—a meaning that might not be experienced in words or even in sound but may come to you as a subtle understanding. Appreciate it, note it, and then pass on. Keep repeating this throughout your walk until you have had twelve such experiences. Each time stop, attend, and intuit (without fishing for a rational explanation) why your attention has been engaged. Then return home and review the omens in the order you experienced them, relating them successively to the months of the year. Next New Year's Eve you can check your findings.

Take a walk as suggested above.

The Meaning Beneath the Meaning

The journey we begin as we answer the call is long, and filled with all that we have been and all that we will become.

—CAIRISTÍONA WORTHINGTON, Modron of the
Order of Bards, Ovates, and Druids

Our spiritual journey leads us through many stations of experience. We feel the need to travel in company with others: we join churches, courses, movements, and groups, learning all that we can from their leaders and exponents. Sometimes sharing the journey is helpful and supportive to our unique spiritual call; other times it is very dissatisfying, causing us to give up and continue our journey elsewhere. This period of spiritual nomadism can be lengthy, as we move from place to place, from religious movement to spiritual group in search of the meaning beneath the meaning.

It is good to realize early on that whatever is spiritually important to us must be identified and made use of, not discarded later in the journey because it does not "fit" our current spiritual practice. It is in the experiences that we have along our way that our spirituality grows and matures. Dancing, catching leaves, meditating in the bath, praying while singing, walking in the countryside—all these are ways to honor Spirit.

In order to live our spiritual path, we cannot leave out *any* part of ourselves or our experience: every single bit of who we are and what we do has to be included. It is in recognizing the mystic we always were rather than in mimicking the pious practices of our faith that we discover the meaning beneath the meaning which has always been calling us.

What causes you to be aware of the meaning beneath the meaning? Begin to incorporate your own innate spiritual responses into your daily practice.

The Pledge of Passion

And Findabair used to lay her hand on every goblet and every cup for Ferdiad, because he was her beloved and chosen wooer.

—*Taín Bó Cuailgne*, early Irish text

The ancient Celtic and Germanic worlds shared the custom of pledging the cup of hospitality to guests. The woman of the house would greet the leader of a company with the guest cup. In certain circumstances, eligible women took the opportunity presented by this hospitable action to check out the guests. Findabair (FIN'a-ba), the daughter of Queen Maeve of Connacht, who was besotted with the hero Ferdiad, evidently took every opportunity to be close to him, using the old custom of hospitality to welcome him home from combat. It is clear that the offering of the guest cup could be an erotic invitation that might, or might not, lead to marriage.

Over the pledged cup, alcohol and sexual desire created their own ferment of intoxication, overflowing mundane barriers of reserve and opening up the gateway to intimate encounter. In similar fashion, it is common today for future partners to meet each other over the holiday season at parties and gatherings.

The love that is pledged at this time is whirlwind and generally physical and nonverbal. There is a kind of ritual alchemy of attraction at work that is intensified within the ceremonial cup of the season. And though this may not be the rational and considered love of other seasons, its passion carries a forceful truth that fixes the unspoken pledge at a deep level of promise.

The pledging of passion is not the preserve of the young alone; passion can arise at any age, in any circumstance, when we least expect it. No one is immune to the kindling sparks of passion that burn at certain meetings.

Pledge your passion to your beloved and welcome ecstasy back into your relationship.

～ 4 JANUARY ～

Restoring the Enchantment

Without the enchantment to kindle the beckoning flame of mystery and wonder, we lose touch with the on-going story of the soul.
—CAITLÍN AND JOHN MATTHEWS, *The Little Book of Celtic Wisdom*

The ancient bards of Britain maintained "perpetual choirs of song" that kept the land harmoniously connected and whole. As long as there was one voice, the land and its inhabitants remained within the enchantment. We now think of enchantment as a malign magical spell, but the original meaning of "to enchant" was "to infuse with song," which is what the ancient choirs of song once did, maintaining the interconnection between this world and the otherworld. When awareness of this sacred link is severed, we lose the enchantment and fall into a sorry condition of disconnection.

Disenchantment happens to us all, taking the familiar forms of depressive illness, addictive behavior, and malaise from which there seems no escape. It is important to act quickly when these states begin to set in, to realize that our soul's story is out of phase with its sacred connection.

How can the soul or the world be re-enchanted once it has lost the enchantment? Only by returning to the story of the soul and retelling it up to the point of fracture; only by placing our own story within the context of the greater song. When Myrddin (MER'thyn), now known as Merlin, is exposed to the carnage of battle, he runs mad through the forest. Many try to calm him and bring him back to society, but only when the Welsh poet Taliesin (Tal-ee-ESS'in) comes and sits with him does Myrddin respond, asking the odd question, "Why do we have weather?" This seemingly trivial query is all that Taliesin needs to help his friend. He begins to recite the creation of the world. At the end of Taliesin's recital, Myrddin is restored as the sacred context of his story is given back to him.

Consider the enchantment that keeps your soul's story on track.

The People of the Gift

Give humble respect to each of the wise people of the gift, for honour is due to them.

—*The Book of the O'Connor Don,* Irish text (trans. CM)

In Celtic society, the people of the gift—the *aos dana* (EES DAH'na), or artists—were given the kind of respect that we now accord to great religious leaders, political leaders, actors, and singers. They were honored because they had the power to go beyond this world, to commune with otherworldly powers and to mediate their inspiration to the community. Respect was given because they represented the unseen reality to our world in a process of mediation.

In our society, the ability to convey sacred reality in living forms has become the preserve of the religious painter, poet, or performer, and only in the highest forms of aesthetic appreciation do we see a comparable attempt to convey the beautiful and simple truths of the sacred. Only when performers and artists come close to the heart of the mystery of their craft do they feel the impinging power of the sacred. Those whom we universally regard as especially gifted, because of their ability to convey something beyond the music, the script, or whatever art form corresponds to their skill, have humility and regard for their sacred art. But today the respect that is due to the *gift* is often accorded solely to the artist and appropriated by her as a personal honor.

People of gifted vision are generally unable to live by their art because so few people are able to apprehend and receive the gift. It is not a question of money but of our interest in and involvement with the gift, with the art itself. This alone creates a climate wherein the gift of the otherworld can be received and welcomed, and true respect for the people of the gift can flourish once again.

Meditate upon your personal relationship with sacred gifts of art, music, performance. Your respect changes everything.

Lord of Misrule

Now, now the mirth comes
With the cake full of plums,
Where Beane's the King of the sport here;
Besides we must know,
The Pea also
Must revell, as Queene, in the Court here.
—Robert Herrick, "Twelfth Night"

The Lord of Misrule governed the celebrations of this January day. He was appointed from the company by drawing the slice of cake with the bean in it and would devise games and forfeits for the company.

The Lord of Misrule governs in the holidays that are outside temporal time, when misrule (or disorder), revelry, and games take the place of order, sobriety, and work. The function of misrule is the mixing up of one reality with another. Within the resultant confusion, we enter the clown's world wherein the proud are humbled, the usual becomes the unusual, the tight-lipped are made to laugh, and the tight-fisted are made to pay up. Societies that do not have the safety valve of seasonal misrule become monolithic, dour, and life-denying.

Lords and Ladies of Misrule are supreme magicians who bring good cheer through a healthy mockery of institutions, both loved and hated. The ability to laugh at what we hold dear is not disrespectful: if we cannot take a joke about precious things, we do not share the divine sense of humor that rules the universe and is probably responsible for life itself. The opportunity to laugh at what we fear is god-given, since it releases us from the shackles of fear itself and lessens fear's powerful hold over us.

The ones who govern the Court of Misrule are truly mediators of freedom, to whom we owe considerable respect and not a few custard pies!

Overturn your usual customs. Do something uncharacteristic. By no means do any meditation today! Find your own freedom instead.

~ 7 January ~

Traveling to Wisdom

I travelled over the earth
Before I became a learned person.
I have travelled, I have made a circuit,
I have slept in a hundred islands, dwelt in a hundred cities.
—TALIESIN, "Câd Goddeu" (trans. CM)

The Welsh poet Taliesin speaks here of his spiritual peregrinations—
not only his physical travels but also his soul's circuit before it became
incarnated in its present form. The way to spiritual maturity is through
personal and interactive experience. We travel to wisdom along the
roads that our soul is drawn to explore, eventually evolving a map that
we begin to understand. Even within formal religions this journey
must take place; otherwise, spiritual stasis sets in.

In the old language of craftspeople, there are three aspects to the spiritual path: first we are the apprentice, painstakingly learning the basics
of our craft; then we become journeymen, trained apprentices who are
able to travel from place to place practicing our craft; finally we become
masters of our craft and are honored as repositories of skill. Our journey
to wisdom, to a mature spirit, must go through all three phases. And
even when we have arrived spiritually, we face the devastating revelation
that the spiritual path is just that—a path, not a destination.

This is a lonely realization for many, yet we are not unaccompanied
on our path. Upon it we encounter others who are traveling our way,
some of whom will become close personal friends because they are
spiritual kindred. These encounters and spiritual friendships mold our
understandings as soul calls to soul, bringing new insights and concepts. By working with such friends, we realize the validity of our journey, we absorb new concepts that modify our own, we become more
practical and less theoretical, and we change and grow in spirit.

Draw an overview map of your own spiritual progress, noting signifi-
cant features and encounters that have helped mature your soul.

The Well at World's End

Those who in youth and childhood wander alone in woods and wild
places, ever after carry in their hearts a secret well of quietness
and . . . they always long for rest and to get away from the noise
and rumour of the world.

—W. B. YEATS, *Letters*

The Well at World's End is one of those secret places of restoration, healing, and beauty that are sought in faery stories. To carry its refreshing waters, we have to overcome obstacles in our path, identify and ask the help of allies who may not be human, and purify ourselves in order that we may be worthy to receive the immortal draught.

The surest doorway to the secret threshold between the worlds lies hidden deep in our experience of childhood. Search your memory for the sweet, essential time of childhood play when the universe was in your grasp: when the dammed-up stream behind your house became a river in flood, when your own body became the horse that you (now rider too) intrepidly rode, snorting and stamping along the path. Remember the dappled jungles of undergrowth wherein toy figures became heroic in their adventures, battling with mighty ants. Recall the stories that you told yourself, reading the landscape with masterful childhood senses that instinctively knew the way between the worlds.

Those stories, feelings, and perceptions are your childhood passport to the realms of the Well at World's End. Those magical waters have power to revoke the march of mortality and to invoke the wild places of the heart. They recall to you the allies that you made when you played unselfconsciously—allies that you have ignored through lack of trust and because you have "put away childish things." When you long to rest from the whirling everyday world, remember your own Well at World's End and drink deeply of its waters.

Recall your childhood allies. (These might be places, toys, books, games,
friends, animals.) Give them thanks for their companionship.

The Kindness of Kindred

Natural kindly human instincts, whose earth-born rudiments exist-
ing among animals and birds, have come to us from Nature herself.
—JOHN COWPER POWYS, *Obstinate Cymric*

The kindness imputed to nature by the writer J. C. Powys might be disputed by those who find her "red in tooth and claw" in a variety of ways, as she turns the seasons and the weather without warning and creates destruction. Yet nature is a mother who teaches all species to interrelate with each other. Kindness is nothing less than the recognition and acknowledge of our kinship with other beings, extending beyond humankind to embrace all that is. Kindness includes all and is cooperative. Kindness enables recognition of kinship in others.

Nature's real beneficence is found not in "random acts of kindness" patronizingly meted out to the web of life but in an ordered dispensation wherein all things touch, meet, and mingle. Kindness, for nature, does not mean the cozy preservation of one life at the expense of all; it is an instinctive cooperation with the larger web of life. Those beings who choose to live outside this law are no longer kindred with life—a fact that human beings would do well to remember if we wish to continue!

Is there someone or something toward whom you find it hard to be kind? What is it that severs kinship between you? How can true kinship be restored?

Reconciliation

Two men can meet quicker than two mountains ever.
—Welsh proverb (trans. CM)

When we have fallen out with friends or colleagues, the way back to reconciliation can seem worlds away. Pride and hurt can cause us to decide that the first approach will never come from our side, but the same sentiments are often experienced by the other party.

To arrive at reconciliation, we may have to explore the avenues of negotiation and compromise. If we can find a sensible and eloquent go-between who can be trusted not to fan the flames of dispute, then the first approaches can be taken by this means. If we have no such go-between, then we have to open negotiations on our own behalf. With tact and sensitivity, we can invite the other party to meet with us on neutral ground, to discuss the causes of dispute and each other's views—an invitation to come down from the lofty heights of separation and agree on a truce.

The aim is not to shame or coerce the other into capitulation, but to allow both parties to bring their differences to the light of day so that they may be seen as they really are, rather than as they are emotionally experienced. This perspective may be difficult to maintain, especially if anger or grief is involved. It may be that the discussion must be carried on through letters, if emotions are too raw.

While both parties are in the healing stage, it is often beneficial to perform some common act together—something that benefits neither party directly but is undertaken for the common benefit of others, such as clearing a stream of rubbish or giving a few hours to a community project. Such acts provide a mutual focus that helps to heal division.

With whom do you wish to be reconciled? If your disagreement is of long standing, write a letter offering to close the gap.

Recognizing the Potential

Three things that should not be despised: a ragged young man, a shaggy filly, and a freckled-legged girl.

—Scots Gaelic triad

The ability to foster potential and encourage the young is one of the great gifts of a mature individual. It gives power and hope to the as-yet-undeveloped soul struggling to find its place in life. When we invest interest and encouragement in someone, we invest her with a level of trust, a belief in herself that may give her the power to blossom and mature in wonderful ways. Every act of encouragement must be sensitively judged, however, for if we invest *too much* hope in people, our expectations become a burden that may cause them to falter.

The recognition of potential is something that all ages need, if we are to flourish. This is especially true for those souls who have been discouraged in their early life or whose potential has been blocked by unfortunate circumstances. The soul damage to people who have been taught to despise their own potential is incalculable; they can speak only slightingly of themselves and their achievements. They need careful, steady encouragement to remind them of their true worth and to reintegrate the gifts that they were born with but that were stolen by the insensitive and manipulative actions of others.

The ragged young man may yet make good, the shaggy-haired filly may win uncounted races, and the freckled-legged girl may turn into a beauty without help and encouragement; but if the beholder can recognize the potential of each, the hidden gifts may develop in a more assured way.

Without judging by appearances, look for the potential in those you meet.

The Twice-Born

To dare the incarnation; to take the road in silence.
To know the ascension; to will the resurrection.
The song shimmers in the golden people.

—AIDAN ANDREW DUN, *Vale Royal*

There comes a stage upon our spiritual path when we stand at the threshold of serious commitment: Do we enter into the unknown mysteries of the deeper way or remain on the safe, known pathway? This process of going within is called "initiation," and the one who enters within is called the "initiate." This is a scary threshold to cross because no one can share the experience or explain it in advance.

Within the Celtic tradition, there have been people in every generation who have gone consenting to the threshold of initiation in order to learn from and be taught by the teachers who are no longer incarnate. It is they who have kept open the ways and been the mediators of the mysteries. Their commitment and avowal of intention to serve their spiritual tradition may have been hidden, arrived at in solitude and struggle, but they have stretched out their hands to the ancestral teachers nonetheless and become the "twice-born"—initiates who have been born anew into the life that is beyond physical existence.

The twice-born, like the bards and druids of old, access the help of spiritual guardians for whom time and space are no obstacle. Over many centuries, to the mundane eye, they have arisen and disappeared, quietly stating and living the ancient wisdoms. These courageous wisdom-keepers have in turn become teachers for the next generation of seekers.

So the old songs have become new: not only by studying and researching, but by crossing the boundary between the worlds and entering into direct, living relationship with the mystery of the ancestral wisdom.

Which initiatory thresholds have you encountered in your life?

The Embrace of Heaven and Earth

The stars speak through the stones. Light shines in the densest matter. Earth and heaven are one. Our physical beings and our heavenly souls are united in the Mystery of Being.
—PHILIP CARR-GOMM, *The Druid Tradition*

The druidic tradition is deeply acquainted with the interrelationship of the apparent and unseen worlds. This interrelational understanding certainly did not originate with the druids, but it was apparent to the earlier megalithic peoples whose stone circles and monuments are now popularly assigned to the druids. If you have ever stood within such a stone circle at night, the relationship between stone and star becomes immediately apparent: in earlier times, when street lighting did not pollute the night sky, the most immediate feature would have been the dazzling stellar canopy overhead. It is unfortunate that our own dazzling technology has diminished the stars with its emissions.

Even nonscientific people suspect that we are part of something greater and more complex than a merely physical universe. It is not only the natural world that speaks to us of an integral but unseen relationship, but also the everyday mystical experiences that elevate us to spiritual insight. In this, we are no different from the deep ancestors of prehistory. Scientists today discern the heavens with more far-reaching sight than ever the druids could achieve, yet many still fail to see the stars within the stones or the light within matter. The continual embrace of heaven and earth surrounds us all, if we become still enough to perceive it.

Go out and look at the stars. As you look up, meditate upon the connection between the matter in your body and the matter in the stars.

Merlin's Isle

She is not any common Earth,
Water or Wood or Air,
But Merlin's Isle of Gramarye,
Where you and I will fare.

—RUDYARD KIPLING, "Puck's Song"

Merlin trains King Arthur to be a worthy king, but long before Arthur passes to Avalon, Merlin retires from his role as prophet and adviser to a tower that has seventy doors and windows. From which he can see the whole realm and maintain his guardianship. It is for this reason that the name Clas Myrddin (KLAS MER'thyn) was given to the island of Britain, for it falls under his watchful protection.

Many countries have a secret, hidden, or poetic name that describes the true nature of the land in a deep, mythic way. When wearing this name, the country becomes a realm that somehow lies beyond its geographical location and given name, leading us into a hinterland that can be crossed only in dreams and visions, perceived only in stories and legends. Something in our hearts speaks to us of the mythic reality of Merlin's Isle, a place that yet abides.

Beneath the history of every country there is a *gramarye*—a secret magical teaching—to be learned: the lore, the stories, the enchantments that only the land can teach us. It is so in Merlin's Isle. There the *gramarye* is written not in the common elements but in their subtle counterparts, which are perceivable at dawn and twilight, at the between-times when color and light merge into sound and distance. Within the folded hills, by the singing streams, deep in the secret hollows, Merlin keeps his school; and there, under his intimate tutelage, we can read the book of nature and of story and know our own land's *gramarye*.

What are the rudiments of your own land's gramarye? Which figures in story and legend are associated with the keeping of your country's secret wisdom and power?

Mediating the Primal

A culture that doesn't have . . . a shaman, that doesn't therefore have access to the potencies of the beginning, is in trouble.
—JOHN MORIARTY, *Turtle Was Gone a Long Time*

The ability to access the primal powers of life, to connect with them and mediate them, is the task of the shaman. Today most of us have forgotten to honor (or even recognize) the primal powers of life. Life is merely the stream of existence in which each of us swims. We move along this stream largely unaware of the larger reality in which we are involved.

The shaman stands at the threshold between the worlds with the duty of honoring the powers of both apparent and unseen worlds. On the druid path, this role is fulfilled by the *ovate:* the vision-seer who walks between the worlds in order to bring the apparent world into harmony with the unseen world.

Without such mediators, who are aware of the primal otherworld, our own world can become disconnected from the larger harmony. A shaman's work is primarily healing the fractures that separate our world from the other so that power can once more flow; this task is performed for people, animals, plants, and places.

The potent, primal world of beginnings is potentially accessible to all of us by virtue of the life within our veins. The spiral ladder of DNA is itself a pathway of life, a circuit of power connected to the primal source of life from which we can consciously draw the healing that we need. But we still need our shamans—our mediators and healers— who can pass beyond physical boundaries to effect the work of reconnection; we need them to maintain an embassy at the threshold of the worlds so that the ways of negotiating remain open.

Meditate upon the source of primal life. How are your body and soul connected to this source? By what evidence do you know this?

Returning to Work

From midwinter's burrow,
Send light down the furrow.
Come forth, hidden sun,
For the year's work's begun!

—Caitlín Matthews,
"Incantation for Plough Monday"

The first Monday after Twelfth Night was called Plough Monday in earlier centuries: the day on which farm laborers returned to work and the plow was honored and paraded around the village. During this week when many people have returned to employment after the holidays, it is easy to either become mindlessly immersed in work or to remain detached from it (depending on how committed we are to our job). For many of us, work is a means to an end rather than a craft or profession that we undertook purposefully and in which we actively delight. How can we return to our work with better spirit?

The customs of Plough Monday offer suggestions that can help reinvest both our work and our workplace with fresh interest and vigor. Meditate upon the nature of your work. What tool or object is emblematic of it? (If you use computers, this might be a pen and paper; if you work on the land, this might be a plant.) Whatever your actual work, what small object might represent it ritually? What is the finished product or effect of your work?

On the day when you must return to work after a period of rest, spend some time in meditation with the emblem of your work enshrined and honored before you: contemplate it and the outcome or final result of your work (even if this is shared by many employees). Make your own dedication to the work of your hands and ask for a blessing upon it.

Create a personalized and suitable ritual of your own based on the suggestions above.

~ 17 January ~

Leaving Home

Dark is yonder town
Dark are those within
You are the brown swan
Going within fearlessly.

—Scots Gaelic blessing for
a child leaving home

The moment comes in every parent's life when his child is launched on the world for the very first time: a moment fraught with hope, fear, and expectation for both child and parent. The invocation given above offers clues to the kind of preparations that can pave the way for the one who is leaving. Chief among these is a self-esteem that comes from the recognition—by others and self—of one's innate qualities, those strengths that every young person has. Second comes the appeal to and recognition of the role models that inspire the one leaving, that encourage and sustain her in times of adversity. Third is the blessing that comes from the heart of the parent to rest upon the child.

In Celtic folklore, the child about to leave home asks the parent for a blessing. The formulaic reply to this request is, "You can have a mother's blessing and half a bannock [loaf] or a mother's curse and a whole bannock." The child who asks for the latter usually does not fare well, but the child who asks for half the bannock is truly blessed. So it is in our own times, when so many children feel driven out by their parents: their leaving is not experienced as a cooperative venture involving both parties, and they feel the blight of the parental curse. Those for whom leaving home is an anticipatory enterprise want to have the parental blessing: they are willing to carry half a bannock with them on their journey as prophecy of their own ability to earn a living, thankfully taking the half that is offered as a token of their parent's continuing support and as recognition of their own new-found independence.

Make your own prayer for those leaving home .

Polishing the Jewel of Craft

NEDE: *"What art do you practice?"*
FERCHETNE: *"Hunting for the treasures of knowledge."*
—Colloquy of the Two Sages, anon.
Irish poem (trans. John Matthews)

When young Nede (NAY'da) hears of his father's death, he returns from Scotland to take his poetic chair. To give himself a semblance of maturity, he sticks on a grass beard. But this fails to fool Ferchetne (Fer-KET'ne), who challenges him to a poetic contest.

Each poet throws challenging questions at the other: Nede's answers are aerobatically ambitious and self-vaunting, while Ferchetne's are sober, modest, and grounded in real practice, his prophetic insight far surpassing that of his junior. The dialogue concludes when Ferchetne asks Nede, "Who is greater than yourself?" Casting off his false beard, tearing off his professional robe, Nede kneels at Ferchetne's feet, asserting that only God and the greatest of poetic prophets is greater. He cedes place to Ferchetne as his elder and puts himself under his protection.

To arrive at a position of mature power and discernment, like that held by Ferchetne, takes much practice and many years of experience. Nede tries to short-circuit the path of his own fledgling art by assuming a maturity that he does not as yet possess and is forced, out of humility and truth, to acknowledge that his elder has a better claim to the poetic chair than he does. The years lie ahead of him which will bring polish to the uncut gem of his inexperience.

It is practice alone that brings a burnished glow to our own rough-hewn skills; it is by continual application of our craft that they become jewels in their appropriate setting.

Consider your particular skill or talent. Visualize this as a gem and meditate upon its appropriate setting and context.

Shutting Out the World

Is it I
From earth and sky
Shut out, or they
From my closed heart?
—KATHLEEN RAINE, *The Oracle in the Heart*

As we become increasingly urbanized and the population rises, people in cities cannot help but begin to exclude parts of the world around them, out of sheer self-survival. We cannot meet and greet everyone in the street, nor would this be entirely desirable. Given the effort we expend on blanking out parts of the world, is it any wonder that we sometimes have the impression that we are shut off from the world? If we are emotionally hurt or physically traumatized, if patterns of depression and disconnection continue, we can end up feeling isolated and unable to communicate with the world around us.

The process of opening our heart after it has been injured is best begun in nature. We can become aware of the beauty, variety, and seasonal changes of the natural world by regular exposure to the countryside. We can also go directly to the sources of nurture that have given us insight and empowerment in the past: music, animals, poetry, books, places, and friends are all able to feed our spirits. Learning and observing fresh subjects can also draw us from depressive introspection into new avenues of communication. Reaffirming our spiritual connection through daily prayer, meditation, or communion with the sources of spiritual strength can likewise reopen closed pathways.

The most profound change comes about if we frequently extend our sincere welcome to the world to be with us in our space. In that invitation we learn that it is not the world that excludes us, but we who shut the world out.

Contemplate times when you have felt excluded from the world. What factors helped you feel included again?

~ 20 JANUARY ~

Spiritual Navigation

O where will I get a gude sailor,
To take my helm in hand,
Till I get up to the ⸱⸱⸱ top-mast,
To see if I can spy
    —"The Ballad of ⸱⸱⸱ ⸱trick Spens," Scots folk song

The art of spiritual navigation is one that few are taught in our era. If we are fortunate enough to have a spiritual director or adviser as companion along our way, then we receive expert guidance when difficulties arise. A sensitive adviser does not attempt to solve our problems but makes suggestions and gives resourceful clues.

The chief aid to our personal exploration is our own spiritual practice. In our meditation, in our prayerful listening, in our silent attunement, we derive a good deal of navigational information. Most of this is likely to go unnoticed if we do not record and correlate it. Like any explorer to an unknown realm, we need to know the contours of the land, its flora and fauna, its friendly and hostile inhabitants. The mapping of our spiritual progress will certainly not be straightforward or easy to record. We will have to be alert to subtle changes and correspondences between what we experience and what seems to be true for us. Like the navigator who steers his ship through the fog, we have to sound the waters ahead of us and proceed slowly, always acknowledging that though we cannot see the stars, they still shine above us.

We each have an in-built aid to spiritual navigation in our dreams. In those nocturnal journeys, we visit new zones and landscapes, encounter archetypal and mythic beings who speak directly to us, often in pun-laden language. Our mapping of the otherworldly shore is based on a set of sequential explorations and recognitions that grow in confidence and trust as we take our spiritual voyage.

Begin to note and map your spiritual journey using a diary, chart,
and/or set of pictures to which you can refer and add regularly.

Superiority

When we let go of believing we are superior, we open ourselves to the experience of living in the community of Nature.
—PHILIP AND STEPHANIE CARR-GOMM, *The Druid Animal Oracle*

In nature there is a pecking order of dominance to which weaker species bow; but the sense of superiority seems to be especially strong in human beings, regardless of any real power we possess. Our culture has told us that our species is superior to all others, that human convenience is at the top of the heap, and that every other inhabitant of earth must give way to us. This view is not held in traditional cultures such as the Celtic, however; instead, all life forms are seen as fellow participants in life's dance.

Superiority separates us both from other species and life forms and from our fellow human beings. To live even one day with an awareness of our interconnected participation in life is a profoundly humbling experience that reconnects us with the community of nature. To experience, say, trees without the barrier of human superiority is to meet and interact with wise beings; to greet a child as a living soul, without adult superiority marring our encounter, is to be aware of primal understanding; to stand in a shower of rain and experience every drop as a kindred being is to be washed clean of separation.

We do not have to walk around feeling mystically merged with everything, devoid of a sense of our own distinct identity; we need only remember that the beauty of life is too precious to be hidden by superior attitudes.

Practice experiencing the world for a short time without allowing your innate sense of superiority into the driver's seat.

Phantom Lovers

Running ever through my head, is an old-time rune—
"Who meets the Love Talker must weave her shroud soon."
—ETHNA CARBERRY, "The Love Talker"

This poem speaks about a faery spirit called the Love Talker, who is said to come to young women and cause them to fall hopelessly in love with him. Such phantom lovers are not mythical. They still affect our world and draw our desires to them.

When we interact with phantom lovers, we draw upon the image of the ideal man or woman to which we naturally gravitate. The problem comes when we either project that image upon a living partner, relating to him in a totally false way, or become obsessed with the projected image and fall in love with it to the exclusion of our health and well-being. Then the characteristic signs of one lured away by the phantom lover are clearly visible: an inability to relate directly to those who love us, a distaste for usual pleasures and recreations, an unhealthy need for solitude. In such cases, we come under the spell of the phantom lover and dance to his tune.

When we project our ideal image upon a real person, we create terrible confusion and heartache. We also expose ourselves to unsuitable relationships and even violent abuse: because we are in thrall to the ideal image, we do not see that its mundane reflection is not worthy of our love. The phantom lover speaks to us of things that are attractive but unrealistic. It is essential that we become aware of the reality of the situation and make a clear separation between the phantom lover as ideal image, our actual human partner, and the true image of our soul—the anima or animus. Finally, we should not confuse phantom lovers with our soul's beloved, the one who is the true friend of the soul and certainly no deceiver. (See 25 December.)

Scrutinize your relationships for traces of the phantom lover. Ask your soul's beloved to give you help in clarifying this matter.

Clearing the Way

The plow must go five times over the site of a wood before it can become a field.

—traditional Welsh saying (trans. CM)

The sun has returned and the light is growing, but the plans we have been brooding upon may show little signs of progress. Now is a good time of year to prepare the ground for the projects and plans that are important to us. Make a list of plans and projects whose unfinished rubble clutters your way forward. These may include long, ongoing plans that are not going anywhere fast and short-term projects that are unfinished due to a lack of resources or energy. Look down your list: Which irritates you the most? Which nags at you as unfinished? Which did not work out according to plan, and why? Do not be surprised if you access deep emotion, and do not be afraid of what you feel.

Go through this list, creating questions that challenge and uncover the roots of the problem. Has your vision for each of the plans changed? Are your projects still workable as they stand? Evaluate long-term projects for significant progress and assess which approaches might loosen things up. Do you perhaps need to break down long-term plans into shorter achievable components, for example? Are there associations with partners or friends that are impeding your progress? If someone else is involved, what contribution has that person made? Finally, go through your list item by item and mark projects for eradication, rethinking, or fresh effort.

This procedure requires hard mental effort, but it can help dig up the soil of our potentiality and prepare it to receive new growth.

Set aside time to clear your way and root out outworn strategies and failed plans.

Selling Our Souls

Very early in the life of every youth there will be . . . the question
of how far he ought to sell his soul for the sake of his life.
—John Cowper Powys, *The Meaning of Culture*

How can we be true to our vocation in situations that call us to sell our souls? We must remember that there are two criteria in the workplace: we work in order to gain a livelihood, and we work in order to honor our soul's potential. It is becoming rare for workers to be able to meet both criteria. Many people who feel that their talents have been used for unspeakable ends have found more satisfaction in menial work well done than in their chosen profession. But to maintain this kind of professional honor is to take the high moral ground, a stance that may not support a home and family.

For many people, work is a compromise between livelihood and soul's honor. They cannot be without work, but they can search out ethical employers and forms of work that do not exploit their skills without proper return. This return is not only monetary, however: there must also be respect for the worker and his rights, and a proper appreciation of the work done. When this return is absent, we feel cheated, short-changed.

When we prostitute our talents to purely exploitative ends, we risk divorcing ourselves from our primal vision. Such a divorce is a separation from the greater reality of which we are a part, and a selling of our souls to those who will wring out every last essential drop of our vocational skills.

Meditate upon your vocational vision, even if you are not actively performing or fulfilling it at this time. What qualities and features characterize it? How have these been employed, recognized, and acknowledged in your life to date? How and why are you dissatisfied with the work you currently do? Are there remedies for the dissatisfaction?

The Gift of Love

Love is drawn to love.

—Welsh proverb (trans. CM)

On this day, the Celtic equivalent of St. Valentine's Day, Welsh lovers celebrate the patron of love, St. Dwynwen (DWIN'wen), by sending each other St. Dwynwen's Day cards. Many legends tell of St. Dwynwen, including one that speaks of her love for Maelon Dafodrill (MY'lon Dav-OD'ril). Things did not work out, however, and one night St. Dwynwen prayed to be cured of her love. God appeared to her in her dreams, giving her a draught that cured her love and causing Maelon to be frozen into a block of ice. But St. Dwynwen was offered—and made—three divine wishes. The first she uttered was that Maelon be unfrozen; the second was that any true lovers whose love was not reciprocated might be cured of their love; the last was that she might never marry.

Love is one of our world's most clichéd words. It has to work hard to cover all kinds of conditions and relationships, from the intimacy of lovers to the filial, parental, and national forms of love that surround us. We look for love and approval everywhere without understanding that love must also be extended by ourselves, that the giving of love is an essential part of the process. There is a lack of grace, a kind of lovelessness, that inhabits the body of someone who has not been a receptacle of love.

The presence of love calls out the gift of love in others. Love's reciprocity is catching if we once allow it in. Unreciprocated love, however, is a curse not a gift—one that St. Dwynwen herself seems to have well understood.

Meditate upon the gift of love. How has it been manifested in your life?

Extremity

Man's extremity is God's opportunity.
—Scottish proverb

When we are brought to the verge of crisis, our well-honed philosophies and careful, controlled strategies fall away. All the spars that make up our life raft, the things on which we daily rely, have a tendency to break up in the force of events. It is usually when we feel our utter solitude and helplessness that we call upon the spirit world for assistance. Even though we may have no well-founded belief, we instinctively know that even if all other things have fallen away, divine providence will not let us down.

Crisis may help kick-start spirituality temporarily, but only a consenting soul can maintain it. Crisis and extremity are not missionaries on an evangelical campaign trail for our souls; they are agents of change able to strip away the inessentials and awaken us to a deeper resourcefulness that is not ours alone.

Like the volcanic force that shaped the rugged landscape of Scotland, extremity scoops out hollows and scours deeply embedded rubble from the surface of our lives, leaving behind deep declivities that only Spirit can fill and temper. The excavation of possibility simultaneously brings the realization of wider capacity. As nature abhors a vacuum, so does Spirit find ways of filling the emptiness of our soul.

We may be aware of none of these realizations in a conscious way during our time of trial, but we can throw the imploring rope of appeal to our spiritual source and ask for it to be safely caught.

Meditate upon a recent crisis situation in your life. What spiritual opportunities were present? Which did you take up, which refuse? Create your own short invocation for help, to be used in a time of future extremity.

Waking the Sleepers

Woe to the coward that ever he was born,
That did not draw the sword before he blew the horn.

—traditional Scots rhyme

There are many stories concerning giants (or King Arthur and his knights) sleeping under a hill. The sleepers are really guardians who should not be woken until there is a great and national need. A foolhardy man discovers their sleeping place, usually when seeking buried treasure that is supposed to be lying with the sleepers. Greed takes him in, but at sight of the awesome warriors and their gear, confusion grips him. He blows the horn to wake them but fails to draw the sword that lies nearby to indicate the real urgency of his need. The sleepers stir and ask, "Is it time?" The foolish man has nothing to say for himself, and is indicted with the rhyme above. He is never able to find the cavern again.

In every country, there is a similar tale of sleepers whose purpose is to be the vanguard of defense in national crisis—ancestral or otherworldly sleepers who are contracted to be guardians and protectors of the land. (See 24 June.) They should not be woken unless we really need them. Those who invoke the sleepers out of greed or curiosity get neither gold nor knowledge. This applies also to those whose spiritual practice is entirely self-serving, who undergo a kind of metaphysical assault course wherein all traditions are ransacked for their spiritual treasures in order to provide soul-credits at the finish line.

There are many aspects of ancient traditions that are in a period of sleep, retreat, or transformation—aspects that are best left sleeping now. Not only atavistic and barbarous practices that are no longer a part of our world, but also deep and abiding truths that will one day awaken and come to aid of those in centuries yet to dawn.

Who are the abiding sleepers in your tradition? Meditate upon the purpose of their sleep.

Transforming Our Rage

It is in bringing the rage of what hurts you personally into the world that you have the power to bring néart, *this active spirituality, out into the world.*

—from a speech by Nuala Ahern, Irish
member of the European Parliament

The Irish word *néart* (NYART') is one for which there is no English equivalent. It means "strength" or "power" in the sense of "the energy of life." This sacred energy is the source of all movement in the universe. People who have been disconnected from the health and harmony of their *néart* for any length of time, lose contact with their essential power. In people who have been disconnected from their *néart,* rage is often a positive sign of returning life and power. People who are totally downtrodden and powerless do not have the energy to be angry. But what do we do with our rage once it is awakened? The transformative aspect of rage is found in reconnection with our *néart:* instead of being stuck in victimhood and persecution, we step out powerfully and acknowledge our strength. Rage can be destructive if it remains in a mentality of victimhood, for it never properly connects with the primal power of life. However, it can become a revolutionary force that rights many abuses when victims decide to band together, to blow the whistle and ensure that others do not suffer in like manner.

But rage can be an important gauge of distress, and neglecting its warning is dangerous. If rage flares out of self-protection or warning and we ignore it, we begin to lose our *néart;* we give it away to others and let them walk all over us. The life-power that courses through us is a gift to be protected and guarded; it cannot be taken from us unless we allow that to happen. If righteous rage arises, listen to its warning voice and act to protect your precious gift.

What kinds of things enrage you? Correlate your findings with the boundaries of your own néart.

Sympathy, Empathy, and Compassion

Can I see another's woe,
And not be in sorrow too?
Can I see another's grief,
And not seek for kind relief?
—William Blake, "On Another's Sorrow"

How involved do we become when misfortune falls upon those around us? Our level of affection and acquaintance may determine our response, as well as our level of responsibility: this will obviously be higher in our immediate family than with our friends or with strangers.

The three main responses to misfortune are usually clustered around expressions of sympathy, empathy, and compassion. We offer sympathy to those whom we do not know well and with whom we have little intention of becoming involved. Expressions of sympathy offer the minimum response that is socially acceptable when suffering arises, and they do little to assuage the suffering. Well-motivated empathy, on the other hand—distinguished from sympathy in that it regards the sufferer more than the self—can ease pain and bring comfort.

Compassion, alone of these three, embraces the needy and acts to meet the need. Because of its impartiality, it is the most difficult of the three to experience and to maintain. It neither remains on the boundaries of the suffering nor becomes emotionally entangled with it. Rather, it encompasses suffering with a love that is universal, respecting the primal core of life and envisioning its relief with heartfelt action. Compassion takes a good deal of disinterested regard. For that reason, it may be easier to maintain compassion among strangers, those by whom we are not known and with whom there are no intimate ties to emotionally cripple our actions.

Consider your own responses to the suffering that is about you.

The Song of the Cailleach

Sad the day, woe is me,
That I sail not on youth's sea!
All my years of beauty gone
And my lusty flesh forlorn.

—"Death Song of the Cailleach Beare,"
early Irish poem (trans. CM)

The Cailleach Beare (KAHL'lee-ak BEE'ra)—the Old Woman or Grand-mother of the Beare Peninsula in Ireland—is remembered in many land features as the one who formed the mountain ranges by tossing rocks from her apron—a titanic figure who rules the wintertide, whose hammer freezes the ground.

This long poem laments the passing of her youth and of the many excitements, lovers, horseraces, and gifts she once enjoyed. In her decrepitude, she no longer savors the company of young people or feasts on tasty food with kings as she was wont. Instead, she is incarcerated with veiled nuns whose only conversation is dull and dreary prayer. The Cailleach sings of her former life as the flowing tide of incoming waters, but she begins to see that her later life is of the ebbing tide.

As youth's vigor passes from our limbs and we enter the wider sea of age, so we all become old ones of memory and experience, the new rememberers and guardians in our turn. We cannot reach that role without relinquishing our youthful grasp on life, however. Only when we become aware of the changing tides of our life can we enter the ebb tide and step out of the flowing tide; only then are the gifts of age available. If we continue to swim against the tide, we will not find them.

Not only for the aged and the wise, but also for the young and the inquiring, the Cailleach sings her song. She is the mistress of winter's heart. Now we can hear her song clearly and understand that the changing of the tides heralds no ending, only a renewal of all that we are.

What is flowing and ebbing the tides of your own life right now?

Imbolc

Washing the hand, the foot, the head: this is the work of Imbolc.
—ancient Irish saying (trans. CM)

The festival of Imbolc (IMM'bolk) marks the loosening of winter's grip upon the land. The feast's matron, Brighid (BREE'yid), brings new energy and light to the world, breaking the spell of the Cailleach's hammer, which has frozen the ground hard.(See 30 January.)

The name *Imbolc* is derived from the lactation of ewes, which begin lambing at this time of year. For people in ancient times, the milk from sheep would have been the first dairy produce after the long winter. All food production and household protection was believed to be under the aegis of Brighid, who was also seen as the primordial midwife.

Imbolc is a time of lustration, cleansing, and purification. It is not without significance that February, into which Imbolc extends, is exactly nine months from the lusty festivities of Beltane in May—festivities during which many women would have conceived children who were born now. Rites of lustration frequently follow childbirth.

The celebrations of this feast include a ceremony wherein young people gather together to sing the praises of Brighid and to fashion a *brídeog* (BREE'jog), or Brighid doll. The company go from house to house, knocking for admittance. At each door the *brídeog* is welcomed and ushered in, since every household wishes to partake of the blessing. The making of a Brighid's cross out of rushes is also part of this festival: this was originally a woven emblem with three slanting legs running sunwise, but now it is commonly a four-footed cross. The power and light of Brighid's protection encircles the household where this emblem is displayed.

Make everything clean for this festival with the conscious intention of purifying your household of all old, stale, and wintry influences. Kindle candles at fall of dark and set them safely in every room. Then go to the door and welcome into your home the protective blessing of Brighid.

Imbolc

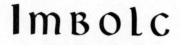

Season of Spring

FEBRUARY

Month of February—scarce are the dainties;
Wakeful the adder to generate its poison;
Habitual is reproach from frequent acknowledgement.
                                        —anon. Welsh poem

February sees the beginning of the season of spring, the festival of Imbolc. The themes this month include beginnings, illumination, recognizing our song, myth and story, disorder and pattern, clear discernment and memory, help and advice, service and sacrifice, the three threads of the soul and their ninefold expression, wasteland, and healing.

Brighid, Mother of Memory

Brighid of the mantle, encompass us;
Lady of the Lambs, protect us;
Keeper of the hearth, kindle us;
Beneath your mantle, gather us,
And restore us to memory
—CAITLÍN MATTHEWS, "A Blessing for Hearth Keepers"

The festival of Imbolc is under the protection of Brighid. The ancient goddess, daughter of the Dagda—or Good God of the Gaelic gods, the Tuatha de Danaan (TOO'a-ha day DAH'nan)—is the matron of poetry, healing, and smithcraft. In the fifth century, her namesake St. Brigit of Kildare took over many of the goddess's qualities and aspects.

The extraordinary fusion of goddess and saint demonstrates how important Brighid is to the Celtic people. So great was her power that even the coming of Christianity could not diminish her influence: Brighid was immediately promoted within Irish Christianity to the role of the Virgin's midwife and Christ's foster-mother, and remains the secondary patron of Ireland to this day.

The mantle of Brighid is continually invoked in Celtic prayer, to powerfully encompass all and protect from harm. As the keeper of the hearth, Brighid and her power are present in the hearth-fire that radiates its welcoming glow throughout the household. (See 5 October.) Poets and craftspeople look to her as their inspirer, householders beseech her to encompass their homes and flocks, and the sick pray to her to cast her mantle over them and bring them again to health.

Brighid is the mother of memory, the one who reminds us of the original, divine, protective motherhood that promotes the individuality of our power and fans its flame to quickening life.

Make your own invocation to Brighid to ask for the encompassment and protection of your household, including all that is dear to you.

Light in Darkness

There are three candles that illumine every darkness: truth, nature, and knowledge.

—ancient Irish triad

Truth has been the mirror and shield of all seekers since life began. The primal integrity of all beings shines out like the light of a diamond, sharp and clear; but when truth is hidden, we are aware only of a dimness and obscurity that cloaks our perception. Our unique sensitivity of soul to truth is inbred. It tells us what is good, well-aligned, and perfect. If we return to recognizing truth in ourselves, our actions, our speech, and our thoughts, we relate to ourselves and to the universe with better respect.

Nature is the shining garment in which all life is clothed. The vigor, strength, and power of life are nature's gifts. We experience nature through our physical senses, and this experience is often ecstatic. We tend these days to rhapsodize nature, after a long era of neglect and abuse. We are each part of nature: if we abuse it, we abuse ourselves and those we love. If we observe and learn from nature's beautiful and balancing continuum, we live lives of harmony and justice.

Knowledge is the glory that arises when truth and nature are properly welcomed and respected. It cannot be given to another; it can only arise when Mother Nature and Father Truth conjoin in union. Knowledge is the glorious child stored in every cell of the universe. If we search for glory in our thoughts, motivations, and experiences, we align ourselves with knowledge. But neither truth, nature, nor knowledge can be owned: this is why they are the eternal candles. Let us always be on guard, therefore, for anyone who attempts to trade these three, for such action heralds the approach of absolute darkness. But with the three candles of truth, nature, and knowledge to light our way, we need never be in darkness.

How do these three candles illuminate your own darkness?

Conception

*It is in the agony and ecstasy of corporeal love, it is under the
ascendancy of this first-born of all the senses that mortals draw
most near to the quivering secret of life.*

—LLEWELYN POWYS, *Earth Memories*

In the Celtic tradition, it was believed that conception took place after
a significant event: when the mother drank water from a certain well or
sat under the moon, for example, or when she ate a magical salmon or
when the shadow of a god fell upon her.

The moment of the soul's entry cannot be heralded or decreed.
Women who yearn to conceive often do so only when they cease worrying about their goal. It is in the secret, unregarded moments that a
soul incarnates.

In the conception of a child or of an idea, there has to be a passionate connection wherein the seed of making can pass from one to
another, whereby life can be kindled and its flame grow secretly in the
dark. Conception is not a solitary or a daytime affair. Our passion must
be stimulated, recognized, and shared by another being: in the conception of a child, by our physical partner; in the conception of an idea,
by a nonphysical partner—a spiritual ally who can penetrate the veil
between the worlds to help convey the soul of a thought into manifestation. The actual conception takes place in darkness, beyond the compass of our conscious thought or participation.

Wrapped in a passionate embrace, in which differences of gender or
form are reconciled in the bliss of union, the ecstatic wellspring of life
springs up.

*Meditate upon some project close to your heart before you go to sleep,
praying that it might come into being. Pass into sleep and let your
dreams reveal their secret magic.*

A Ruler's Rules

Do not be too wise, nor too foolish,
do not be too conceited, nor too retiring,
do not be too haughty, nor too humble,
do not be too talkative, nor too silent,
do not be too hard, nor too weak.
—*The Instructions of King Cormac mac Art* (trans. CM)

The Irish King Cormac's instructions can be applied to anyone with benefit. If we give the impression of being wise, much is expected of us; if we give the impression of being naive, we are taken advantage of. If we are full of ourselves, we annoy people; if we hide our achievements under a bushel, no one notices us. The overloquacious soon lose their audience; the silent are never asked their opinion. Those who act harshly are broken on the rock of their own flinty hearts; those who act like victims are crushed.

Avoiding the extremes of exaggeration or underemphasis, we allow the true self to be expressed. Finding our own proper balance is the work of years of practice, however. Since we reflect and respond to each person in an individual way, we are occasionally thrown off course or present ourselves awkwardly.

It is not the duty of any human being to appease or permit inappropriate behavior out of misplaced politeness. It is possible to stand firm in our innate integrity and not be swayed by persuasive and manipulative people. We can achieve this stance by holding to the core of our own being and discovering the power of our soul.

Check your demeanor with people today. Did you come on too strong to some? Did you feel ignored or manipulated? Meditate upon how you can be more adaptable, especially with those people and in those situations that cause you to feel out of balance.

The Healing at Hand

May healing be near to our hurt!
—EOGHAN RUADH MAC AN BHAIRD,
in Osborn Bergin, *Irish Bardic Poetry* (trans. CM)

At moments of crisis or action, there is no time for long-winded utterances or beautifully written invocations, only for a swift arrow of prayer to pierce the veil between the worlds and beseech assistance. The prayer "God between me and all harm!" and the observation "God is nearer than the door" are examples of the Celtic trust in the immediacy of help and spiritual assistance.

The help or healing that is near to us may not always be obvious or seem available. But even if we do not know who our spiritual allies are, they know who we are and will find us soon enough. The important thing is to ask for help or healing, so that we create a pathway down which help can come.

Many of us feel that we are personally and solely in control of our lives, that we should be able to manage without intervention, that we are capable human beings who do not need help.

The healing that lies near to our hurt needs our assistance to be manifested: we must be able to ask for it without setting limits on its action. Rarely given in an instantaneous miracle, healing makes us whole over an organic period of time. But we must cooperate with and trust the healing, not pick off the band-aid every hour to see how the wound is doing! To trust the help or healing, we must learn to trust the spiritual allies who provide it.

Make your own short invocation for help or healing. Meditate upon the help that you need and upon your own receptivity to healing. Make an act of trust in your own spiritual allies and their ability to heal.

Concentration

Traditional training laid great stress upon . . . observing the motion of the breath, concentrating on a tree or a stone, hearing the environment and observing the traditional cycle of the year in plants, animals and the earth itself.

—IAN G. REES, *The Therapist's Chair and the Siege Perilous,*
in R. J. Stewart, ed., *Psychology and Spiritual Traditions*

The preparation of bards, ovates, and druids included training not only in the memorization of knowledge and practices but also in the stillness of attention that we call concentration. If you have ever tried to learn a new skill that requires the memorization of long lists or subtle correspondences, you will know that modern memory can be often unprepared and evasive when it comes to remembering on command.

The traditional Celtic method of concentration is learned in stillness and in the contemplation of the natural rhythms and cycles, involving the whole of our body, not just our intellect. In this deep stillness, poets discern metaphor, musicians music, architects primordial design, thinkers archetypal patterns and relationships, and seers truthful visions. We too can achieve this kind of concentration if we slow down and exercise our deeper faculties into a robust vigor that sustains whatever we wish to learn. (See also 16 September.)

Find a quiet place where you can contemplate some aspect of nature: a stone, tree, plant, or star, for example. If you are indoors, concentrate on the sky you can see from your window, or on a plant growing in your home. Be aware of the object of your contemplation. Gradually become aware of the space around the object. Now switch your attention from object to space and back again, backward and forward repeatedly. Finally, become aware of both object and space at once, and then include yourself in the relationship and remain in stillness and waiting, entering into a deep communion. Record your findings in a poetic or artistic way.

Willingness

Ae man can lead a horse ta the water but twenty couldna gar
[make] him drink.

—Scots proverb

If you have ever tried to give strong-tasting medicine to an animal or child, you have encountered (probably with some frustration) the full extent of unwillingness. The same frustration sometimes arises when we try to persuade someone to our way of seeing something; no matter how many times we explain our perspective, the listener's understanding does not come to the place of realization. It is just not within range of his will.

In our lives we must do many things contrary to our consent: out of duty, expediency, or consideration for others. Our ability to show willingness is often a measure of our maturity, a skill honed by circumstance, upbringing, and experience. But these very factors often have the reverse effect; that is, they detach us from our own will.

When we do spend time trying to define our will, it is often a shock to find how much of what we think of as our own opinion, our full consent, our true will is formed by the opinions, wishes, and desires of others. Sorting the grit from the grain takes a lot of perseverance.

Will without maturity is of no service to us; we must know when we can compromise it and when we should defend it.

Consult your own will. Where are its boundaries, and when must you defend them?

The Mythic Present

It is not the literal past, the "facts" of history, that shape us, but images of the past embodied in language. . . . We must never cease renewing those images; because once we do, we fossilise.

—BRIAN FRIEL, *Translations*

For contemporary society, history has become factual and finite, an index of deeds done and words spoken. This literal past grips our imagination, disabling our vision from ranging wider and seeing the infinite variety of possibility, shape, and pattern that could be revealed.

Finding the living context and eternal resonance of the past can deliver us from the bondage of history. This means allowing the silt of history to fall and the living metaphors and images to rise up buoyantly to the surface so that we can understand the mythic present. True myth is a living entity that clothes the present in wonderful ways. It comprises both the received awareness of popular consciousness and the archetypal metaphor of history, being a collection of symbols, images, and metaphors that abide beyond the context of history.

The mythic present is continually reshaping events, whereas history alone merely chronicles the tides of time. History deprived of its mythic context becomes petrified into sound-bites of the timeline; but when myth inspirits history, we hear the voices of the past with our own ears, see the images with our own eyes.

Remember an incident in your past in which you were actively involved. Now retell that incident as if it were a folk story or myth, putting it in the third person and allowing the parallel story to unfold in its own way. Draw upon the metaphors, symbols, and images that the incident evokes for you. Note the differences between your myth and your history. What is changed by this process of narration? What is made clear, and what new insights do you have?

Disorder

The three oppressors of the wise are drunkenness, and adultery and bad disposition.

—triad from *Laws of Hywel Dda*

These aspects of disorder are thieves that break the sacred contracts upon which society is based. The misuse of intoxicants creates a muddled perception of reality, resulting in disorderly behavior. When we misuse sacred substances for mundane recreation, we poison ourselves and lose the pathways to bliss.

Sexual desire has its own sacred contract, grounded in the consent of two hearts together. Adultery attempts to steal the affection of another person's partner and violates this sacred contract.

Those who set their faces against the tide of the society in which they live are thieves of the common good. All societies are based upon the contract of good order. Those who exclude themselves from upholding the common good parasitically bleed the resources of their society.

The contracts that we make within our society are what keep it orderly. When these are subverted, turned aside, or appropriated, we do not merely hurt other people around us; we also sever pathways of connection between ourselves and the spiritual allies who interface with our world.

What contracts have been severed by disorder in your life? Ask help of your spiritual allies to reconnect what has been broken.

Innocence Abused

Who is it that laments in this house of stone? . . . It is Mabon, the son of Modron who is here . . . and no imprisonment was ever so grievous as mine.

—Culhwch and Olwen, from *The Mabinogian*

In the story of Culhwch and Olwen, Mabon, son of Modron, is a primal being of innocence, abducted from his mother's side when he was only three nights old. No one knows whether he is alive or dead, as the young hero, Culhwch (KIL'ook) discovers when he goes to liberate the Child of Light from his long imprisonment.

The gifts of innocence are eagerly sought by those who have lost their own. Those who have spilled and wasted in hideous ways the hope, freshness, vigor, openness, directness, and joy of youth seek to replenish their stores, and so the cycle of the abused preying upon the innocent goes round.

How can the cycle of abuse be short-circuited in our society? Only when each of us decides to break the circle that keeps us imprisoned as victim, in fear of the predator. It is only by liberating the Mabon of our innocent selves that we can find the strength to overcome abuse and violence: we need the primal help of our innocent, lost, and imprisoned soul-fragment, which was overwhelmed in childhood.

How has your innocence been abused or lost? Over a period of time, begin to create the components of your quest for the Mabon of your own lost soul-fragment. Where does the crying come from? In what circumstances do you access the memories and pathways? Follow these until you find the place in dream, meditation, and soul-flight. Envisage the innocent becoming the strong liberator.

A Life Deferred

Too long a sacrifice
Can make a stone of the heart.
—W. B. YEATS, "For Anne Gregory"

We all know someone who has put her own life on hold for the benefit of another person or for a project. This is a fine thing if there is eventually a turning back to the heart's desire and one's own way of life, but too often this does not happen.

Deferred life inevitably means lost opportunity. We can stand only so much of this. To refrain from action, from personal engagement, from practicing skills and talents, from the formation of satisfying relationships is to marginalize our power. Never being attuned to our power, never being able to cooperate with it, sends the message of despair to our soul.

If our life's purpose is not to curdle within us after a deferment, we must set to fostering it again and learning how to move from the place of imprisonment into a wider place. This may mean relinquishing our service to another, or delegating or sharing it. It may mean a total change, a turning of the back upon the service in question, the opening of a new door.

Before the heart becomes a stone, we must seek out the cause of our joy and integrate it fully into our lives, or else discover the joys within the way of service.

What is the joy of your life? How are you serving it? If you are not, where has the joy gone? Take steps to engage with it.

Finding Our True Song

Only when I gave
my fame to the Hazel shade
did the true song come.

—PAUL MATTHEWS, "The Hazel Shade"

Finding our true song is about relinquishing the burden of ego and the false choruses that it sings. Self-importance causes us to dance to strange tunes that our feet find unnatural. When we act out of self-importance, we trip ourselves up, make Freudian slips, inadvertently revealing to ourselves and others how far we are from our soul's circuit.

The false songs that we sing are out of tune with our soul; they are merely the responses we have adopted from others, not utterances from our own deep core. Our uncertainty and lack of conviction echo in them. The solution to these false songs is to forget ourselves and concentrate upon what we are doing, refusing to engage with fear and self-disclosure. It is not that we should ignore ourselves, but rather that we should attempt to step out of our own way. The Irish poet W. B. Yeats noticed this for himself: he discovered that whenever he went out of his way to create something purposefully beautiful, he sabotaged his poem.

The same is true of our own deep song, which is forever singing its beautiful melody beyond the reach of our ears. When we act sincerely, when we speak from the heart, when our passion is engaged, the true song is heard in all its glory.

Meditate upon who you truly are—not upon what you have achieved, nor upon your background and antecedents, nor upon your social status or reputation. Where is your true self allowed to express itself in your life? If you do not like what you find, do not suppress your realizations; invite your true self to sing its own song and help the false personas step out of the way.

The Cosmos of the Soul

One soul in the immensity of its intelligence, is greater and more excellent than the whole world. The ocean is but the drop of a bucket to it, the heavens but a centre, the sun obscurity, and all ages but as one day.

—THOMAS TRAHERNE, *Centuries*

The druids believed that the soul encompassed the far extents of time and space, uncircumscribed by temporal dimensions. For the Celtic peoples, the physical world was seen to be made up of three elemental dimensions: the depths of the sea, the breadth of the earth, and the airy regions of the heavens. Fusing these three dimensions together was the fiery sun, whose diurnal circuit maintained the life of the apparent world. Each ensouled body lived within the dispensation of these dimensions. But the soul was regarded as yet greater than these, able not only to move through water, earth, air, and fire but also to travel beyond these modes into the wider domain of the unseen world. For the soul, the passage of ages is but a day in cosmic time; there is no sense of time passing, only an eternal present to soul-travelers who enter the otherworld.

When we begin to pay attention to our soul, rather than ignoring its needs and urgings, we experience a sense of inclusion within the universe. If we learn to pass beyond the limits of our body as soul-travelers, we discover that the constellations and planets that spin within the soul are qualities, intelligences, and allies we have always longed for.

Look into the depths of your soul, as into the immensity of inner space. How is the cosmos reflected within your soul? What constellations and planets are featured therein? Within the solar system of your soul, what major features do you recognize?

Unrequited Love

To luve unluvit is ane pain.
—ALEXANDER SCOTT, "To Luve Unluvit"

Unrequited love is painful to both the lover and the putative beloved. It is an urging that comes unbidden and makes a wasteland of the heart. The lover's longing for reciprocation and union is met with the beloved's disdain and separation. All offers of affection are distasteful, all gifts returned. Nothing can change the heart that is not pledged.

Unrequited love, though overwhelmingly powerful, usually is of finite duration simply because the beloved does not respond. The one who attempts to persuade the beloved to attend, who goes beyond the normal limits of trial, courtship, and persuasion, merely makes himself a nuisance.

When someone with whom we have had a long-standing relationship leaves us suddenly, there is little time to retract love: one side of the bridge of partnership is just no longer standing one day, but the old traffic of love does not suddenly come to a halt. The lyrics of songs of unrequited love now have a dimension of their own, as love enters the twilight zone of bereavement.

Send greetings of affection to your beloved. If your relationship has come to a sudden end, express your love and sorrow in verse or song.

The Service of the Grail

Go, heart, unto the lamp of licht [light],
Go, heart, do service and honour.
　　　　　—anon., "Go, Heart, unto the Lamp of Licht"

The traditional concept of service is based upon the honor of the soul and the respect that we tender to other souls. In the Grail legends, the sacred vessel of healing and restoration can be accessed only by questers who are sufficiently attuned to their soul to ask the "Grail question," which is said to be "Whom does the Grail serve?"—a question that, once asked, accesses the healing that it freely brings. It is only when we are able and willing to look beyond the boundaries of our own concerns and inquire what is wrong and to what extent we are involved in putting things right that we truly understand service. Then the realization that *we* are not the source of help, grace, or service becomes clear to us: we are truly cooperating with the spiritual source of our life and made mediators of healing.

The Grail is a lamp of light, life, and love that brings its solace only when someone is willing to serve. When we align our heart with need and honor, the heart itself becomes a lamp at which light is kindled. When the heart is alight with service, the flame can pass freely from heart to heart.

What is the nature of your service within the universe? What are the terms of the contract between your service and the spiritual source whom you serve?

Books for the Soul

That I might search all books and from their chart,
Find my soul's calm!

—St. Columba's "Song of Exile"

When St. Columba went into self-imposed exile on the Island of Iona off the west coast of Scotland, he borrowed a particularly fine volume of the psalms from Abbot Finnian of Moville and had it secretly copied. When Finnian discovered what had happened, he demanded not only his book back but also Columba's copy, on the principle that "to each cow her calf." Columba, whose enthusiasm for the dissemination of knowledge often outran his ethical judgment, had to comply.

In the early days of book transcription, only sacred texts were considered important enough for an illuminator and scribe to spend several months working on them. Today printed books are widely available; we are able to read a variety of writings, from sacred scriptures to poetry, from biography and history to philosophy, from legends to novels.

If we look along our shelves, there are certain books with which we would never wish to part, dear to us because they provide us with soul-food. These are not always sacred texts: they may be myths, folk tales, or other stories whose narratives inspire us with their abiding wisdom; they may be poems or songs that reflect the music of our own soul; they may be biographical accounts of people whose lives and works have been inspiring to our own soul's circuit.

Which book comes nearest to being your soul's chart? Meditate upon a passage from it today. Make your own blessing for the author.

Parenting

*Children begin by loving their parents; after a time they judge
them; rarely, if ever, do they forgive them.*
— OSCAR WILDE, *A Woman of No Importance*

The things that we hold against our parents seem to remain larger than
life in our imaginative memory for the duration of our adult years. It is
a fact that makes parenting especially poignant and exasperating, since
our own childhood experience potently informs us how our own children are likely to judge us in later years.

The twentieth century has gone through several models of acceptable parenting, from the highly disciplined and formal models (in
which children are expected to behave well or receive strict punishment) to the more liberal models (in which parents and children have
contracts for allowance and self-discipline). Since these extremes each
have their faults, most parents today aim somewhere in the middle in
an attempt to provide a moderate and tolerably workable system.

We seek the love of our children, but we should not expect their
gratitude—at least not until they are grown up. Parenthood is a
responsibility, not an obligation. We will make mistakes—sometimes
the very mistakes that our parents made with us—but we remain parents out of love.

*How do you judge your parents? What still rankles with you about
your upbringing? If you have children, what is their judgment of you?
Where do you need to exercise greater sensitivity with them?*

The Druid Circle

In Druidry, we come together in circles . . . to experience that we are
in communion not just with our present-day companions, but with
the spirits of the animals, trees, stones, stars, ancestors and children.
—PHILIP AND STEPHANIE CARR-GOMM, *The Druid Animal Oracle*

The breaking of hierarchy was the idea behind King Arthur's Round Table, at which worthy guardians of the land could sit without order of precedence getting in the way, at which counsel could be given and taken without offense. The old stone circles that predate the Celtic era by centuries were the first meeting places, erected to put people into correct alignment and spiritual communion with past, present, and future, and with all the beings no longer living as well as those yet to be born. In our own time, people are learning these wise yet ancient ways of relating to the universe.

The change of emphasis that spiritual practice undergoes when people meet together in a circle is radical: no altar rails, no pulpit, no them and us, no priest and congregation. Suddenly there is an equity we have never before experienced. We are one, not only with those gathered about the circle with us, but also with beings in ever-wider concentric circles of relationship that set the universe in a different order and break the old hierarchies forever.

The whole universe is symbolically seated about a communal fire called life—a fire that we all share in the darkness of our isolation, that courses through all veins, that maintains the life of even stones and plants and all that we seldom think of as living. It is a fire that burns in all times and places.

Light a candle and invite other beings and allies—from the spirits of
stars to the spirits of stones—to gather in a circle around the candle
and meditate upon the life of the universe. Thank all your invited
guests and extinguish the candle. What happened, what changed when
you did this? What have you learned?

The Red, the White, the Black

Peredur stood and compared the raven and the whiteness of the snow, and the redness of the blood, to the hair of the lady that best he loved, which was blacker than jet, and to her skin which was whiter than snow, and to the two red spots upon her cheek, which were redder than the blood upon the snow.

—Peredur, from *The Mabinogian*

In his adventures, Peredur (Perr-EDD'yr) comes upon a scene that transfixes him so completely that his companions are unable to gain his attention. He sees a raven stooping upon a wild duck in the snow; and the fusion of the three startling colors—the redness of the blood, the whiteness of the snow, and the blackness of the raven's feathers— causes him to fall into a reverie of his best beloved.

These three colors—black, white, and red—appear in worldwide folklore as heroes and heroines long for the beloved of their heart. A kind of soul-alchemy surrounds these colors, which are considered to be the sacred colors of many spiritual traditions. Within the Celtic tradition, these colors appear in triadic fusion as the colors of the spiritual quest, which has its easy, difficult, and inspired phases. These respective fair, ugly, and strong phases of our soul's circuit are the central core of our personal pathway: all phases are important; none can be excluded. As we follow our personal quest for meaning, we can draw upon the wisdom of each phase.

Obtain three balls of wool or reels of cotton in the colors discussed above and cut three arm-lengths from them. Meditating upon your spiritual path to date, consider the difficult times, the easy times, the inspired times. Weave together these three colored threads into a braided cord. Decide which color represents each strand of your life. This sacred cord now embodies the three most important strands of your soul's pathway. Keep it safe.

The Doors of Perception

If the doors of perception were cleansed, everything would appear as it is, infinite.

—William Blake, "A Memorable Fancy"

The doors of perception are the senses—not only the physical senses of sight, hearing, smell, taste, and touch, but also the subtle senses of inner vision, resonance, instinct, discrimination, and empathy. Without the cooperation of these two sets of senses, we cannot perceive truly.

To be able to perceive everything as it really is means retraining and exercising senses that we have often neglected. Meditation can hone our subtle senses, as we reach beyond the physical for the unseen reality and its meaning. Using a range of senses, we rely on our tactile and empathetic senses to combine with our hearing and resonance so that, like a bat or a whale, we have a sense of space, distance, and mass. Or we may find that our sense of smell/taste combines with our instinct and discrimination to give our visual field a sense of color and quality that is both accurate and surprising.

When the doors of perception are cleansed, we receive earlier warning of matters that are likely to be dangerous or problematic for us; we are subsequently able to make better decisions, draft more accurate forecasts, and read the character of the universe in an altogether better way.

Practice using your subtle senses in combination with your physical senses today. Your eyes tell you one thing about a person, but what do your ears tell you? Is the message different? What do your deep instinct and discrimination have to say?

Inspirers

I draw my knowledge from the famous cauldron,
The breath of nine muses keeps it boiling.
—Preiddeu Annwn (trans. CM), anon. Welsh poem

The cauldron of Annwfn (ANN'uvn), the Welsh Underworld, was guarded, warmed, and inspired by the nine sisters of the cauldron—the primal inspirers of the Celtic world. The ninefold sisters were understood to take the threefold thread of each life and amplify it till its full potential was realized. (See 19 January.) They were seen as the Gifting Mothers by the Celtic world, and later as the faery godmothers of medieval tradition. (See 15 November.) Actual sisterhoods of priestesses played an important part in the sacred and inspirational guidance of the ancient Celtic world. The sacred flame within the enclosure of St. Brigit was tended by nineteen sisters—two shifts of nine nuns and their abbess.

The relationship between ourselves and our various inspirers is complex and subtle. We rely on the teachers and inspirational people of many ages whose craft we follow; the practitioners of our own life-skills who preceded us; the places, animals, plants, trees, and land features that have become central to our symbolic and metaphorical understanding of our vocation; the music, books, art, and skills that feed our soul; the stories, songs, texts, and teachings by which we live our lives. All of these come together to heat the brew in our cauldron of life. Our inspirers pull upon the thread of our soul's circuit to remind us where our vocational duty lies.

Which nine major influences in your life keep your own cauldron of inspiration boiling? Visualize each of these, appreciating them and focusing upon those aspects that most inspire you.

Loss of Mythic Place

If the full, rich, mythic sense of place is finally taken out of our cultural compass, then we will mentally inhabit a spiritual wasteland.
—PAUL DEVEREUX, *Revisioning the Earth*

In the Grail legends, the loss of primal harmony between the worlds causes the apparent world to become a wasteland. A similar process is at work within our own world at this time: the demythification of the earth. The long-held stories and understandings about the land are being eroded by forgetfulness and active neglect. Each region has its own stories and traditions, fusions of legends and stories that cluster about the nexus points of sacred sites and prominent land features. They tell of the creative acts of giants, gods, or spirits, the deeds and quests of heroes and heroines, the wise advice of animals and trees. These points are thresholds of connection between our daily temporal world and the eternal timelessness of the otherworld.

The erosion of such myths in our landscape arises when we begin to view the land as inert and spiritless, as a commodity of financial value, when we separate ourselves from the greater community life of our own country, when human beings are understood as the summit of creation and are encouraged to take its bounty as their own, without thought of return or reciprocation.

If this process is continued, we will indeed begin to inhabit a spiritual wasteland, a place of separation wherein we have no intercourse with the abiding soul of the land.

Find out about the area in which you live. What history, myths, stories, and legends are wound into the soil? What do these tell you about the nature of your region?

Rites of Passage

How can we help our young
Who wait to cross the frontier
Between child and adulthood?
—CAITLÍN MATTHEWS, "Conference of the Trees"

The transition from childhood to adulthood is a time of emotional upheaval not well supported in our society. The preparation for adulthood requires sensitive rites of passage that actually mean something. In Celtic society, children were frequently given in fosterage to neighboring families so that this transition could be overseen by adults who were not blood kindred, who had good sense or some special skill into which the child could be inducted. The custom of fosterage also put a buffer zone between child and parent, thus avoiding the worst of the acrimonious generational confrontations that plague families during adolescence. Poorer children would receive the initiation of solitude when spring was well under way, for then the herds and flocks could be taken out of lower pastures and driven up to higher ground. There, some distance from their homes, adolescents would tend the animals, living by night in a *sheiling,* or temporary structure.

When a much-loved child crosses into the harsh frontier of adulthood, there needs to be a sense of achievement and celebration, a paving of the way, a marking of the transition. Rites of passage need to welcome the new adult into the community and value him or her.

Think back to your own time of adolescent transition. What would have made your transition easier? What ceremony would have given you a sense of achievement and self-worth? If you have children, meditate upon ways to enable their transition.

Advice

He who won't take advice will take the crooked track.
                                        —Scots Gaelic proverb

It is often said that advice is a two-edged weapon: it can both harm and help, depending upon how and whether we take it. Young Peredur (see 19 February), who was brought up in purposeful woodland seclusion by his mother, sought to go to the court of Arthur. Peredur's mother gave him advice so unworldly and indiscriminate that it subsequently led him into discourtesy of the grossest kind.

Without discrimination, advice can be worse than useless. When good and thoughtful advice is offered to us, we must have the wit to weigh it for its worth and implement it as sensitively as we can, balancing it with the prevailing circumstances that surround our case. When we offer advice to others, it must always be set within the context of our experience rather than based on someone else's criteria.

Age and wisdom tend to give advice to youthful inexperience, but it is not always welcome. The reactionary stubbornness of youth often chooses to take the longer road of personal example in order to gain wisdom. The crooked track that then unwinds may be like that traveled by Peredur—a road fraught with obstacles and difficulties. Only when we have traveled such a road and labored to clear the obstacles can we finally have a true context for advice that is offered.

From the experience of your life to date, what are the three best pieces of advice that you could offer someone about to make her way in the world?

A Cheerful Household

The house without a dog, a cat or a baby: a house without cheer and laughter.

—Scots Gaelic triad

The spiritual quality of a house is derived from its inhabitants. When the owners are away, the house seems soulless and unhappy. Those who live alone are particularly aware of this. When they arrive home, there is no one to greet them, no meal on the stove, no one with whom to share the day's activities. The presence of a pet within the house changes the whole atmosphere. Whether it be a dog, cat, goldfish, or bird, a pet charges the house with life throughout the day, and the homecoming of the solitary dweller is thus a happier one. The interdependence of animals and humans is a two-way process: not only do we care for our pets, but they also care for us, often giving us companionship when our fellow human beings do not.

A house without children is often a very formal affair, with everything preternaturally neat and totally geared to the occupants' pleasure. A house *with* children, on the other hand, is rarely either tidy or static: everything from disorder and muddle to outright chaos can typify such a home. There is a sense of nesting when babies are present, a sense of transit when the house is full of teenagers about to launch themselves on the world.

The cheerful household is one wherein love is present. As long as love inhabits the home, the spirits of neglect, solitude, and sadness are absent. We all need someone to love and someone to love us. In a house where love is absent, there is little cheer. All homes need the kindling of love; only with that kindling can the spirit of the household welcome us to its hearth.

Where is the love invested in your household?

Fallowness

All Nature seems at work.
Slugs leave their lair—
The Bees are stirring—birds are on the wing—
And Winter slumbering in the open air,
Wears on his smiling face a dream of Spring!
And I the while, the sole unbusy thing,
Nor honey make nor pair, nor build, nor sing.
    —SAMUEL TAYLOR COLERIDGE, "Work Without Hope"

When fallowness strikes, it is important to place it in the context of the creative cycle. After the period of conception—an exciting period during which we sparkle with ideas—comes the time of gathering and preparation, when things get moving. This is followed by a period of growth, which cannot be hurried, and then by the moment of ripeness, when the idea must manifest or the project get off the ground. This is followed by a time of enjoyment and appreciation, when we can share our manifest idea or plan with others. Then we must let our idea go to make its ways through the world. After all that has happened, we come to the time of fallowness.

To honor our own creative cycle and patterns, we must respect this period and learn to be as empty and receptive as we can. After any birth and manifestation, we are too tired to immediately reconceive: we need this time of rest when we lie as fallow as the unplowed field that the farmer sets aside for several seasons to regain its fertility. Let us honor our fallowness, our uncreating emptiness, by cutting ourselves some slack and giving mind and heart time to recover their former savor in a new season. Fallowness is the ground of our conception: when the soil is ready, the seed will fall and germinate.

Consider helpful strategies to sustain yourself through these empty times in ways that honor fallowness creatively.

The Between-Places

*Celtic mysteries occurred in twi-states between night and day, in
dew that was neither rain nor river, in mistletoe that was not a plant
or a tree, in the trance state that was neither sleep nor waking.*
—ELIZABETH SUTHERLAND, *Ravens and Black Rain*

For every one of us there are moments of revelation at the nexus point
where opposites meet: dark and light, joy and sorrow, knowing and
unknowing, keeping and losing, making and unmaking, silence and
singing. In these days of growing light, when spring is still far ahead
and the grip of winter is ever present, the opportunity to sample the
opposites and stand at their still center is potent. These experiences do
not have to be sought after; they arrive, magically blending elements
together to seek us out. These are thresholds of power where *néart* (see
28 January) and soul are fused in one vision of wholeness, unity, and
often ecstasy. These between-places are the creative nexus at which
vision and craft come together in embrace; this is where poetry, song,
art, beauty, and inspiration uncoil from their hidden domain.

The between-places are neither fearful nor horrific, as popular opinion has so often depicted them, nor are they filled with monsters and
demons; rather, they are thresholds of awakening where the soul is
alert and watchful for omens of change, auguries of joy, promises of
belonging.

*Be attentive to the thresholds and boundaries of your life—the places
where change happens. What is your most ardent need for transfor-
matory and revelatory change right now?*

Stories Against Ourselves

And the penance that was imposed upon her was . . . that she
should relate the story to all who should come there.
    —Pwyll, Prince of Dyfed, from *The Mabinogion*

On the night that Rhiannon (Hree-ANN'on) gave birth, her baby was stolen by an otherworldly former suitor. In the morning, the nurses were terrified of being punished for their lack of vigilance, so they killed a litter of puppies, spilled the blood upon Rhiannon's bed, and threw the small bones about in such a way as to cause onlookers to believe that the mother had devoured her own baby. Her husband, Pwyll (POO'ilh), was reluctant to condemn her, but condemned she was. Her punishment was that she stand at the mounting block in the courtyard for seven years, to stop all comers and tell them her terrible deed and to offer to carry the guest into the hall on her own back. When her child was eventually restored to her, she was released from her undeserved punishment.

For many, telling untrue stories against themselves is a daily experience. This may begin unconsciously. A parent or teacher may start the process in the early years with an observation such as, "You'll never come to any good." If this message is reiterated often enough, the story becomes self-fulfilling, accepted and believed by the person who might originally have denied its truth. Whatever the cause, the false story that we tell against ourselves can poison our lives and embitter our relationships with others. As the exemplar of those who have been burdened with false report, Rhiannon is the lifter of burdens and the singer of the true song. She can help restore self-esteem and allow a new story to shine forth.

Examine closely the "never" and "always" accounts and all the sorry
untruths that have become part of your own story. Begin to tell a new
story about yourself, taking every opportunity to detach yourself from
the old, unhappy stories that you tell against yourself.

MARCH

Month of March—great is the forwardness of the birds;
Severe is the cold wind upon the headlands;
Serene weather will be longer than the crops.
                                        —anon. Welsh poem

March gives us proof that spring has really arrived. The themes this month include observation and sensitivity to subtle messages, spring cleaning and restoring, tribal and individual consciousness, constancy and change, power and its abuses, creation and increase, public service, creative fire.

The Harp

Healer of each wounded warrior,
Comforter of each fine woman,
Guiding refrain over the blue water,
Image-laden, sweet-sounding music!
    —*The Book of the O'Connor Don,* Irish text (trans. CM)

The harp is one of the most characteristic instruments of the Celtic tradition. The harp of the Dagda (the Good God of the Gaelic gods) was magical. In it the Dagda had bound melodies that would not sound until he summoned them. It had three properties or "strains" that all harpers in ancient times used in their music, each property having a different effect. It had the *suantraigh* (SWON'tree) or "sleep strain," which lulled people to sleep. It had the *goiltraigh* (GOYL'tree) or "sorrow strain," which caused people to weep. And it had the *geantraigh* (GEON'tree) or "joy strain," which caused people to laugh.

These three harp strains are still the property of harp music today—music that can lull us into a restful state, bring tears of beauty to our eyes, or enliven us and set the foot tapping. With these three strains, harp music affects the soul: it pours comfort, balm, and rest into the soul laden with cares, burdens, and anxieties, giving it rest with the sleep strain; it plumbs the depths of sorrow and grief, of loneliness and bereavement, with the sorrow strain; it reconnects those who are lost, stressed, and humorless with the primal joy of life with the joy strain. The playing of the harp confers a special privilege upon all harpers: the ability to unlock the doors of the soul.

Choose three pieces of music that represent for you the three musical strains outlined above. Play them when your soul needs rest, relief, or uplift.

Desire of the Eyes

What is it that will not stand lock nor chain?—The eye of a person in the company of a friend: it will not abide shutting nor restraint, but only looking upon.

—from the riddle contest between Fionn
and Grainne, Scots Gaelic lore (trans. CM)

The riddling courtship of the aging Irish hero Fionn mac Cumhail and the young and lovely Grainne (FINN mak KOOL and GRAWN'ya, respectively) comes to nothing when Grainne sets eyes on Fionn's best companion, Diarmuid. Instead of marrying Fionn, Grainne runs away with Diarmuid. The desire of the eyes that they both feel cannot be tamed; they are helplessly bound to each other and have to retreat from Fionn's sight or suffer in a terrible eternal triangle.

Desire of the eyes is an affliction from which we have all suffered, whether the desire be for a person or an object. In any love affair, desire of the eyes is the first signal to those close to the couple that something is sparking, for they cannot tear their eyes away from each other. The desire that links two people together in a mutual bond is a beautiful and potent force that other people do well to avoid: it has its own attractive energy with the power to short-circuit any interference. But the unreciprocated desire of one person for an unwilling one is an unhappy bondage that sometimes leads to a series of possessive inter-ferences: stalking, interception, even soul-theft or rape. The doting parent who gazes unsparingly upon the apple of her eye with more pride than discretion inflicts the desire of the eyes upon her child; the lonely man who yearns after a woman who is ignorant of his existence inflicts unwanted attentions upon her. Despite these potential distor-tions, desire of the eyes sometimes leads to a great love that (if it is mutual) no one may sunder to the world's ending.

How does desire of the eyes affect your life? Is the attraction mutual or unreciprocated?

The Therapy of Nature

Common experience tells us that a solitary walk by the river or
ocean, a few calm hours in the woods restore the spirit and may
produce more insight . . . than the best labours of the professional
analyst.

—THEODORE ROSZAK, *The Voice of the Earth,*
cited in Paul Devereux, *Revisioning the Earth*

Now that the light is growing stronger and the first signs of spring are becoming apparent, it is good to explore the countryside and see its beauty with our own eyes. Nature is the best therapist for putting things into perspective. When we go purposefully outdoors, we enter our true, living context, becoming once more part of a world that is always there but whose gifts are excluded when we live entirely within walls, under a roof. Early Irish poetry speaks again and again of Spirit as the thatcher who roofs the sky with stars and keeps all things under divine protection. When we exchange a tiled roof for the roof of the heavens, our soul has more room to expand.

The ancients understood about taking problems for a walk: the measured pace of walking, the juxtaposition of the problem against natural surroundings, the submersion or abolition of worry in the face of the beauties and wonders of nature—all these factors enable us to discover a new perspective. Being under the mantle of nature, we receive a truer reflection of help, a more tolerant understanding, a more profound solution that encompasses not only our labyrinthine mental contortions but our physical discomforts and our emotional longings.

Take your own problem for a walk and be open to wider solutions and
perspectives.

Confederate with Eternity

*If through the channels of our homely senses we learn to envisage
with imagination the movement and murmur of life in our moment
of time, we become confederate with eternity.*

—LLEWELYN POWYS, *Earth Memories*

The many branches of science that observe the physical world and its
relationship to the cosmos are profoundly privileged in that they bring
their exponents into a close relationship with the teeming varieties of
life. Since the Age of Reason, it has been customary for science to remain
separate from what it studies and to ignore the spiritual connections
between life on either side of the veil between the worlds. Fortunately,
many scientists have discovered that the patterns revealed within the
universe show an intelligent consistency and order that is both beautiful
and implicit.

We do not have to be forever open to unseen reality or credulous of
every wonder to appreciate the implicit order of the greater universe.
This is revealed every day through our ordinary, physical senses. When
we keep the vision of nature's revelation before our eyes and imaginations, each moment becomes loaded with eternal potential. To be confederate with eternity, we need the practice of life that gives us a special
cynosure through which to view the whole universe in every precious
instant.

*Go out in nature and be present to another life form. Using each of
your physical senses, observe that life form. Now try being present to it
with your subtle senses. What different kinds of understanding do you
have? What differences are there between you and it? What similarities do you share?*

The Colors of the Winds

*North European wind-lore teaches that the quality of the wind at
the moment of the first breath determines the character of that life.*
—Nigel Pennick, *Celtic Sacred Landscapes*

In every land, the winds have different folklore associated with them;
even within the same land mass, winds bring different gifts and messages. In inland areas, for example, the wind has a different quality to
that which blows along the coast. Certain winds are thought of as
bringing luck, health, sickness, disquiet, and so on, because they blow
from a direction associated with those qualities. But there is no fixed
lore on this matter. We can discover the qualities and gifts of the winds
wherever we live in the world, seeking out their regional meanings
from our own observation rather than relying upon findings and traditions from other lands and cultures—findings that have little relevance
to our own situation.

The weather vane of our own emotions and moods is very much
attuned to the winds. Even in places where seasonal variation is less
differentiated, the subtle changes in wind speed and direction, the
change of tides and other subtle indicators of weather have an effect
upon us. Our living breath is seen as pertaining to the nature of the
winds that prevailed when we were born: our first breath gave our
bodies their initial contact with the greater world around us when we
emerged from the womb. No matter how the winds blow thereafter,
our bodies will have memory of that moment and carry certain predispositions of character.

*Make a point of checking the direction of the wind against your own
prevailing mood each day. Stand where you can feel the breeze flow.
Note your findings and record the weather that each wind brings with
it. Use this as a compass of your own behavioral swings.*

The Underground River of Creation

Apart from sleep where the creative act seems involuntary and instantaneous, it does appear that a creative process goes on all the time beneath the level of conscious thought.
—NEIL GUNN, *The Atom of Delight*

The underground river of creation curves on beneath the surface of life, its inspiring waters ever available to refresh and bring sparkle to daily life. People who feel that they are uncreative often complain that they do not know how to get access to these waters. Surely, these people assert, creative waters run through particularly gifted people only.

The way to find the ever-flowing creative river is to dig an artesian well by means of engaging actively and consciously with our creativity. By so doing, we allow the water to rise swiftly. The moment of creative conception happens in the dark, in sleep, in moments of forgetfulness, in lapses of concentration when we have been beavering to bring something wonderful to fruition—but to no avail. As we continue to work, suddenly our project starts taking shape, though progress is still gradual, inching forward day by day. The creative process cannot be hurried without loss or miscarriage of our project. However much we want it to manifest, it has to have organic space and time. It has to rest, like the dough of good bread "proving" in a warm place to double in size. The frenzy of kneading and pummeling will not hasten its arrival. The moment of manifestation, when we share our creation with others, is only one among many moments of deep satisfaction, wherein we have drunk of the sweet waters that flow deeply through us.

What are the processes of the plan you currently foster? At what stage are you at the moment?

Mysteries

The three things which surpass understanding: the work of the bees, the mind of women, and the flow and ebb of the tide.

—ancient Irish triad

Much of our world is mysterious to us. However much science explains to us about our surroundings, there remain many mysteries that still evoke wonder. Though the beekeeper is close to the work of the hive, for example, she remains essentially an outsider, able only to exploit the bees and their honey-making skill. The thought processes of women, totally congruent to the feminine understanding, are mysterious to men. The ebb and flow of the tide can be reckoned by mariners and the Coast Guard, but they are mysteries to those who have not observed them.

These unmapped terrains of mystery do not yield themselves easily to us; they are not apprehensible or quantifiable after short study. Only by observing the movement of migrating birds over many seasons, for example, do bird-watchers understand a little of that process which is natural yet deeply mysterious to the casual observer. Even our own mysterious processes are graspable only when we give time and meaningful attention to them. This means long, patient observation and notation of our dreams, our intentions, our relationship to the world. When we become more sensitive to the subtle messages that are clearly transmitted to us, we come to a deeper understanding of ourselves and our place within the world.

What intrigues you about your life? Begin to gather information by observing and tracking your inner workings; then meditate upon your findings.

The Threefold

The Sacred Three
My fortress be,
Encircling me.
Come and be round
My hearth, my home.

—Alistair MacLean, *Hebridean Altars*

The reverence for the threefold is deeply engrained in Celtic culture. This threefold conjunction is implicit within the creative process of beginning, middle, and end; in the three sacred seeds of wisdom that flash out of the cauldron of knowledge as primal sparks of inspiration; in the human family as mother, father, and child; in the apparent world as sea, land, and sky. Each of these threefolds offers an essential understanding of the nature of life itself and is recognized and revered as one of the supreme supports of the cosmos.

Ancient Celtic wisdom was encapsulated in triads, tersely gnomic renditions of precedents, proverbs, historical incidents, and knowledge that could be remembered by everyone. (Many triads are scattered through this book.) Triple-headed gods and threefold coteries of goddesses are also common in Celtic religion: a triplicity that is reflected in the Trinity—a concept thought by some scholars to have been developed by the Celtic St. Hilary of Tours in the fourth century.

Today the ancient respect for three has become part of our concept of luck: "The third time's lucky," we say. Or, if we have had two unfortunate happenings, we may wonder what the third misfortune is likely to be. Three is the number that comprises creation, destruction, and maintenance of life. For all these reasons, the Celts could not revere a greater or more encompassing number than three.

What are the three sources or supports of your life—those people, things, or places without which it would have no meaning?

The Seanchaí's Art

Lest he should lose command over the tales he loved, he used to repeat them aloud when he thought no one was near, using the gesticulations and the emphasis . . . as if he were once again the centre of a fireside story-telling.

—Alwyn and Brinley Rees, *Celtic Heritage*

The Irish traditional storyteller Seán O'Conaill, a farmer and fisherman in County Kerry who died in the 1920s, was a repository of ancient lore and story, an acknowledged *seanchaí* (SHAN'a-ky) whose memory held a fund of delightful tales. These would have been recited in the evenings after work, or at special occasions and gatherings, but especially in the dark days of winter. People have attested to listening to the same storyteller nearly every winter's night for fifteen years and hardly ever hearing the same story twice.

The memory remains a formidable tool for the transmission of teaching and stories; however, it needs not only a memorizer but also an audience or pupil to hear and receive the story. This second component alone gives life to what is memorized, which is why Sean O'Conaill needed to tell his stories to someone, even if it was only to the back of his old gray mare. Today many people are returning to storytelling and learning its skills in story groups or within their communities. Love of story is something that does not die. Perhaps as storylines and scripts in film and television become ever more mediocre and disenchanting, we will return once more to an appreciation of the *seanchaí's* art.

Memorize a story that you love well. After you have learned it, be aware of the nuances of voice and gesture that spontaneously accompany your recitation. Notice how your recitation alters among different audiences. What new meanings has an audience helped constellate for you?

Empowerment

Power of sea be yours,
Power of land be yours,
Power of heaven.

—West Highland blessing

When the life-force of the universe and the vigor that runs through our bodies are aligned with our spiritual core, then we experience our true power and live with it. The difference between *living* with power and simply *behaving* powerfully lies in one thing: those who inhabit their power by aligning with the universe freely let power pass through them, whereas those who behave powerfully hold onto power like a commodity. When the power of the cosmos is restrained, unable to come and go like a tidal current or a mighty wind, it merely inflates the holder, it does not empower her. And when it is hoarded to aggrandize the holder, she risks disease, want, misery, and a host of ills.

We all have times when we feel powerless and insignificant, but the theft of power from another person or place cannot ultimately assist us. We may have a temporary sense of strength, but it does not last. It is only when we relinquish our fearful grip that our own power comes back to our core, empowering us again. Learning how to live with our power involves living close to the truth that is within us and not deviating; it involves periodically checking out how we are behaving, how we are giving power away to things that do not need or deserve our intervention or assistance, how we are retaining or stealing power to create a cocoon of protection.

Power cannot be owned; it is only on loan to us all.

Check your own use of power in your life. What element of power that you have does not rightfully belong to you? Give back the power that you have held onto so that the tides can flow again.

Horizons New

Look, a mirage, like a round rim, a strange
Wizard's masterpiece about us:
An old line that's not there,
A boundary that never ends.

—David Emrys James, "Horizon"

Just as physical horizons lie just out of reach of our observation, so spiritual horizons stretch beyond our imaginative vision. The new navigators and explorers of our times are those who wish to map the territory that lies beyond spiritual horizons. The neat compartmentalization of the study of human consciousness into psychological and spiritual disciplines has brought us awareness of the paucity of our knowledge of those domains. Investigators who use the criteria of the physical world to investigate the spiritual world are somehow deflected from the evidences of unseen reality that people experience, claiming that those evidences are not objective or finite enough. It is obvious that such explorers will never travel beyond the narrow horizons of the physical world.

The mapping of spiritual territory can never be a scientific colonist's task; it must pass into the care of navigators who use their own experience of the shimmering horizons to draw personal conclusions. When hundreds of such experiences are collated, certain understandings begin to form—understandings that may not lead to finite physical maps but will aid us in finding our way through lands that still bear the legend "Here be dragons" in our imaginations.

What shimmers on the horizon between the worlds when you meditate?

In Our End Is Our Beginning

Our final bliss, perfectly passionate, perfectly kind:
It is our first love, long since left behind.
—Ruth Pitter, "Good Enthroned"

The surprise, delight, or astonishment that passes over the face of the dying as they glimpse what lies beyond is frequently remarked upon by those who attend a deathbed. Those who have kept vigil feel a sense of shared privilege when they observe this, a feeling of exaltation that rises up above sorrow, weariness, and bereavement. What has happened here? At the very verge of consciousness, the dying see briefly beyond the horizon that lies between life and death. What they recognize there is not a barrenness or an absence of everything; rather, it is more life, a recognition of whatever they once thought lost to them forever. That which they relinquished or neglected in years past, as well as the very potential of the soul, is rediscovered in an instant.

The wise treat death as a friend who will restore them, not only in body but also in spirit, to everyone and everything they have ever loved. Living with death as a friend, as a daily companion, is not a morbid practice. It helps to reconnect us with our beginnings, when our hopes and potential were still strongly flowing; it casts aside fear and strengthens the life that we still enjoy. If we substitute the image of our soul's beloved for the popular image of death, we will immeasurably help ourselves. (See 25 December.) Death is the soul's friend, the turner of the key, who liberates us to inhabit new freedoms and who reintroduces us to old loves so that we can find our way back to the primal beginnings of our soul's story.

Consider what hopes you have for your own death, even though hopes *is not a word you would normally apply to dying. If you have a strong fear of death, ask help of your soul's beloved—your deepest spiritual source of assistance and support—in redefining your view and creating a more confident attitude.*

Refusing Evil

And Balor begged Lugh, shortly before his beheading: "Set my head on your own handsome head and so earn my blessing. The triumph and terror that the men of Inis Fail recognised in me: I would they might be recognised within my daughter's son."

—Dunaire Finn (trans. CM)

The primordial god Balor (BAY'lor) had only one eye, but it could sear and shrivel all that it looked upon so that few could overcome him. His grandson, Lugh (LOO'kh), was destined to overcome Balor and his magic. But even at the point of death, Balor attempted to subvert his bright grandson. Threatened with beheading, he saw a way in which his stolen power could live on: he bade Lugh place his grandfather's head upon his own in order that the young man might inherit Balor's deadly powers. In a dialogue reminiscent of that between Darth Vader and Luke Skywalker, Lugh does not submit himself to "the darkening of the force"; he resolutely beheads Balor and casts his head into the deep waters of the western ocean.

The ability to refuse evil and not be swayed by its persuasions is not strong in us if we are not in the habit of attending to the integrity and virtue of our soul. Evil does not always have a baleful eye, greedy teeth, and a dark cloak; it can appear in attractive forms that sway our opinion before we have given it heed. To work against the purposes of our soul, against the harmony of the universe, is to place ourselves in league with those who serve only themselves, who are interested not in preserving the web of life but in making life serve them. Evil can be increased if we give power to it; its diminishment lies in our refusal to serve it.

Where has evil touched your life recently? Meditate upon how its power steals the power of the universe. Ask your spiritual allies to show you what protects you from evil.

Spring Cleaning

Old loves, old insults, old wrongs, old hates, old prides, old con-
tempts, old horrors, old taboos, old totems. . . . [C]an I shed these
worm-skins of remembrance?

—John Cowper Powys, *Obstinate Cymric*

At this season, we are often driven into a bout of spring cleaning, throwing out the unwanted and bringing new order to our household. But what of the deeper hurts, the old anguish, the festering wrongs, and the immovable obstinacies of our very being?

Select one such malingering obstruction to be removed from your mental attic by asking and answering the following questions:

- What past wrong or hurt embitters you the most?
- What past relationship still lingers painfully?
- What childhood horror shadows you?
- What irrational prejudice still clouds your horizon?
- To what or whom are you still shackled by hate?
- What long-dead voice of authority still has you leaping?
- What old story against yourself still rankles?

Now take a walk in nature, meditating upon the issue at hand. Let your eye fall upon things that seem to speak to you about your own case: these might be fallen leaves, pieces of rubbish blowing about, feathers, berries, bark, mushrooms, flowers, and so on. Without damaging the landscape and its inhabitants, collect some of these things and assemble them into an emblem of your issue. These collected items can be tied together with string or woven together with grasses. Create something really beautiful. When it is complete, make a small fire outside. Relinquish your issue to the cleansing flames and burn the emblem you have made, visualizing its influence passing away from you. Stay and watch the emblem turn to ash and be borne away.

Make an emblem and burn it, as suggested above.

Solitariness

It is a good thing to be happy alone. It is better to be happy in company, but good to be happy alone.

—THOMAS TRAHERNE, *Centuries*

Among tribal and traditional peoples today, few choose to be solitary. Purposeful periods of solitude or seclusion are normally experienced only by young people facing their rites of passage—times during which they are taken from their families to be instructed in tribal lore and adult responsibility. In such rites, each young person generally endures a short period of isolation wherein he encounters the spirits of the tribe in a visionary way. Awareness of the otherworld and the way it impinges upon our own reality is one of the fruits of solitariness.

When we are far from the interaction of society, when the chatter and comment of our minds is stilled, then it is possible to enter into a deeper relationship with the universe that we inhabit. The revelations of solitude are often profoundly moving, and though we may share them in conversation with friends afterward, we do not find it easy to reach into the depths that we have inhabited within our solitude once we return to company again.

To be content with one's own company is an art that cannot be taught; it is something we each have to learn as our lives unfold. When there is nothing to distract us, we return to the primal ground of our being, where we can begin to learn who we truly are and discover our context within the rest of the universe.

Whether you are naturally solitary or gregarious, enter the spaciousness of solitude and be aware of your true self and its context.

Change

Now ebb, now flood, now friend, now cruel goe;
Now glad, now sad, now weel, now into woe;
Now clad in gold, dissolvit now in ash;
So dois [does] this warld transitory go.

—WILLIAM DUNBAR, "O Wretch, Beware"

The alternation of order and chaos are natural frequencies that balance our lives. Custom and change are but their children, who allow new influences and possibilities into the world. When things become too formalized and ordered, they become stale and static, lacking the life and energy that only change can bring. Yet when change strikes, we feel out of control, disordered, even attacked by its sudden overturning of all that we have known. Despite that, change is not, of its essence, antagonistic to *us*, only to our habitual and clinging notions. Long periods of change and fluctuation can be very wearing, however, because we have no order or pattern to give context to our living.

The period leading up to the spring equinox is similarly a time of great upheaval in nature: the first full moon of March usually heralds high tides and strong winds that enliven the long-dead period of late winter. The change of spring is one that we welcome with all our hearts, but we appreciate it warmly only because of what has gone before it. Our ability to cope with change will improve if we discover the art of living in the present moment, of being at home where and when we are.

What strategies do you use for coping with change? Meditate upon the fresh opportunities and energies that change is currently bringing to your life.

Privilege

There are three sorts of privilege: natural privilege, privilege of office, and privilege of land.

—triad from *Laws of Hywel Dda*

In our time, many people are resentful of privilege whenever they encounter it, seeing only one half of the contract that privilege entails. Yet privilege is nothing less than the taking on of responsibility and guardianship. Those who enter professional occupations take on onerous public duties and have a responsibility to those whom they serve, not to themselves. To whom more is given, more is required. Privilege of land is a special responsibility, whether we have only a garden to maintain or a large estate. The responsibility of caring for and not abusing the land under our charge is a heavy one.

Keeping to our own part, to our own duties, enables us to be part of the whole. It is not one person's task to do everything. With our emphasis on the nuclear family, we have lost the close sense of community whereby everyone contributes something and has his or her place. Instead, we aim to be superpeople. The privileges that are accorded to each of us depend upon our contribution to the whole. In modern terms, natural privilege now applies to each person: we each receive the privilege of respect as a living being according to our responsiveness to our place in the world.

Carefully consider the tasks and roles that you are currently maintaining. Are you contributing to your community, or are you taking on too many tasks?

The Gifts of the Awen

Then Ceridwen began to boil the cauldron. . . for a year and a day until
three blessed drops of Inspiration had been obtained from the brew.
—HANES TALIESIN, Welsh text (trans. CM)

When Ceridwen (Ker-RID'wen) brewed her cauldron of inspiration, she set a boy called Gwion (GWEE'on) to tend it. Three drops leaped from the cauldron and burned his hand. As he sucked the scalded spot to cool it, knowledge came to him in an instant. He hid in a variety of shapes, but while hiding as a grain of wheat he was eaten by Ceridwen, who was in the form of a red hen. Resuming her usual form, she conceived him in her womb; nine months later he was born and sent forth upon the waters in a skin bag. Eventually he was discovered in a salmon weir, where he was recognized as Taliesin (Tal-ee-ESS'in).

The three drops of inspiration—the *awen* (AH'wen)—are encryptions of primal creative power, having the ability to change our lives. Their impact upon Gwion was such that he had to be literally born again in order to assimilate the knowledge he unwittingly gained. The *awen* is not merely an old myth, however; it is a living possibility. It arises when the rays of experience glance upon and inspire the dormant seeds of knowledge within us. The connective energy of inspiration runs through our being, bridging areas of ignorance, reconnecting areas of neglect, bringing into one teeming mass of imagery, metaphor, and understanding all that we are about. The assimilation of this experience can take the rest of our lives, or we can welcome the manyfold experiences of our lives to help ripen our understanding from day to day.

The gifts of the *awen* lie dormant within each of us, to inspire, connect, and creatively empower all that we touch. From the creative soup of our personal experience, we can leap out to play in the teeming waters of the river of life as wise ones who are able to assimilate all that befalls us.

What are the three main inspirations of your life experience?

Clearing Ill-Report

Unfortunate the one whose name has been linked to ill-report since youth.

—Welsh saying

Once a story attaches to us, it is hard to shift. Gossip and hearsay usually run ahead of any good repute we have. It is particularly unfortunate if a story attaches to us when we are young. Once it is believed that we are difficult, unreliable, or badly behaved, this "information" has a way of following us around and becoming a self-fulfilling prophecy that sabotages all that we attempt.

How do we make good our reputation once ill-report has done its work? Many people attempt to clear their name by starting again in a new place—a place where their actions will not be prejudged by others who know their story.

Those who choose to remain where they are and attempt to make good need at least one ally who will support and encourage them, someone who will be an advocate in the community, someone who will witness and support their intention to start again. But the final change of reputation will take place only when others observe the fruits of change with their own eyes—and it may take a very long time for marked improvement to become visible. People who have an old story thrown into their faces again and again need to reiterate, "That was then; this is now. I'm changing, but I can change only with your help and support." (See also 16 November.)

Consider an old story that attached to you when you were younger. Think about how you have struggled against or overcome its spell. If the story still sticks to you, meditate upon the way you want to be now.

The Apprenticeship of Love

Seven long years I served for thee,
The glassy hill I climbed for thee,
The bloody shirt I wrang for thee,
Will you not waken and turn to me?
—*The Black Bull of Norroway,* Scottish Folk Story

The Scots folk story *The Black Bull of Norroway* tells of a young woman who goes to a seer to get knowledge of her future love. Her furture husband comes to her in the enchanted shape of a black bull. They become separated, and the woman has to suffer many trials to find and win him again: she must climb a hill of glass with shoes of iron, apprenticing herself to a smith for seven years to make them, and in the end must wash her lover's bloody shirt to disenchant him.

This story is nothing less than a tale about the apprenticeship we each serve to love. Although it is told about a woman's love-quest, it would apply equally to that of a man. The first stages of love are often as uncertain and headlong as the heroine's flight on the bull's back: neither partner is sure of the other, and there are many unrealistic expectations on both sides. Love may not be equal at the beginning, so one partner may need to be patient while the other discovers a similar depth of affection. The ability to be constant, consistent, and reliable is one learned over a long period; during this period, many relationships falter or come to grief. The glassy hill of love presents a great challenge to the faithful lover. The spiked shoes of iron are not made overnight. And many a shirtful of wounds may have to be laundered before old loves and hates learned in past relationships are leached out of the present one. Constancy, perseverance, and patience are the skills we learn in the apprenticeship of love.

Meditate upon your own apprenticeship to love. Where has your story got to? Which qualities need more development?

The Prayer of the Spring Equinox

*With the first rays of the sun on the plant's leaves its ethereal spirit
is strong enough to summon our convention-blinded souls to this
primitive worship.*

—LLEWELYN POWYS, *Earth Memories*

At last we have a clear sign that the year is rising from the enclosing
darkness of winter into a warmer, brighter world. On this first day of
spring, the sun is at its midway mark, halfway between midwinter and
midsummer, when its glory will be greater still. This is a good day for
beginnings.

Make a gift of this day, dedicating it to the beginning of a new phase
of your life, or to a new plan or enterprise, rather than doing your
mundane work. Begin the day by greeting the sunrise, if you are able,
becoming aware of the passing darkness of winter and seeing the sun
as the herald of the light that will grow from now on.

Stand in the light of midday, facing the sun, and tune your heart to
the season of spring and all that it means to you. Be aware of how your
own soul's circuit and the circuit of the sun are being aligned and
attuned to each other. Make your own prayer for this spring quarter on
behalf of all beings. Then turn and face your shadow, feeling the sun
upon your back. Your shadow is shorter than it was at midwinter and
will shorten even more as the year grows.

Project your thoughts and intentions forward over the next few
months. Over what activities, plans, and events is your shadow going
to fall? Draw the light into your body and allow the sap-rising spring
to penetrate to your soul. Be aware of the fusion between body and
soul, of their unity with the light and the season. Open your eyes,
becoming aware of your surroundings and your life's purpose. As you
prepare to sleep, be thankful for the darkness and the rest that enable
everything to grow.

Stand in the sun at midday, as suggested above.

The Increasing Year

Three things which are always increasing: the light of fire, the intelligence of truth, the life of existence—these are victorious over all things and are the end of darkness.

—Welsh triad (trans. CM)

From this day on, the sun is climbing toward its zenith at midsummer in the northern hemisphere: a good day on which to consider the optimistic triad printed above and the many things that are growing and increasing in our own lives and in the unfolding history of the world.

The radiant spark of light is at the core of every creative being; it leaps from place to place, from heart to heart, changing and forever growing. Nothing can stop this spark from spreading through the world like flame through a piece of charcoal. It is becoming harder and harder to pull the wool over people's eyes, to deceive others for more than a short period of time. This is predominantly because of better education and the discernment that derives from it.

The many associations around the world that uphold human rights are in the business of protecting truth and justice. Countries and regimes that give truth nothing more than lip service are increasingly having to fight off criticism from without and dissent from within, as consciousness and truth increase.

Our whole consciousness of what life is, of how we live it and how we ethically deal with it, is the next challenge that will increase the boundaries of our understanding.

Meditate upon three wonderful things that have increased within your own lifetime. How have these increases changed the world?

Power of the Word

Tongue is weak and tongue is woe,
Tongue is water and tongue is wine,
Tongue is chief of melody,
And tongue is thing that fast will bind.
—"Prophecies of Thomas of Erceldoune,"
Scottish text (trans. CM)

It is probably impossible to fully realize these days the power of the word in the Celtic world. In a society that used no writing, the word had a primacy that can scarcely be now imagined. The poets, druids, and judges were highly respected, because what came out of their mouths was not only the lore of the tribe; it was also the *truth*. Like Thomas the Rhymer, the Scottish poet who entered the world of faery and won from the Faery Queen "the tongue which cannot lie," the gifted ones of the Celtic tradition could use their skills both mundanely and magically.

While the poet most often used his skill to praise patrons, recite genealogies, encourage, and enchant, he could also call upon formidable verbal powers to initiate change. A poet's satire was not just a painful lampoon that others would snicker about; it could actually raise blisters upon the face of the subject, bringing shame. It is said that a well-placed satire could even cause death.

In many people, the tongue is untrained and weak, and some use it only for spreading gossip and for scaremongering. While speech can be workaday or poetic, it can also be the music that enchants and inspires, the wine of praise; it can be used as a weapon to bind, both in truthful promise and in smiting satire.

Strengthen the power of the word in your mouth by speaking only truth today.

The Greater Good

Three things for which a person might hazard his/her life and lose
it: the search for truth, the upholding of justice, the performance
of mercy.

—Welsh triad (trans. CM)

The eternal search for truth engages many people in a dangerous quest, whether that quest be research into life-threatening diseases in an attempt to find a cure, the struggle of writers, poets, and activists to maintain the voice of truth in the face of restrictive regimes, or any of myriad other pursuits.

The upholding of justice is a worldwide concern. Although we may complain that judicial systems are antiquated and need reform in the West, at least we have a system of justice, however poorly we may believe it to function. In parts of the world where dictatorship, war, and other evils reign, justice is a gun in the hand, and there are many daily who die in attempting to bring an end to unjust governance.

The performance of mercy endangers life every day: wherever the land, the weather, or the prevailing conditions are dangerous, there are teams of rescue workers and health professionals who hazard their own lives in order to save those of others.

Those whose view of humankind is a very low one, who believe humans to be intrinsically selfish and greedy, need only look at the lives of the defenders of truth, justice, and mercy to change their opinion. If we cannot venture our lives in defense of the three principles named in the above triad, then there is indeed little hope for our species; but there never seems to be a lack of compassionate people who put their own concerns aside and risk their very lives in defense of the greater good.

Make a blessing of protection for all who hazard their lives in defense
of lofty principles.

Young Love

Oh that I and my choice of partners were in yon glen up there, no witness beneath the white sun, save the bright star and the planets; no simple infant with no sense, no gabbling one there nor lying one to spread about the story.

—*Carmina Gadelica* (trans. and ed. A. Carmichael)

The sexual passion that wells up in young lovers is akin to the urgent energy of spring. It is vibrant and undivertible, a deep sap that rises irresistibly to the surface. The need to be private, to experience the ecstasy of young love when it is running, is one that we all understand well. Within the family home and community, there are always people to snoop and spy, and soon the story goes around that a certain girl is going with a particular boy. Only in the broad expanse of the natural world is there any privacy for lovemaking.

Regardless of the moral upbringing children are given, most find ways to express their potent sexual urges, whether they are mature enough to form lasting relationships or not. This period of sexual experimentation is one that all animals undergo. In humans, it rarely leads to marriage or a committed relationship.

The fears of parents for their children around sexual matters are very real ones. Sexually-related diseases and life-wrecking consequences haunt parental minds at night, as do fears for emotional vulnerability and spiritual health. No amount of sex education can prepare young people for the immense power of physical desire, as life itself begins to pour through their bodies. We might as well try to push plants and saplings back into the earth as forbid all sexual activity. Life will find its way through our children, as it did through us. All we can do is ensure their well-being in the best ways we know how.

Consider your own sexual awakening. What advice can you offer the young and their parents, based on your own experiences?

Trees and the Life of the Planet

Every tree is a living watercourse; its roots, trunk and branches conduct water up from the soil to the leaves, from which it then passes into the atmosphere.

—NIGEL PENNICK, *Celtic Sacred Landscapes*

The interdependence of all living things is something we often take for granted. It goes unnoticed in the daily round, so we forget that what happens in one place has its effect upon another place. It is only now that deforestation has been revealed to be a terrible legacy to our children that we begin to appreciate the contribution of trees to the life of our planet.

At this time of year, the spring rains have an important function in the revivification of the land, especially around the full moon. Trees are able to draw up the rainfall from their roots to their highest branches so that the canopy can become green again. As the leaves emerge from their buds, we notice a corresponding unfurling of spirit in ourselves as we respond with gladness to the annual regreening of the world.

As those leaves unfurl, they exude oxygen, so vital for our planet's atmosphere and our own living breath. The carbon dioxide that human beings exhale is absorbed and transformed by trees. Our lives and those of the trees are beautifully and aptly intertwined as we share and replenish the atmosphere for each other. Our breath and the exhalation of trees have a symbiotic link that is necessary to our very life.

Verdancy of spirit comes when the sap rises in our souls, when we return to a state of thankfulness and welcome the spring with joy.

Attune to the life of a tree that grows near you. Meditate upon the life that you share. Even better, plant a tree.

Invulnerability

I am an indestructible fortress,
I am an unassailable rock,
I am a precious jewel.

—from an ancient Irish prayer
for long life (trans. CM)

To be invulnerable means never to be wounded. Yet it is the nature of life for human beings to suffer assaults from many quarters. Our bodies endure various accidents and illnesses; our emotions are roiled by fierce winds; our minds are subject to doubt, fear, delusion.

For those on the druid path, death is not the end. The soul passes into other forms to find rebirth again and again. Similar beliefs are still held around the world in many cultures. It is only in the West, where we have disbelieved in any other reality than the apparent world, that we have an awesome terror of death. For many people today, this life is all there is or will be. No wonder they live without joy or expectation!

Only the soul is deathless. It is indeed our indestructible fortress, our precious jewel, our unassailable rock. So where, then, is the eternal vigilance in our care of the soul? Where are the limberings, the workouts, the exercise programs, the efforts at beautification and enhancement of the soul? If we truly wish to share confidently in the invulnerability of the soul, we need to polish our jewel and peer deeply into its primordial and unassailable facets to find the beauty that cannot die.

What are the gifts of your vulnerability?

~ 28 MARCH ~

Defending Ancient Springs

Where her head was lifted, a spring was found . . .
Healing for every disease is within it . . .
Making body and soul whole.
　　—*Life of St. Gwenfrewi,* anon. Welsh chronicle (trans. CM)

The communion with the holy waters of a well or sacred spring is intrinsically part of Celtic tradition. All natural places of water have their own indwelling spirit, but many wells and springs frequently have holy, curative properties.

The way in which we approach these sacred waters matters a great deal. The tendency among many people now exploring and discovering the sacred sources of land, heritage, and culture is to act as consumers, demanding that the sacred otherworld give to us unstintingly. We do not participate in the sacred by such action; rather, we disconnect ourselves from participation. We can so easily become takers rather than givers. The act of sacred participation always requires us to give the gift of ourselves, to honor the sacred presence, to respond and reciprocate with our very best. This means behaving appropriately when we visit: not using the sacred place as a site for mundane refreshment, for example, smoking or picnicking or listening to the radio. When we come within the compass of ancient springs, we are on holy ground. When we take the waters, it should be prayerfully and thankfully, engaging spiritually with the guardian spirit of the waters.

By not allowing ourselves to become consumers of the otherworldly gifts that present themselves so generously to us, by reciprocating with thanks, we permit those gifts to work their own healing, reconnective magic upon us.

Find out where your own nearest source of sacred water is to be found.
What are the traditions surrounding it? Go and visit it if you can, and
experience the waters for yourself.

The Green Fire

Aengus is a deathless comrade of the Spring, and we may well
pray to him to let his green fire move in our veins.
—Fiona MacLeod, "The Birds of Aengus Og"

Aengus mac Og (ANN'gus mak OGE) is the Irish deity whose spirit inhabits the megalithic monument of Newgrange in the Boyne Valley of Ireland. (See 21 December.) His hostel on the banks of the Boyne is a traditional entrance to the otherworld, a place where souls congregate and rest. In their soul's circuit, several Irish heroes and heroines have become lost or disoriented. It is within Aengus's care that they are given time to recover.

Birds and other animals begin to choose their mates as the growing year burgeons strongly in the strengthening sunlight. The green fire that runs over all the earth is sparked by this very sunlight and the deep germinating power of the earth. When plants reach toward the sunlight, the red, violet, and blue bands of the light spectrum activate the chlorophyll pigment within each leaf so that it reflects green. This pigment alters as the year progresses, causing the leaves to change color, but from this time forward a medley of greens is apparent.

This green fire is also within us—not in our physical bodies, as it is in plants, but in our emotional and creative lives. Spring fever has many manifestations, some almost hormonal. The creative urge of spring brings into being much verse, for example, as our emotional upheavals reach out for fresh life and vigor. To experience the green fire and answer its call is to commune with the green vigor of Aengus.

Where is the green fire in your own life at this time? Take your emo-
tional and creative temperature; then give yourself over to something
pleasurable and enlivening this week.

The Hidden Truth of Dreams

Your dream tells a truth about yourself. A truth you hide from while you are awake. A truth you need to know about yourself. For your . . . wellbeing.

—DAVID RUDKIN, *Penda's Fen*

Dreams are messengers of the soul. Every one of us has dreams, whether or not we remember them. Dreams speak of hidden truths in oblique ways—truths that we have not been able to understand or assimilate in our waking lives. Their enigmatic symbolism cannot be decoded by books of dream interpretation that give pat or plausible answers for standard dream themes; dreams must be decoded entirely by the dreamer and scrutinized for their personal symbolism.

What is the truth that we need to know about ourselves? Whatever we have covered over or hidden from in our daily lives has a way of breaking through in self-disclosing (and often pun-filled) ways in our dreams. For example, we may dream of putting an annoying but senior colleague at work into the garbage, while in waking life we seriously wish that we could put a lid on his snide remarks.

In a society that defines dreams as wacky or illusory, it can be hard for us to realize that they reveal to us the nature of our waking self-delusion. Dreams not only warn of dangers; they also reveal areas that we have never dared explore because of their power or wonder. Dreams bring us to meet the potentialities of our soul in a remarkable manner: we may dream that we are flying, dancing, shining, meeting—deep truths that are the very essence of our well-being, that we can find, court, and assimilate if only we listen to our soul's messengers.

Take one dream fragment from this week. Without giving it a psychological spin-dry, look at it honestly and see what truth it has to tell you. What emotions does your dream evoke? Where is your power free or suppressed? What is the overall impression or message it conveys?

Seeding the Wasteland

Learning the mysteries whereby wasteland
Becomes wheatland: grains must fall
Into the hungry earth and be swallowed whole.
—CAITLÍN MATTHEWS, "Avebury Easter"

When wasteland has become an ever-present reality, when something stricken has lain barren for many years, it takes special grace to recover again. It is not a matter of snapping back into normal mode or of pulling ourselves together. It is usually a matter of picking up the pieces slowly and painfully, an organic process that can take a long time. This reassembly is like a gathering of precious seeds and fertile fragments, a putting-together of the essential selves that form our soul, so that life's flavor and savor can return.

The scattered seeds that hold the potential of our lives must come home and rest once more in the familiar soil of everyday living before the grain can germinate and send its long shoots toward the sun. This mysterious return is begun by preparing the soil to receive the seed. The farmer must remove all obstructions from the ground; the hatreds, fears, lies, and treacheries have to be relinquished. Then the plow must turn over the soil; all the deep needs of the soul must be acknowledged and an urgent request for help and return be sent up. This is a time for singing over the ground of loss in consolation, and a time for singing for the scattered seeds to come back, letting them know that they are welcome.

The mysterious sowing happens in silence and unknowing: the soul seeds return and lodge in the deep earth. There they will rest, germinating in their own time, until the once-barren wasteland becomes fertile again.

Look at the causes of your wasteland; then let go of the fears, hatreds, and other obstacles that impede your return to full health and wholeness. Now begin the work of welcoming back whatever qualities have fled. Be patient, persevering, and hopeful.

APRIL

Month of April—aerial is the horizon;
Fatigued the oxen; bare the land;
Common is the visitor without an invitation.
                                                —anon. Welsh poem

April sees the full flush of spring. This month's themes include friends, opponents, and spiritual allies; healing and care of the body and soul; the variety of spiritual approaches; bridging and mediating the otherworld; walking our own path.

Good Friends

I pledge my oath without boasting,
For how ever many good people we might name,
A hundred of them would not match Cerna's goodness—
If we could even call so many to mind.
    —The Metrical Dindshenchas, ed. Edward Gwynn (trans. CM)

What constitutes a good friend? Someone who is insightful, like-souled, tolerant of our failings, someone who says the right thing at the right time, someone who blesses us by her quiet support, someone who helps us laugh at our inflated notions, someone who mourns with us in our sad times. Friends are the sisters and brothers of our soul. But friendship is a two-way street; there are obligations on both sides.

Although the rules of friendship are unwritten, it is clear to both partners when they are broken. If we transgress against trust and confidentiality, if we allow the friendship to become one-sided or without meaningful exchange, if we fail to communicate about a misunderstanding over too long a time, if we keep something of our friend's and forget to give it back, if we presume to speak on behalf of our friend without authority, then we break the rules of friendship.

The bond of friendship is shaken by neither time nor distance. It abides beyond temporal boundaries, necessities, and unseen contingencies in profound and beautiful ways.

Meditate upon friendship as a friend and as one who is befriended. On what are your own friendships based; how are they sustained? What do you value most in your friends?

Bringing the Peace

And have you brought the wisdom
That we have near lost?
Or have you brought the peace
That we're all aching for?
　　　　　—MARY MCLAUGHLIN, "Bring the Peace"

Peace begins at home. Many of us have peaceful intentions regarding the world at large, but what is the use of feelings of cosmic peace if our own heart is troubled and we cannot keep peace within the family or between neighbors? Conflict should be set aside as we lie down to rest, since it blocks the path to peace. (Toward that end, the self-clarification shown below can be used at the end of the day, before sleeping.) Only by the surrender of forgiveness can conflict finally and completely be resolved, however.

This surrender is hard to achieve, because it means giving up pride, boundaries, territories, rights, and many other issues that we instinctively defend. Peace does not require us to tear down natural defenses or let the other party invade our domain, but it does require us to extend hospitality of spirit. Peace will sprout only when we ourselves spill tears of release upon the hard ground of our hearts.

Meditate upon the following questions.

- *Is there peace between me and my soul? my family? my neighbors? my environment? my country?*
- *Is there peace between my faith, race, and generation and those of others?*
- *Is there peace between my country and the world?*
- *Is there peace between me and Spirit?*

Finally, make your own blessing upon those with whom you are currently in conflict: "May there be peace between me and _____; and may Spirit breathe peace into every breast."

Spiritual Sentinels

The inner warriors and sentinels that give us the steel to stare into the night and look the unknown in the eye are there for everyone to call upon.

—MARK RYAN AND CHESCA POTTER, *The Greenwood Tarot*

Many people now consider themselves to be separate, alone, autonomous, put on earth to live this life and this life only. This has created a curious self-dependency: they rely upon themselves alone, upon no other agency. Yet in the Celtic world, every enterprise, however humble, would have been preceded by an appeal to the watching spirit or guardian angel for protection.

Many people today are as unaware of their own guardian spirit as they are of any other source of spiritual help. To contact our guardian spirit, we have only to ask for it to be made known to us, and then spend a short period each day in meditation as we wait for it to make itself known. For those who have ignored or neglected their spiritual allies, this process of attention is very important. Just going to the threshold between the worlds and waiting, patiently, hopefully, welcomingly is an act of love that signals our readiness to cooperate.

We can envisage ourselves going to the place where we best love to be and waiting, perhaps holding some special concern in our hearts, with a view to meeting our guardian at this location. Whatever comes to your place to meet you, do not accept it unquestioningly; ask it if it is your guardian spirit. If it is not for you, do not engage with it, but neutrally let it be. Do not be surprised if your guardian spirit is not in anthropomorphic form. It may appear to you as either some kind of creature or being or a mixture of two kinds of being. When you have met it finally—and this may take several attempts over several months, so be patient—ask your guardian spirit for help about something that concerns you, not out of curiosity but out of need.

Spend time discovering or communing with your guardian spirit/angel.

∽ 4 APRIL ∽

The Art of Mediation

I am in the place between sun and moon, where the lightning-flash strikes.

—ROSS NICHOLS, *The Book of Druidry*

Mediators stand "between sun and moon," ready to heed the messages of the sacred sources of traditional wisdom from ancestral depths and to help bring through the ideas and blueprints that originate in the otherworld. Mediators are the burden-bearers and shock-absorbers of our world. They do not ask for this responsibility, but they are called to this work by their spiritual allies and shown how to handle the vital power that can transform and bridge worlds. Their work is done not for personal gain or spiritual aggrandizement, but for the benefit of all life. All spiritual traditions have their mediators, but the world does not usually know them. While the work of mediation is not secret, it is usually performed behind the scenes.

Mediation is not analogous to channeling or mediumship, which often put one in touch with nothing more than the chatter of unclarified spirits. Great mediators do not produce many manifest works. Instead, their work is like that of a satellite, which receives signals and transmits them to the world at large. For most of us, the function of mediation is to be in the right time and the right place simultaneously. The purposes of spirit are not known to us, but we do sometimes have the feeling of being at the place where lightning strikes, the sense that we are called to conduct a feeling or meaning that is greater than our personal comprehension. It is then that we stand briefly in the shoes of the mediator.

Make your own prayer for all mediators who help bridge realities for the greater needs of the world.

Walking the Earth Sacredly

It is all sacred. Every hill and every valley. Our land is a living thing, not a grave of forgetfulness under our feet.

—OWEN M. EDWARDS, cited in Emyr Humphreys,
The Taliesin Tradition

The way in which we walk the earth matters greatly, but our feet do not always remember this. Instead of walking the earth sacredly, we tend to stamp with proud disrespect in every stride. How can we remember the sacred dimension of the earth? Only when we realize it as a living entity does this understanding come home to roost. Nearly everyone has at some point experienced the impinging of a greater living presence when we have seen a beautiful view or stood at a powerful land feature through which the earth's soul is clearly discernible, but this feeling fades away once we are back in our home surroundings.

To get a sense of the living presence of the earth as an ensouled being, we can chose to purposely notice the abiding life of the earth by sitting in nature and focusing upon its breathing, its rhythms, and its soul. This requires that we filter out our own concerns and presence and focus instead upon the earth's. Whenever we give up this kind of time and attention, the rewards are striking. We learn, at first hand, the beauty and presence of the sacred earth; we hear its ancient stories, songs, and myths; we become aware of the humbling fact that we are a part of the earth, not the earth of us.

With this realization, we can take up a new relationship with our planet, walking gently and with remembrance, dancing the song-lines of the living mythic landscape in our soul's circuit.

Today, wherever you walk, be aware of each step as a blessing upon the earth.

An Opponent's Criticism

What is sharper than the sword?—The reproach of an adversary.
—from the riddle contest between
Fionn and Grainne (trans. CM), Scottish lore

There is nothing like the sting of an opponent's criticism to needle us into reaction. Such criticisms trespass upon our self-esteem and dent our pride past bearing. We find ourselves retaliating with scornful rejoinders, and we think up vengeful scenarios that will teach the opponent a well-placed lesson, even though we do not intend to implement them. Leaving aside unjust, outrageous, or malignant criticism, most criticism has a kernel of truth, which is what makes it so painful to receive. We are aware, even as we are hurt by the words, that there is some justification for complaint or reproach. The criticism of friends strikes us with less force, since it is usually framed in a kindly way, but the criticism of enemies—who see with the deadly eye of knowledge what we are all about—is threateningly penetrating.

For Fionn, the sting of Grainne's reproach lay in the fact that he was old—something that he could do nothing about. In courting a woman several decades his junior, he laid himself open to such treatment. There is no fool like an old fool, they say, and certainly Fionn experienced the full shame and reproach of rejection here.

We can learn from our opponents a good deal more about ourselves than we will ever learn from forbearing friends.

Consider a recent incident in which one of your opponents criticized you. What truth emerges from your reflection? What does your reflection tell you about yourself and how you conduct your life? What resolve springs up in you as a result?

Nature's Power to Heal

Your pain and sickness
Be in the earth's depths,
Be upon the grey stones,
For they are enduring . . .
Be upon the clouds of the sky,
For they are the rainiest,
Be upon the river's current
Cascading to the sea
—Scots Gaelic prayer for healing (trans. CM)

A common treatment of illnesses in Celtic tradition involved invoking the help of the elements—the sky, the earth, the sea—to disperse illness harmlessly. For mysterious or persisting conditions, the patient would seek out a sacred site and ask for spiritual assistance from the guardian of that site—a saint, spirit, or deity. This custom still endures throughout the Celtic countries, where it is believed that pilgrimage to a sacred site, in conjunction with prayer, is a sure form of assistance. On arrival at the site, the pilgrim makes a *turas* (or sunwise circuit) around the perimeter, with prayer or invocation. If the site is a well, then the pilgrim takes the waters and anoints the afflicted part, again very intentionally and prayerfully. Then, if a tree hangs over or near the well, it is customary to tie a piece of cloth to a branch and pray, "I leave a portion of my illness in this place." As the cloth fades and withers in the sunlight and wind, dispersing in the elements, so fades the illness.

Applying to the wider web of the universe, to the spiritual sources of help, is an eminently sensible course of action: the powers of spiritual allies—from the great elements to our own personal helpers—have a wider influence than those of doctors. Their power to transform pain, disorder, and infection into health is miraculous.

Ask your own spiritual allies to help heal your infirmities.

Many Mansions

The Son has spoken of the Father's many mansions: he has succes-
sively stripped the bark of revelation in each age of the many-
coloured world.

—CAITLÍN MATTHEWS, *The Celtic Book of the Dead*

The coming of Christianity to the Celtic peoples overturned many ancient traditions—not all of them desirable or sustainable—and brought a new way of traveling the soul's circuit. The new teachings were received through a Pagan consciousness that found the idea of universal redemption—the welcoming of all, regardless of social condition or gender, into the family of God—both astounding and appealing. The fusion of Pagan and Christian elements can be seen in the quote above. The poet, using the imagery of bark, expresses a connection between the cross and the otherworldly tree—a tree which penetrates all ages and upon which can be seen seed, blossom, and fruit simultaneously. In druidic belief, there was a strong sense of the way in which souls pass through sequential worldly time and through the timelessness of the otherworld. Some of these ways could be identified as exemplars of great power.

The poet sees Christ as a Celtic exemplar: one who has seen the rise and fall of the many-colored ages and who, like a vision poet, has stripped the bark of the otherworldly tree to read its revelations. It is in the bridging of these two beliefs that the poet derives power and comfort. As we enter a time of religious pluralism, our own consciousness is full of the metaphors and symbols of Christian belief. They frame and shape the ideas and beliefs that we hold, even though we may not be practitioners of the faith. Because of this grounding in Christian thought, we sometimes experience doubt and confusion when we encounter other belief systems. If, however, we remember the concept of many mansions, many manifestations of spiritual truth, we will not be in error.

Meditate upon the beliefs that have power for you.

The Five Streams

Our violated senses yearn back to the flow
Of Segais' well: five pure streams
Bridging the worlds with wonder.

—Caitlín Matthews, "Avebury Easter"

When King Cormac visited the otherworld, he saw a shining fountain bubbling up, with five streams running out of it. Nine hazelnut trees grew over the fountain, dropping their nuts into the waters; and a salmon swam in the pool, eating the nuts and sending the husks down the streams. Cormac found himself transfixed by the melodious singing of these waters, which was sweeter than that of any singer he had heard. Manannan mac Lír (MAN'nan'NAN mak LEER) told him that this was the fountain of knowledge and that the five streams were the streams of the five senses through which knowledge is obtained. He said that only those who drank of the five streams and of the fountain would gain knowledge, and that all the gifted people—the poets, artists, and craftspeople—drank from them both. (See 23 September.)

The five senses that are our windows upon the world have both mundane and spiritual functions, although we all too often utilize only their mundane mode. These doorways of perception can also be channels of direct inspiration if we dedicate them to the fountain of knowledge and become more sensitive to the ways in which we receive information. This increased sensitivity will result in a direct awakening of our subtle senses: insight, resonance, discrimination, instinct, and empathy. These are the correlatives of our mundane senses: sight, hearing, taste, smell, and touch. When both sets of senses are consciously connected, otherworldly knowledge flows directly into our sensors, causing our creativity to become active and visionary.

Meditate upon how your own senses are fed by the five streams of the otherworldly fountain.

The Mythic Truth

The mythic truth is the whole truth.

—P. L. TRAVERS, interview

For some people, the juxtaposition of the words *mythic* and *truth* may take a lot of swallowing. Myth has become so devalued by our society that we fail to see how there could be anything remotely truthful about it. We have substituted news and history for myth in our society, giving them the primacy of factual truth; myth, on the other hand, has taken on connotations of wild and woolly believing, of unsubstantiated rumor or the warped understandings of ancient peoples. Myth is not just about ancient stories of spiritual beings, however; it is the current and ever-living dimension of things that are happening now, to us, to the land, to the world. Myth is the concordance of life's meaning, the story behind the story.

The mythic truth represents nothing less than the totality of a thing: it is all that we can know about something, its essential core and being. Our daily self-deceptions and contradictions cannot hide from the light of mythic truth, which illuminates the truth or error of our lives. The psychological application of myths to the human condition is very interesting and often enlightening; we do indeed share many truths from world myths. But the greatest enlightenment comes when we understand our own mythology, within the context of our own lives.

What is the core of the myth that you are living at present?

Perspective of Age

I could have told much by the way
But having reached this quiet place can say
Only that old joy and pain mean less
Than these green garden buds
The wind stirs gently.

—KATHLEEN RAINE, *The Oracle in the Heart*

It is said that youth loves autumn best because it promises the fruits of maturity, but that age loves spring best because it recalls the freshness of beginnings. When we have come into that quiet place that age opens us to, into the secret, walled garden of remembrance, the deeds of our lives seem of less moment than the miraculous spiral of life. The old pains and joys, the treacheries and rejections as well as the sweets and pleasures, find their resting place. It is at such moments that we find windows to accept or bestow forgiveness, to forget injuries, to fully appreciate the riches that have come to us, and to accept and cease to regret the things we have not done.

From the perspective of youth or middle life, none of these resolutions may seem currently possible or ultimately achievable, but our time will come. The returning cycles of the year bring us ever nearer to the heart of things, to the core of ourselves, wherein all things cease to spiral. At the perfect heart of the still center which is the soul's home, there is a different vision—not the view of the traveler along the way, but the intimate perspective of age, which at last understands the motions of life from the heart's stillness.

Recall moments of stillness that have given you a brief glimpse into or perspective of your soul's circuit in this lifetime—moments of convalescence, times of crisis, periods of mystical introspection. What eternal truths have you learned from such moments?

Including the Soul

Excluded soul is the great calamity of our age.
—JOHN MORIARTY, *Turtle Was Gone a Long Time*

Wherever we look, we see a lack of sensitivity to the soul's needs. In the race to eliminate world starvation, we have forgotten that the soul can also suffer from lack of nurture. On the way to world literacy, we have forgotten how to read the book of the soul. The temptation to go beyond what is humanly feasible, to drive our energies to the breaking point, is often irresistible. In conventional health care, the needs of the soul are often secondary to the needs of the body (if they are consulted at all). In the building of housing, little attention is paid to the aesthetic and psychic needs of those who will occupy the structures.

When soul is excluded, we instinctively and unconsciously recoil from the implicit rejection, seeking out ways in which soul-satisfaction can be simulated. This simulated satisfaction often takes the form of shallow gratifications that give us a quick-fix sense of satisfaction, but when this feeling passes—which it soon does—we reach for even less nurturing things. When soul is pushed right out onto a limb, we grasp at addictive things: not just substances—drugs or foods—but forms of behavior and crablike ways of living that scurry around the real need. These addictive ways of life are on their own continual loop, giving us nothing and eroding soul ever more at each turn. Addictive fixes are merely self-sabotaging. The needs of the soul are not just religious: they are cultural, creative, and inspirational. When we pay attention to these, the soul is able to give scope and dynamism to our lives.

Meditate upon the needs of your soul and how they are being met currently. Where are they being encroached upon or neglected?

Commonsense Spirituality

Once a monk questioned Abbess Samthann about how he should pray: should it be lying down, sitting or standing. She replied, "A person should pray in every position."

—Saying of St. Samthann (trans. CM)

There is an unfortunate tendency in those who are interested in spirituality to completely abrogate their common sense. Many people truly believe that a different set of ground rules apply in the spiritual life and that these are known only to gurus. The credulous or uncertain need to realize that, just as we would not tolerate abuse in daily life, so we do not accept the manipulative or misleading advice of any teacher or spirit.

Constancy, perseverance, and questioning are the three requisites of spiritual life. Constancy to our self-respect, to our spiritual quest, and to any true teachers whom we meet will encourage and support our progress. Perseverance in prayer, meditation, and the implementation of spiritual practices will maintain our quest; and if certain of those practices are not working for us, perseverance until we find a practice that does will return us to the right path. A questioning tongue and heart are also essential as we seek to stay on that path: regular self-clarification and the self-questioning of our motives, the questioning of teachers and spiritual allies regarding things that concern us, and the questioning of anything within our tradition that is not manifesting the spiritual message will ensure that our path is a clear one, that we are not merely accepting the unclarity of others.

Meditate upon constancy, perseverance, and questioning within your own spiritual path.

The Grail Messenger

When you were in the court of the Lame King and saw the youth bearing the streaming spear from which drops of blood flowed in streams . . . you did not ask their meaning nor their cause.
—Peredur, from *The Mabinogian* (trans. CM)

These words are addressed to Peredur (Perr-ED'yr) by the Grail messenger, an ugly maiden who comes to berate him for not having asked the "Grail question." (See 15 February.) She publicly rebukes Peredur for his lack of resolve. The Grail procession passes through the hall, but Peredur, who has been warned about curious questions, keeps silent and so loses a wonderful opportunity to transform the stalemate suffering of the Wounded King and the wasteland.

The function of the Grail messenger is to remind putative Grail winners of their responsibilities. Within our own lives, we need such figures to goad or shame us into behaving ethically and appropriately. Strong advice is not always forthcoming from our friends, who may love us too well to speak out for our good. Only our very close friends have this license, and it is a privilege they do not often exercise. Our spiritual allies may also bring to our attention important things we have neglected or the effect of actions that have set things awry; but unless we are in close relationship with them, we do not always choose to heed their words.

The one Grail messenger whom none of us can avoid is the voice of the soul—that thing which many people call conscience. The word *conscience* literally means "with knowledge." Our unwitting actions do not go unregarded by the soul, which reminds us where we have contravened its codes of behavior. Its voice can be an ugly reminder of things that have to be put right.

Consider the things that blemish your soul. Change or put right the consequences of your actions wherever you can.

Treasures of Solitude

To get the full impact of all the elements, within and without, one has to be alone.

—NEIL M. GUNN, *The Atom of Delight*

The physical impact of the elements upon our earliest ancestors must have been considerable. It motivated them to build shelters in which to hide from the weather; it caused them to construct clothing that would protect them from extremes of heat or cold. Human beings have gradually adapted to their climate and habitat in distinctive ways, until only the adventurous still face the challenge of the elements regularly. These days, most people are accustomed to living predominantly indoors rather than outdoors, seldom exposing themselves to the elements long enough to be affected by them.

Yet there is a more subtle way in which the elements affect us, a way that passes beyond their physical impact: the way in which the elements play upon our emotional response and spiritual understanding. If we listen to the subtle messages of the elements, we can become aware of how they illuminate bridges between our conscious and unconscious awareness of what moves our inmost heart.

To be alone in nature is not to be lonely. The companionship of the elements surrounds us on every side, enveloping us in a living web of vitality and movement. Within that mantle, we are enabled to find our own place, uninfluenced by the demands and bustle of everyday life. We are able to hear the wisdom that wells up from our unique perspective—wisdom that the elements alone can amplify loud enough for us to hear and understand.

Allow yourself to experience the elements of wind, rain or sun, earth, and sea or sky at first hand on a solitary walk today.

Consumerism

With the desire for possessions the very nature of man alters.
—LLEWELYN POWYS, *Earth Memories*

The human desire to possess is threatening to consume the world's resources. How do we rediscover a way of life that is more simple and respectful? Few people wish to return to baking their own bread, typing on a manual typewriter, or washing clothes by hand, so how can greater simplicity emerge, how can our consumption be reduced? Taking a leaf from our grandparents' generation and from traditional peoples around the world, we can begin by living within our income rather than running up our credit cards. This means shopping carefully and thoughtfully, and buying goods that are well made so that we do not need to replace them often. It also means considering the kind of impact that the object we want to purchase will have on the world when we have finished with it. Knowing that today's consumer durables are tomorrow's antiques or cast-offs, that we will not be in possession of them after we breathe our last, will help moderate our life-style.

The pleasures of shopping bring color and variety into our lives. If ease of purchase is weighed against our actual needs, the satisfaction of possession will find its own golden mean.

When you next go shopping, balance your actual needs against the world's good.

The Religion of the Heart

Forced prayers are nae [no] devotion.

—Scots proverb

Too often, religion is a forced devotion, coercively thrust upon unwilling souls, used to keep people submissive and obedient—an approach that smacks of the reformatory, the orphanage, or the prison, a mode that infantilizes and imprisons the soul. Wherever we are in our spiritual search, we must each worship according to the needs of our heart and nature. To do other than this is to betray our soul. But it is not an easy path. Many confusions arise, especially when we find helpful clues within spiritual traditions and writings whose primary tenets we abhor, or when we discover that our chosen way of worship, though satisfying to others, has become savorless to us. Who or which is right? Those who want ultimate certainty and reassurance in their spiritual lives often choose fundamentalist modes of worship; those who want to be always right choose dogmas that exclude everyone who is remotely wrong.

It is worth realizing that the many factors that comprise our religion of the heart may be shared by different spiritual groups, and that our most potent spiritual experiences and clues may lie not in scripture but in nature. The fact that there is not only one (or even any) *right* way and the possibility that our spiritual questing may not have an ultimate solution or destination are hard to accept. We can only follow our heart's leading to our soul's home.

What is the religion of your heart? Of what factors is it comprised?

Manifesting Our Dreams

Dreams grow holy put in action,
Work grows fair through starry dreaming;
But where each flows on unmingling,
Both are fruitless and in vain.
May the stars within this gleaming,
Cause my dreams to be unchained.

—CAITLÍN MATTHEWS, *Celtic Devotional*

We live in a world where the divorce of dreams and their practical implementation is almost complete. How can we weave the two strands of dreaming and working together? By attending first to our dreams and visions, and by allowing a space to appreciate and develop them. Unless we take these steps, our dreams fall barren into the rocky soil of our unconceiving imagination. Dreams will not manifest without our active help, or without the energizing grace of the spirit. And while that grace is generously available to us, it will not accomplish our dreams without our hard work.

When our dreams manifest through this process, the whole world is recreated in that moment, for we have been cooperators in the work of creation, not merely passive creatures who crawl upon the earth. It is then that the stars dance where we step and the song of joy issues from our spiritual allies, for we have made holy the daily ground of our working.

Before sleeping, hold your inspired plans and visions in your heart as you recite this prayer. Be attentive in the days that follow to the clues and pathways that open to your dreaming.

Our Spiritual Kindred

The soul of each one of us is sent, that the universe may be complete.
—PLOTINUS, *Enneads*

When mystic meets mystic, when we recognize our spiritual kindred, the common emotion is one of joy and validation. To discover someone else who feels, thinks, and believes as we do is a great privilege in this world, especially when we find our *spiritual* kindred. Though we may have been born continents or generations apart, we know and recognize the features of our spiritual family by our likeness of soul.

When one soul meets another kindred soul, a great surge of energy rushes through the weaving of the universe as an important connection is made. In the unexplored regions of human consciousness, another light has come on, revealing shared territory. This is the work of dedicated souls on the spiritual path: their individual light illumines the universe for everyone, brings hope, and keeps open the pathway to understanding. This sacred trust is maintained by all who have consecrated their existence to spiritual wisdom; it is a kinship that runs like a golden chain from one age to another. That golden chain comes now into our hands, a sacred trust not only to our ancestors but to our descendants and every inhabitant of the universe. It is our turn to make the next link, trusting that others in turn will complete the circle until the whole cosmos is connected in one bond.

Who are your spiritual kindred? How have you recognized each other? What binds you in a common soul-bond?

Herbs

After Miach had been buried by his father, from the joints and
sinews of his body there grew three hundred and sixty-five herbs,
one for each joint and sinew. Then his sister Airmed opened her
mantle and separated these herbs according to their properties.
—The Second Battle of Moytura, in *Lebor Gabala Erenn* (trans. CM)

Each of the healing herbs that grew from the body of the healer Miach
(MEE'ak) has its own special properties. The lore surrounding healing
herbs has been handed down from healer to healer since earliest times,
when herbs were the only medicine anyone had. The way in which
this wisdom was originally obtained is a method that we can also use:
working with the spirit of the plant allows us to discover its uses and
properties. Not only can preparations of leaves, flowers, or roots bring
cure, but they can also convey the wisdom of the plant's spirit. The
most helpful herbs are usually those that are common and plentiful,
and it is respectful to the spirits of our own land to seek these out and
allow their local and immediate properties to help us.

Walk in nature, asking to be shown an herb, plant, or tree that can
bring healing to an ailment that you currently have. Let your attention
be drawn only to the plant in question: you will begin to notice that
one particular plant almost waves at you. Go and sit with it, without
touching it. Greet the spirit of the plant and intuit from sitting with it
what kinds of things it is good for. Ask permission to take a sample
from the plant, and take a very small part if this feels all right. In
return, sing a song, pull out a hair and leave it nearby, or breathe your
blessing upon the plant by way of thanks. Identify your plant, if you do
not know what it is. Check your findings in a book of herbal properties.
Do not use the herb in any preparations to ingest or anoint, however;
this is the work of a professional herbalist, whom you can consult.
Work only with the spirit of the plant. Visit the spirit of the plant to
ask what actions or rituals can help bring healing. Give thanks.

The Lady of the Lake

Beware and do not stir the lake
Untimely, lest she take offence.
Bring gifts of gladness well bestowed,
No sadness for your recompense.

—CAITLÍN MATTHEWS, "In Avalon"

The Lady of the Lake stands at both the beginning and the end of King Arthur's story, as fosterer of his youth and as healer of his wounded body. She gives Arthur his sword and the scabbard that goes with it. When Arthur first receives these gifts, Merlin asks him which he regards as more important. Arthur, musing upon his sharp blade's ability never to fail him in battle, names the sword. But Merlin informs him that the scabbard, which guards him against loss of blood, is equally important. The sword that Arthur wields all his life is raised in defense of the land, but it is not his personal property, nor can it be passed by him as an heirloom to any successor he might choose. Wounded at the battle of Camlann, he demands that it be thrown back into the lake from which it came, that the Lady might take charge of it again.

The Island of Avalon, the home of the Lady of the Lake, is one of the deep guardians of the land, to whom all heroic defenders must return for healing and restoration. The island is an abode of bliss where the weather is always temperate and where those who are overburdened by their sorrows or wounds can find recovery. Like all parts of the other-world, it is accessible to those who make the soul-flight thither.

Building on yesterday's meditation, take a soul-flight to visit the Lady of the Lake to seek for healing, taking with you the herb that you found. Give the herb to the Lady of the Lake and let her use the plant to bring healing to you. Give thanks for her help and return to your own time and place.

Equality

The finger tops are not equal in length;
nor are all men equally strong;
there's no gaming-board without its king,
no litter born without its leader.

— MUIREADHACH O DÁLAIGH, in Osborn Bergin,
Irish Bardic Poetry (trans. CM)

Celtic society recognized and appreciated all individuals for their particular strengths and abilities. The many skills and professions were seen as pillars that upheld the land, at whose center was the king. Complete equality is very rare. According to the qualities, strengths, and abilities that we possess, each of us will find our way in the world. Dominant traits and abilities will come to the fore, whatever anyone does, whoever tries to diminish them. The advantages of certain people will always appear better to us than our own. But from those who are richly endowed, more is required.

We cannot accommodate everyone, nor can we bring total equality to all. Some will inevitably win high achievements and others will lack them. If, however, we appreciate every single person for him- or herself, if we give respect regardless of age, color, education, gender, or religion, we come as close as we can to equal opportunity. Having committed to that, we must accede to the fact that, in different places, states, and conditions, each of us will have different and particular needs.

Meditate upon the differences between equality and equality of opportunity in your own life.

The Gateways of the Heart

Ancient power spots, and sacred sites . . . are gateways. The real openings lie in our own hearts, minds, and lives.

—JO MAY, *Fogou*

The whole of our lives is a bringing together of our inspirational and power sources. These are like the stones that form the gateway of our spiritual path, creating thresholds to which our spiritual allies in the otherworld are drawn; they come close to us when we recognize and visit our inspirational and power sources. Our efforts and their efforts combined make these thresholds real gateways between the worlds, through which vital energy can flow. The reciprocation between the worlds passes through these thresholds. When we finally come to die, our fear will be lessened because we will already be familiar with these thresholds of passage.

The ancestors who once visited sacred sites were acutely aware of these things. They would doubtless prepare themselves before visiting by prayer, fasting, and purification and be interviewed by the guardian of the site before they approached it, to ensure that each visitor was truly attuned and prepared. If we also cleanse the gateways of our heart before we approach sacred sites, we will come fully prepared for the encounter between the worlds: to greet our ancestors with peace and our spiritual allies with love.

Before you next visit a sacred site, meditate upon the preparations you may need to take before visiting.

The Gospel of the Grass

I am the author
written into the
greenbook of the grass,
the primal scripture.

—BILL LEWIS, "The Skyclad Christ"

The idea of a document's being "scriptural,"—that is, having authority—is integral to Western thought. We no longer remember that wisdom, knowledge, and teaching were conveyed primarily by oral means, that in early Celtic times it was the *word* that had authority, not what was written. The druids did not write their teachings down; they conveyed them by word of mouth directly to the ear of the hearer. Nothing intervened.

Beyond oral traditions of transmission is another level of understanding that human beings have largely forgotten but that animals still live by and understand—the gospel of the grass. The connective principles of the green world have their own authority and primacy in the transmission of living wisdom. The *Book of Job* compares all life to grass, and speaks of the way in which the upspringing green shoot that withers away is cast into the fire to be burned. Yet this green shoot feeds the human and animal worlds. The green grain ripens into the golden harvest that makes our very bread.

Before people spoke, or wrote, or even existed, the grasses were growing and swaying in the wind. If we are able to listen to the wisdom of the green world with our instinctive senses, we may hear the primal scripture that has its own spiritual language and understand the knowledge that transcends all religious boundaries.

If you can, sit with the grass and listen to the wisdom of the green world today. What does it tell you?

～ 25 April ～

Helping Others

One should give only what people need or want, and in the way they need or want it.

—Peter Levy, *The Flutes of Autumn*

It is a good and natural thing for us to want to help and support others. But it can also be a very difficult thing, as we may have already discovered. There are a number of factors we must consider before we step forward to assist someone. In the first place, help may not be wanted. In the second place, if help is wanted, we may not be the best people to bring it. The one we wish to help may not want our assistance or be able to receive it. This inability to ask for or receive help can be very frustrating to the would-be helper, but for the one in need, personal control over her life—even to the extent of refusing help—may be all that she has left. To persist in helping in the face of downright refusal is a way of further disempowering that person in need.

When we help others in order to help ourselves, we are on a slippery slope of self-delusion. Sometimes, after discovering something wonderfully efficacious to our own condition, we press that something on everyone we meet in a fit of convert fervor and excessive zeal. People find their own ways to ask for help. Our part is simply to be sensitive to the signs (whether obvious or indistinct) that they make in our direction. Then we can look into what kind of help is needed, what nature of support and backup is desired, when to back off and let well enough alone so that nature can heal wounds. If our personal help is inappropriate or inexpert, we must leave the helping in the hands of those better capable than ourselves and not press our attentions where they are not wanted.

Is there something you need to ask help with at this time? If so, is there someone you know whom you would like to have help you?

Soul-Protectors

For you took what's before me and what's behind;
You took east and west when you wouldn't mind me.
Sun and moon from my sky you've taken,
And God as well, or I'm much mistaken.

—"Donal Og," traditional Irish folk song

The betrayal of love and trust is not entirely avoidable in this life, but we can reorient ourselves better after such a hurt if we are aware of our soul-protectors and their help. These can be discovered by meditating upon the nature of our spiritual allies according to the directions of the compass. By identifying, meeting, and working closely with these allies, we gain a better sense of our way.

The allies who walk ahead of us are the scouts on the trail of our life—the leaders, path-clearers, and forerunners who show us the way. The allies who stand behind us are our parents, motivators, and teachers—the ones who have prepared us to go forth in life.

The allies who are on our left are the challengers, caution-givers, and questioners. It may seem strange to regard challengers as allies, but without the hindrance and help of the allies on our left and right, our progress would be strangely crooked. If we think of the allies on our left as those who question our motivations, we will steer aright. The allies on our right are the encouragers, dare-setters, and friends; they give us unfailing support.

The allies who are beneath us are the ancestors and the ones who give us power, the allies of the natural world; without their example and sacrifice we would not even be alive. The allies who are above us are the inspirers, deities, and spiritual teachers whose wisdom keeps us on our path.

Meditate facing each direction in turn and begin to meet your own allies. Finally, make your own protective blessing, visualizing the allies about you.

～ 27 April ～

The Vehicle of the Circle

The entire space of the circle becomes our sphere of inner work-ing—it becomes a sacred area in which, like a magic carpet, we can travel to other states of being.

—Philip Carr-Gomm, *The Druid Tradition*

Whenever we sit in meditation or do any sacred work, it is good to hallow or bless the area in which we are working. That blessing signals to the spirit of the place and to ourselves that what happens within the circle is special and holy. The demarcation of our sacred space is easily accomplished: we can walk around it and describe the circle with our body; we can point at the ground while walking; we can *sain* (bless) our circle with emblems of air, fire, water, and earth; we can welcome our soul-protectors and spiritual allies to make our place of working safe and protected. (See 26 April.)

Some people shy away from the idea of a "magical circle," but the cir-cle that surrounds us when we meditate is not a place where wonders or manipulative things occur. Rather, it is a holy and intentioned place wherein we acknowledge the coexistence, in one spot, of our apparent world with the unseen world. Within our small circle, the whole cos-mos is microcosmically present.

Our circle can become a vehicle in which we travel to the other-world. Within it, we speak to and meet our allies, we consider our con-cerns and ask help about them, and we have communion with the life of the universe. When it is time to return to mundane life, we thank our allies, unwind our circle by walking round it in the opposite way, announce that our circle is concluded for this time, and return to our ordinary lives, refreshed and empowered with the help, wisdom, and blessing that we have experienced within the circle's protective space.

Practice making your own circle before you meditate. Find out what procedures work best for you. Use your own words and movements, doing everything simply and with intention rather than for effect.

Aisling

O'er mountain, moor and march, by greenwood, lough and hollow,
I tracked her distant footsteps with a throbbing heart;
Through many an hour and day did I follow on and follow,
Till I reached the magic palace reared of old by Druid art.
—AODHAGÁN O RATHAILLE, "Gile na Gile" (trans. J. C. Mangan)

This poem is an *aisling* (ASH'ling), a vision experienced by a person in a lonely place who becomes aware of an otherworldly or beautiful woman who comes for a purpose, usually to invite him to visit her, find her, or perform some service for her.

The ancient *aisling* poems show the Goddess of the Land appealing for a champion to right her wrongs. One of the last poets to write a genuine Irish *aisling* was W. B. Yeats, whose poetic and dramatic writings depict Ireland as Kathleen ni Houlihan, an old woman wandering the road in rags, prophetically uttering words of transformation.

These later poems are expressions of the poet's vision of the land; he is able to envision the appearance of its spirit and the condition of the group-soul of the land. Within our own lives, we can also become aware of the problems that beset our country by seeking out an *aisling* vision of our own.

Envision your country laid out before you; in soul-flight visit whatever part of it seems to you to represent its sacred heart. Stand there and ask for an aisling *vision of your land's condition. How does the spirit of your land appear, and what things does it show you? Remember that your land may be either a mother- or fatherland—that is, its indwelling spirit may be either female or male. Do not get hung up on gender, but attend with all your attention to the vision that you have. What needs to change? What attention can you help throw upon the problems you have been shown?*

Faeries

We are from the beginning of creation
Without old age, without consummation of earth.
—*The Voyage of Bran*, early Irish text (trans. CM)

The faeries are the race of beings who live between the worlds, making their home upon the earth but usually apprehensible only to otherworldly vision. Every country in the world has stories about the faeries as the "people between" who inhabit quiet country places but occasionally interrelate with human beings, exchanging favors for small gifts and courtesies, such as gifts of milk or food.

Within the Celtic countries there is still a great respect for the faerykind. People and faeries are considered to be neighbors who must live in mutual respect. People are careful to build their houses away from routes frequented by the faeries, and refer to them only as "the good folk."

Many stories relate how musicians have learned tunes from the faeries, or how humans have wandered into faery domains and lived with them there. Such tales may seem fabulous to those who have clichéd images of tiny, gossamer-winged faeries who flit about from flower to flower; but faeries within the Celtic tradition are considerably more robust, some being even taller than humans.

As Beltane (BEL'tenn-a) approaches, faeries become very active. It is believed that now and at Samhain, the doors to the faery hills are open, and that the faeries make their progress through the land. It is a time to be sensitive about our movements and intentions so that we do not disturb the fair folk about their business.

Discover the faery traditions of your own part of the land. What spots are associated with faeries? What courtesies are customary? Respect their ways; leave them to their own affairs.

Beltane

Unite, unite, let us all unite,
For Summer is a-come unto day
And whither we are going we will all unite
On the merry morning of May.
  —*Padstow Night Song,* traditional Cornish song

At twilight this evening, May Eve, the great festival of Beltane begins, a great communal celebration that excludes no one from its embrace. Ancient Celtic celebrations involved the kindling of bonfires at this time—indeed, the name of the festival derives from "bright fire." The Beltane fire itself was kindled in a special way: evidence from nineteenth-century Scotland reveals that the wood had to be of nine different kinds, that it had to be gathered by men with no metal about their persons (metal being inimical to the faerykind), and that it had to be kindled without metal. The ancient method of fire-raising involved a fire spindle and a small piece of wood to create friction or by the rubbing together of two oak poles. This arduous task was traditionally performed by nine teams of nine married men—eighty-one firstborn sons.

Once the fire had been kindled, people danced sunwise round it and jumped through the flames. As the fire was dying down, the animals that had wintered over in barns and local pastures were driven, on their way up to summer grazing, between the parted fire to ensure their fertility. Before the coals died out, people took fire from the ceremonial blaze to rekindle their hearths (which had been extinguished in every household prior to the festival).

Welcome in the May by making your own fire or lighting a candle and singing May-time songs. Honor the coming of summer in your own way. Rise before dawn and wash your face in the dew tomorrow morning, to receive the blessing of Beltane. If you have a partner, this is the best time for sexual fun and frolic.

Beltane

Season of Summer

MAY

Month of May—wanton is the lascivious;
Sheltering the ditch to everyone who loves it;
Joyous the aged in his robes.

　　　　　　　　　　　　　　　　—anon. Welsh poem

We welcome May and the coming of the summer season, the festival of Beltane. This month's themes include meditations upon safety and assurance, times of light and darkness, familiarity and the unexpected, holiday and recreation, plenitude, guardians of life, and the green world.

∼ 1 May ∼

May Day

The true man sings
gladly in the bright day,
sings loudly of May—
fair-aspected season.
—John Matthews, "From the Isles of Dream"

Since before dawn this morning, many people all over Britain and Ireland have been up to greet the May, to sing to the rising sun, and to gather greenery and flowers. Others have been preparing to celebrate with May-pole dancing and community festivities, which may include the election and crowning of a king and queen of the May. Most often the holiday royalty are a boy and girl from a local school, but once they would have been the lustiest young man and woman of the district.

This is a day that is still honored in every part of Britain. Despite many efforts to quell its rowdy good humor and lusty enjoyment down through the centuries, it has survived in very good shape up to our own time. The sheer exuberance of May overwhelms the restrictive and humorless reformers who have tried to stop it.

The explosion of May-blossom, sunlight, and burgeoning life needs expression at this time, when workday commonplaces can be thrown to the four winds and the bright joy of living can bubble up within us with natural ecstasy. All who have waited at dawn to welcome in summer have felt the sudden burst of brightness that ignites the deep happiness of the living earth as the sun rises. This brightness is the sign of the ancient Celtic god Bel, whom the Gauls called Belenos—the Shining One—the bright-faced splendor of green summer whose glad arising spreads a shining honey of golden light over the waiting earth. It is hard to witness this sunrise without feeling part of it.

Cancel work today. Go and enjoy May Day by doing something that gives you great pleasure. Try to be outdoors all day if you can. Leave formal meditation alone and let your natural joy find its best outlet.

~ 2 May ~

Care of the Land

Spiritual orderliness originates in harmonious care of the land as sacred.

—Nigel Pennick, *Celtic Sacred Landscapes*

For the Celtic peoples, the land was inspirited, able to reflect whatever was done upon it. The concept of land as inert, unable to respond, was foreign to them. There was also a sense that not every inch of the land could be used for human purposes, that some was to be set aside as sacred to the spirits of the land.

The prosperity of the land, the abundance of flocks and herds, the fertility of fields and orchards—all these were dependent upon the sacred ordering that gave respect to the spirit of the land. This intrinsic knowledge arose from the land itself and was mirrored in the way people behaved and believed. In an age when few of us actually work the land with our own hands, this knowledge is now retreating and we begin to see the products of the soil as commodities rather than as inhabitants of the natural order.

The very land and its inhabitants speak to us of spirit and sacred order if we will listen to them. It is in the patient tending and listening that those who have worked the land for generations know when a plant or animal needs particular things, and when some profound wisdom is being conveyed. If we make the spaces for these moments of transmission, create opportunities for communication between ourselves and the land, we may begin to embody the sacred orderliness that maintains our whole ecology.

Go and listen to the land sometime this week. Be sensitive to its needs, your appropriate response to those needs, and the spiritual lesson that it has to teach you.

～ 3 MAY ～

Growing Up

*How many inner umbilical cords connecting me with the depths
and heights of all that is . . . were severed and knotted in me in the
course of my education?*
— JOHN MORIARTY, *Turtle Was Gone a Long Time*

The freedom we experience in the country of childhood is very special. Most deep childhood bonds are never severed entirely, only stretched so that they can help us through our adult years with more flexibility. These bonds are those of wonder, play, and simplicity. The jaundiced perceptions of adulthood allow little room for wonder: the ability to be deeply moved and reconnected with the wider world. When wonder leaves us, our childhood senses are finally fogged up and we no longer see the world as part of ourselves. A renewed sense of wonder awakens our ability to be responsible as adults and helps us bequeath an unspoiled world to our own children.

The child's ability to play, to be completely involved in the game, can be ours if we make love with life enthusiastically. Childhood simplicity gives way to adult sophistication, which seeks how to please others and is self-aware in a way that childhood is not. The ability to retain a measure of simplicity enables us to perceive things without worrying about other people's opinions, beliefs, and ideas, to be guided by the innocence in our soul.

*In which areas of your life do you feel that you are still "growing up"?
What facets of your childhood wisdom have you retained?*

～ 4 MAY ～
Accepting Our Purpose

Help me to find my happiness in my acceptance of what is my purpose: in friendly eyes; in work well done; in quietness born of trust, and, most of all, in the awareness of your presence in my spirit.
—ALISTAIR MACLEAN, *Hebridean Altars*

The dull or continual round of life can set up a pace that gives us little space to appreciate and enjoy it as it turns. We yearn for some new stimulus or a change of pace to help us escape the grindstone that feels as though it is wearing us down. We do indeed need holidays and rest times during which we can refresh ourselves, unscheduled changes from routine that give us new breath, but these are not always possible when life is very demanding. To continue without becoming broken or burned out, we must change the way we perceive our lot in life.

Without entering the trap of resignation, we can focus instead upon our own life's purpose and see how it sits with our circumstances right now. If our life's purpose is at odds with our present life-style, then a complete change is needed for the sake of survival. But if, as is usually the case, our purpose and our life-style (while not perfectly harmonious) are walking together in the same direction, we can make a renewed dedication to our purpose and tread with better spirit down the road.

We can refocus, not upon our own dull state but upon what is happening around us, in order to express our life's purpose in our work and actions with generous hearts and to live in the moment without chafing at the passage of time. Suddenly, dramatically, the daily round of life becomes a place of revelation that we have not envisaged. Where once we harbored a grudge in our hearts, there is now an entirely different spirit. The daily round no longer seems dull but has its own tides and rhythms. We have become aware of Spirit's presence in a new and wonderful way.

Meditate upon your life's purpose. Make your own prayer of dedication and implement the suggestions above.

~ 5 MAY ~

Safe Return

May my strength be increased,
May my tomb not be readied,
May I not die on my journey,
May my return be ensured to me.

—early Irish invocation (trans. CM)

Whenever we set out on a journey, fears and anxieties beset us. We repeatedly check our money, passport, and plane tickets, and we leave instructions for the smooth running of the household in our absence. Even while we are busy with those details, part of us fears the dangers of travel—dangers that are perhaps no worse than those our ancestors faced. We are now more concerned with material things and less concerned with the spiritual support that accompanies us wherever we go.

Because some difficult journeys are unavoidable and come upon us suddenly, it is good to have our own ritual sequence to help us deal with the anxieties of travel. My own ritual procedures for departing and returning are to bid farewell to my home and household and to speak to the spirit of the land to explain that I am going away. I seek protection and direction for my journey. At the airport, I say a final farewell to the land on takeoff and commit myself to the spirits of the air; on landing, I greet the spirits of the land I am visiting and ask their help during my stay. I use my free time to explore the place I am visiting and to greet the local spirits of place. On leaving, I bid farewell and give thanks to all who have helped me. I reverse my procedures on coming home, greeting all in my own land and giving thanks to them.

I cannot say that this keeps me invulnerable from the dangers of travel, but it is a good way to travel, with its own cyclic unfolding and continual support. It also banishes homesickness and enables me to truly engage with each land I visit.

Meditate upon your own procedures for departing and returning.
Make your own invocation for a safe return.

Death of a Loved One

Though I live, yet am I not,
since my sweet hazel-nut has fallen;
since my dear love departed,
bare and empty is the dark world.

—MUIREADHACH ALBANACH, in Osborn Bergin,
Irish Bardic Poetry (trans. CM)

Directly after the death of a loved one, we no longer walk the same earth as everyone else. Part of us lingers at the frontier of death's domain, looking into its unknown distance for signs that the soul is safely over, or for comforting messages that will assure us that we are not really, finally alone.

The sudden loss of someone vital to our life's story means that our own story may be whirled out of context into total disorientation or petrified into a stasis wherein time no longer runs at the same speed as it does for others. Since every daily action, every piece of forward planning, necessitates the painful realization of how different life will be from now on, how lonely, how impossible, time and our progress through it alter our perceptions completely.

A loss must be fully recognized. The old custom of the wake—which kept vigil about the bed, included the body of the deceased in a communal celebration and farewell, and encouraged tears and laughter to freely mingle—was healthier than the relegation of the corpse to a mortuary or the chill obsequies of a "professional" funeral.

Our support of the bereaved is best shown in our willingness to talk about the deceased in a warm and natural way when appropriate, by acknowledging and sharing the loss rather than hurrying to cover over the aching gap, and by understanding that our compassion must extend beyond a few months' passage of time. (See 2 November and 28 December.)

Make your own blessing for all people facing bereavement.

Fullness

*The three most beautiful things in the world: a ship under full sail,
a woman with child, and a full moon.*

—Scots Gaelic triad

These three fullnesses are eulogized throughout the Celtic world; they define aspects of daily life that were very important to the ancients. Among the Celtic peoples, mothers were held in special awe—not only because their fertility increased the tribe, but because each mother was also under the protection of the Mothers, the triple goddesses who were depicted in statues and inscriptions as women with loaves, baskets, and babies on their laps. Abundance, stability, and power were their strong message to any who gazed upon them. The woman with child was seen not as frail or ill, as is often the case in some places today, but as strong and fulfilling her purpose. The full moon had a special meaning to the Celts as well, for it marked the twofold division of the month into the bright or waxing half and the dark or waning half. The full moon marked the day of the festivals, since the Celts did not use the modern calendar or reckon things by exact date. For them, the moon was the guide to each month's shape.

In our own time, our standard of values places the fullness of wallets, shopping bags, and gasoline tanks ahead of the natural triad above. Our lives are abundant with so many good things that we do not have a conscious awareness of fullness and emptiness (unless our paycheck is late). Yet there are many other kinds of fullness that are important and beautiful to us: the burgeoning growth of our creativity, the increase of sexual passion, working at the fullest stretch of our abilities. All these take us deeply into the abundance of our human lives and give us a sense of true beauty and fullness.

What are the three most beautiful things in your world?

The Grace of the Grail

The Grail, whether chalice or cauldron,
Gives of its grace unstinting
To gentle and simple, wise and wanting.
— CAITLÍN MATTHEWS, "Avebury Easter"

The Celtic mythic tradition speaks of the vessels of grace that restore the life of the world. In the early legends, we find the many cauldrons that nurture heroes, initiate and inspire poets, and bring rebirth to those slain in battle. In the later stories, the cauldron has become the Grail—which is sometimes associated with the cup of the Last Supper. Grail and cauldron have similar properties: they provide the food that people most desire, bring revelation and wisdom to those on spiritual quest, heal the sick, and revive the dead. The Grail is a vessel of divine grace that appears upon the earth at times of greatest need (though only if help and restoration are sincerely sought). No action of ours can bring it into operation.

What causes the Grail to appear? A large factor seems to be the concerted hearts of many individuals who realize that their personal quest is part of a larger one. It seems that the thing that individuals cannot achieve alone—peace, harmony, healing—becomes possible whenever like-minded people are gathered together to discuss the problems that beset their land and all beings living within it; then something profoundly mysterious happens. The concentration of hope and desire upon the object of need creates the ability to see the Grail and hear its message. (See 2 July.)

Meditate upon the Grail as a vessel of grace and healing. Present your needs and those of the world to its grace.

Overfamiliarity and Neglect

The blacksmith's mare and the shoe-maker's wife are aye [always]
worst shod.

—Scottish proverb

Habit and overfamiliarity can cause some strange neglects in areas where we would least expect them. The things and people that we know best often prove to be furthest from our consideration, sometimes becoming so familiar to us that they feel like extensions of ourselves. This happens if things are unwinding equably like clockwork: when we become used to the easy rhythm, the habitual can become neglected. If our own self-respect is low or we frequently abuse our body and energy with overactivity, we may have a tendency to treat familiar things with the same neglect or contempt.

This is a dangerous pattern. Whether it is the tools of our trade or our partner who is misused in this way, sooner or later something is going to snap. Before a critical tool breaks or we come home to an empty bed, we need to reappreciate the familiar, lest we lose touch with it altogether.

The ability to truly see our familiar surroundings, possessions, and loved ones can be stimulated by an act of will or by looking through the eyes of a stranger or visitor whose remarks and body language tell us about our environment in ways we have forgotten. Recreation is the best freshener of stale perspectives, because it takes us out of the rut of work and daily usage. It is then that we are able to see that the things we most value are on our own doorstep.

Reappreciate something or someone who is really close to you. Look
with the eyes of the "visiting anthropologist" to see how you are living
in your environment and community.

The War with the Green

O if we but know what we do
When we delve or hew—
Hack and rack the growing green!
. . . even where we mean
To mend her we end her,
When we hew or delve:
After-comers cannot guess the beauty been.
—GERARD MANLEY HOPKINS, "Binsey Poplars"

This poem was written by Hopkins in response to the felling of the poplar trees at Binsey in Oxford—a place where he often walked and found inspiration. The felling of trees and the destruction of wild green places is always a sorrow. When green life is cleared for housing or landfill sites, we feel strong resentment. Human beings have been clearing the earth for agriculture and habitation from early times. Desertification began to replace habitation long ago.

It is easy to wax sentimental about the loss of particular trees and green places, but the war on the green world is now a world issue, as tree cover shrinks from year to year. It is not primarily our own human survival that is at issue, but that of the many species that rely upon the green world for their livelihood and habitat and the complex food chains that stem from the plants and the soil. For humans and their fellow creatures, it is a question of whether our descendants will have sufficient vegetation to sustain the continuance of life.

Plant something in your garden or in a pot inside your home, to help
replace the loss of the green.

~ 11 MAY ~

Light in Darkness

O Greatness, hear! O Brightness, hark!
Leave us not little, nor yet dark!
—JOHN MASEFIELD, *The Box of Delights*

From the beginning of time, people have been appealing to the Power that lies beyond their comprehension when they are in trouble. This Power has been invoked under many names by many people. In our current postreligious age, there is some uncertainty about this Something we appeal to. We know that it is Big and that it sheds Light, but we are often at a loss to name it.

As we began to disbelieve in the lode-bearing stories and lose patience with the ancient metaphors for the Divine, we entered a no-man's-land where the most authoritative images are scientific or cosmic. The rumor in that land is that there may be no Big Something. But never fear, say some: in the last event there is ourselves, after all!

This sad, lonely place is inhabited by many who no longer reach toward the beautiful, the glorious, or the holy in a daily, connective way. For them, there is not even a metaphor to put in place of the sacred. Whether for us the Greatness is understood as immanent, transcendent, or actually present, it contrives to protect us when we ask for protection. Whether the Brightness is seen as a candle, a lamp, or a planetary body, it contrives to leave us less dark.

To comprehend the enormity and illumination of the Divine, we must look into our own hearts and perceive the metaphors that define for ourselves the immensity, the friendship, the beauty, and the eternal brightness, using words and images that are meaningful upon our own urgent tongues.

To what or whom do you appeal when you are in crisis? What metaphors define the Divine for you?

Awakening the Dragon

Love is the power to feel through the feet
into Earth and through the spine into heaven
to mingle into motion the inner wheels, to
awaken the sleeping Serpent.

—DEI HUGHES, "Sacred Loyalties"

As the glory of May-time unfurls in every leaf and flower, we begin to feel a new well-being in our bodies, a sense of vigor and energy that we have lacked over the cold months of winter. In terms of Celtic understanding, we are experiencing the *nwyfre* (NWIVE'ry) of the earth in our own bodies. *Nwyfre* is a Welsh word that means the subtle energy field of the earth; it is also often used poetically for the sky or heavens.

Every sentient being has its own energy field or *nwyfre* as well. The symbolic representation of *nwyfre* is the dragon, which is a very important emblem in Britain (the red dragon being the guardian beast of Wales and appearing upon its flag). The awakening of the dragons of the land traditionally happens about the time of Beltane. The *nwyfre* of the land rises up at summer's approach, and the dormant dragons, emblems of the land's power, rise from their dark earth caverns upon powerful wings.

To experience the awakening of the dragons of *nwyfre* in our own bodies, we need to take ourselves out into the open air, to stand without concrete between our bare feet and the earth, to experience the daily miracle of life within our bodies. If we make this our practice, our *nwyfre* will not be lacking.

Stand on the green earth and close your eyes, soaking up the light of the sun and the warmth of the earth at the same time. Be aware of the nwyfre of the earth. Now become aware of your own. As you breathe in, experience drawing up the subtle energy of the earth. Give thanks for renewed energy and life.

Blodeuwedd

I was made through the ninefold elements:
From fruit trees, from paradisal fruit;
—TALIESIN, "Câd Goddeu" (trans. CM)

When the Welsh goddess Arianrhod (Ar-ee-ANN'hrode) is tricked into bearing a son, she retaliates against her scheming brother Gwydion (GWID'yon), who has taken the boy into his fosterage. She states that the boy will have no name or manly arms unless she gives them to him, nor will he ever have a wife of human stock. Gwydion contrives to trick Arianrhod into calling the boy "Lleu" (HLY) and into arming him but even Gwydion's magic cannot circumvent the problem of a wife. With the help of Math (MAHth), he brews flowers to create a woman: Blodeuwedd (Blod-EYE'weth), the "flower-faced." Lleu loves her, but he neither seeks nor wins her consent. Blodeuwedd takes a secret lover of her own choice who, under her tutulage, fashions a deadly spear designed to kill Lleu at his most vulnerable moment, though he escapes death. The vengeful Gwydion, distraught at the injury to his nephew, turns Blodeuwedd into an owl, shunned forever by the birds of day.

In this complex tangle of immortal vengeance and magical trickery, Blodeuwedd emerges as the one most manipulated. Conjured from the essences of flowers and plants, she does not consent to be a human woman, nor the wife of a man she has never met. Her beauty and sexual urges are those of a plant, not those of a woman. The profligacy and bounty of Blodeuwedd are abroad at this time of year as the blossom gives promise of fruit to come. The coming of Blodeuwedd to every bough reminds us that if blossom is picked now, no fruit will result: it must stay upon the bough, unless we would reap a barren autumn. When the blossom is ready to depart from the growing fruit, it will send its soft, owl-feathered petals of snow over the earth in its own time and season.

What elements make up your own sexual nwyfre? (See 12 May.)

～ 14 MAY ～

The Living Ancestors

When we know about our ancestors, when we sense them as living and as supporting us, then we feel connected to the genetic life-stream, and we draw strength and nourishment from this.
—PHILIP CARR-GOMM, *The Druid Tradition*

Theoretically, we each have two parents, four grandparents, eight great-grandparents, and so on, back in time. In practice, though, if each person alive continued that exponential progression for, say, thirty generations, we would come up with more people than were on earth at that time. Genealogists tell us that if we each went back about seventeen generations, we would find many family relationships between ourselves and people of our acquaintance. It follows, then, that we are all intimately related to each other, that our personal ancestors are shared with many thousands of people alive today.

These shared ancestors are the ones with whom we can relate, even though we may not have details of their names and places. Not all were wise or clever or happy, for all human beings make mistakes and bad decisions. But the ones who were wisdom-bearers and way-showers in their lives have not ceased from these roles. By asking our spiritual allies in meditation to take us to meet one or more of our wise ancestors, the living ancestors, we can travel to the timeless otherworld and visit them. We can discover new spiritual allies in our living ancestors, consulting them about matters to do with our family, our way of life, and ways of respecting the spiritual core of all things.

Ask your spiritual allies to help you meet one of your wise ancestors in meditation and soul-flight.

~ 15 MAY ~

Entering the Charmed Circle

"Open the portal!"
"I will not open it."
"Wherefore not?"
"None may enter Arthur's hall but the son of a king of a privileged
country or a craftsman bringing his craft."
—Culhwch and Olwen, from *The Mabinogion*

This dialogue is between the porter of King Arthur's hall and Culhwch (KIL'ook), a young kinsman of Arthur's who arrives after the feasting has begun. He seeks to enter the charmed circle of the feast to gain his uncle's help and has to persuade his way in past the resolute porter, who has been given orders that no one may gain admittance. (See 1 August.)

We each draw upon a network of people and things to fuel the power circuit of our lives: environment, habits and familiar things, relationships to people, our job, family, and personal connections are all important factors in our lives. We base our power network on many things. Finding out where our power lines are truly strong and where they are based on dependency or appropriation is an important task. Claiming kinship with things with which we have no actual personal association, boasting and exaggerating our links with these things, can give us a fine feeling of strength; but that feeling is illusory. When our bluff is called and we attempt to call upon those strengths, they prove to be unsupportive and the whole facade tumbles down, leaving us exposed.

We earn the right to enter the charmed circle of acquaintance or association only when we show proper commitment, when we prepare ourselves and make the trial. Wanting to be in the exclusive club is a terrible hankering for some. Nothing can replace the sense of fellowship and belonging that results when she is truly welcomed as a kindred spirit.

Which charmed circles and associations am I attempting to enter? By
what right?

Creative Ingredients

Four things are needed by every work of art: a place, a time, an author, and a cause.

—*The Martyrology of Oengus*, ed. W. Stokes (trans. CM)

There are many ideas and inspirations wandering throughout the world. They seem to be shaken like stardust over everything, to be caught in handfuls by those who are ready to receive them, or missed by those who have not got a cause in their sights. The extraordinary way in which an idea seems to proliferate in the air is remarkable: several inventors invent the same thing simultaneously; several writers are inspired to write similar books; several musicians compose and record similar tunes. All inspirations must find an author to express them in some form. From the unseen depths of the formative otherworld, many ideas may go forth, but only a few will fall to earth, only a handful will actually find their mode of manifestation. If the author, musician, artist, scientist, or inventor is not receptive to the ideas that flow, nothing comes into being; the idea passes on, waiting to be received by someone who is ready and willing.

Yet even readiness and willingness are not enough: time and place must also be right. Both opportunity and space must be found to bring the idea into manifestation. Timeliness is about the attunement of opportunity and creative impulse to each other. Place is not only about location but about correct placement of our idea.

The struggle to make our ideas manifest must account for all these ingredients. If we try to avoid or omit any of them, we quickly face frustration and dissatisfaction. The coming into being of a creative piece of work is an act of birth that results from many secret unfoldings and preparations.

Check the progress of the creative spark within your own act of making. Are you ready and prepared; is this the right time; is the world ready?

Plenty Enough

My chosen husbandry I'll reveal, without concealment:
Fresh leeks, hens, speckled salmon, bees.
Sufficient clothes and food from the King of fair fame,
And chance to sit at times, praying God in each place.
—ST. MANCHÁN, "Prayer" (trans. CM)

The fantasy of future perfect conditions, of how life will be when we make the big time, often hides the fact of our present plenty, which we take for granted. In a consumerist society, we are tempted to go after more when we actually have enough of something, becoming hoarders or collectors rather than users of a commodity.

And yet, even when we have every good thing that money can buy, if we do not have the simple commodities listed in Manchán's poem—clean water and air, fresh food free of contamination or toxicity, the company of like-souled people to share our plenty—then we are truly impoverished.

How can we truly appreciate what we have? Learning to live with enough, rather than with indulgence, may help us balance the availability of all good things, help us refrain from using more than we need.

An indwelling sense of scarcity may derive from feelings of inadequacy and our desire to make good the deficiency, or it may originate in fear of poverty. To obtain a sense of plenty, we have only to appreciate the things we enjoy and own on a daily basis to be glad of the way that they sustain and support our lives.

Take time to contemplate your present life-style. Where do you need to rein in your consumption? Appreciate the plenty that you enjoy and give thanks for it.

Restoring the Web

May there be peace in the North;
May there be peace in the South;
May there be peace in the West;
May there be peace in the East.
May there be peace throughout the whole world.
—Druidic blessing given to the four directions

The giving of peace to the directions symbolically and actually changes the whole ambience of a circle of meeting and the relationship of the people within it to each other and to all that lies beyond its limits. It is a calling together or re-formation of a primal web of unity and harmony that individual and corporate acts have torn or fragmented.

When we open to sacred space and focus spiritually, we first need to put ourselves in right relationship to the whole world, in both its seen and unseen aspects. To proceed without some act of truce, some easing of earthly anxieties and expectations, is to proceed unprepared, to view the sacred heart of the ceremony, prayer, or meeting through the eyes of our fears and disquietings.

The circle itself is a restatement of the web of life, of connection and unity. Whenever we meet together in this way, we potentially recreate its delicate networks of connection. Even within each encounter with another person, we have to carry this intention of peacefulness, to send over to that person a thread that can become a pathway to peace. If we meet in anger, disgust, or scorn, we sever all possible connections that can exist between us. When we have learned what maintains us within the circle of life, then we are able to be in right relationship to its supporting web.

Create your own act of reconciliation with the apparent and unseen worlds, for use before you open sacred space.

Courting the Inspirer

The Muse, nae poet ever fand [found] her,
Till by himself he learn'd to wander
Adown some trotting burn's meander,
An' no think lang [long].

—ROBERT BURNS, "Epistle to William Simpson, Ochiltree"

We frequently read about the muse, the female form that inspiration takes for men. She is courted by artists who know that they cannot create alone, who need to be folded within her embrace before the creative spark leaps the synapse of potentiality. We hear less about the forms that inspiration takes for women, who are no less inspired as artists and creators than men, although the inspirer most often appears to them in male form. The inspirer of women is the *daimon* (DYE'-mone), the quicksilver spirit who, like the golden muse, brings the wealth of the imaginal realms of creation to our world.

Sometimes the qualities of our muse, or *daimon,* are seen to temporarily reside in or become superimposed upon a living person, someone who shows us how desire, joy, love, and inspiration fuse together in creation. Sometimes the muse or *daimon* is seen not in a person but in a place.which fires us with inspiration. The embrace of nature becomes the embrace of the inspirer. In an act of participation as intimate as making love, the creator walks with the inspirer in the place of making.

When the inspirer is absent from us, we feel as empty as if a lover had gone. To woo the inspirer, we must go faithfully, time after time, to the threshold places where our soul is exposed to beauty—go without expectations to cloud our coming, without demands or extortions to coerce the erring inspirer to visit us again. Venturing into the frontiers of creation, we come to meet with the one who makes our heart's wish leap into verdant life again.

What are the forms of your inspirer? Who most resembles your muse or daimon *in the world?*

Everyday Love

Too late I understood
That love is not in the blood,
But in every simple kindness I denied
To those to whom I owed humanity,
Just because they were day by day beside me.
—KATHLEEN RAINE, *The Oracle in the Heart*

We have no word except *kindness* for the love that we use every day. Kindness is a courtesy that we owe to all, an act of inclusion that notices the human condition and its needs, however rushed we may be. But kindness is not a custom that comes naturally. Concern, politeness, attention—all these have to be noticed and learned as we grow up.

Those who are most often with us can become so much a part of the furniture, so much an extension of our life and household, that we often forget the basic courtesies of kindness, treating them with the same kind of forgetfulness that we may have for ourselves. This may trigger the revelation that we have little self-respect, only a cold contempt that arises from a deep personal unworthiness. If we feel that we stand beyond the inclusive circle of regard, we will not be capable of generating much kindness toward others.

Loving-kindness is not innate. It has to be practiced with everyone we meet, friend or stranger. The obligation of humanity is to give respect to those to whom it is due; each of us, though, has someone who stands outside that circle, someone whom we exclude as unworthy, some group or association that we feel does not merit our kindness or our attention, never mind our love.

Whom do you include within your circle of kindness? Whom do you exclude? Where is respect due to yourself; where do you stand in the circle?

The King Who Will Come

*He is remembered in the stars—Arcturus and Telyn Idrys—
and the mountains do not forget.*

—JOHN MATTHEWS, "The King's Moon Rite"

The title that medieval legend gave to King Arthur was *Rex Quondam Rexque Futurus*—literally, "the King Who Was and the King Who Shall Be." If we look at the unfolding story of King Arthur as he moves from Celtic warlord to medieval king, from a figure of myth and legend to the refiguring of the archetype within the many novels and stories of our own era, we recognize a potent legend that has given Arthur's name long life and glory beyond the days of his actual existence.

The need for the truly heroic is one that seizes every generation. We hunger after heroes who win through great odds, titans whose stories bring hope in dark and difficult times. Those who have heroic capability soon pass beyond the limits of their own lives; they become invested with the regalia of sovereignty—the weapons, tools, and emblems of the qualities by which they are known and to which they are entitled by right of intention, deed, and common consent. Even if heroic qualities are innate in someone, however, that person becomes a hero only if he assents to live beyond the limits of one existence.

Those who have experienced the inspiration of heroes in their lives know the reality of these deathless ones, those who stand by our side and show us how to go through the motions of heroism when we stand friendless and in need. There is an undying sovereignty in every heroic heart that causes us to say, "The king is dead!" and "Long live the king!" in the same breath.

From what unimagined futures will Arthur come among us again? He who is not dead, but resting in Avalon, is not a done-for king but a king of all our futurity. (See 25 October.)

Which heroes—male and female—inspire you? How do their deeds and qualities live in you?

The Holy Earth

There is no state or condition more holy than the Earth.
—R. J. STEWART, *Power Within the Land*

The British writer R. J. Stewart makes this firm and startling claim to counter the ways in which the physical world has been disregarded and disrespected for so many centuries. He does not state that there is nothing but the earth, only that we should regard it as *equally holy* with every other realm.

This is quite a difficult thing for many people to do, especially those raised in the belief that the earth and all its works are somehow spoiled from the outset and that the only holy condition is the heavenly one. This concept and others like it have soured our relationship with the earth, causing us to abuse it as a commodity, a provider of resources, and a place to live our mundane lives as we wish.

What is holiness, and how can the earth be said to be holy? Holiness is nothing less than a condition of wholeness, completion, and attunement. The earth is holy in that it is the womb of manifest life, the partner in holiness with the otherworld, which is the originative fructifier of life. Both sides of this alchemical partnership are equally important; we cannot leave one of them out of the equation.

Awareness of the earth's holiness and partnership with the otherworld is still possible, especially when we stand at a place upon the earth where the veil between the worlds is thinner. In such a place we can still intuit earthly holiness. Even though the earth's surface has been abused, it is nonetheless a living womb of holy life, and we are its children.

Meditate upon the earth as a holy place, and your own human state as a holy condition.

The Security of Home

A house where rain does not pour,
A place where spear-points do not threaten,
As bright as a garden but with no fence about it.
—"Suibhne Geilt," anon. Irish poem (trans. CM)

The security of home is something settled people gladly take for granted. For the nomad, home is the place you happen to be. For the traveler, home—and the longing to be there again—is the spur to a speedy returning. For those made homeless against their will, home is the Holy Grail of their desire. But even those of us who have a home, one that we are streetwise and alert in protecting, sometimes long to be in a place of greater security and safety, a place where we simply cannot be got at.

The security of being at home with oneself, at home in one's being, can never be forgotten once it has been experienced. This sense of ease, insightful understanding, and peace provides a new kind of security. Although people often reach this state through a sudden shock or realization, it is also accessible through a daily regime of meditation or regular contemplation alone in any place where we feel empowered. In this time alone, we make friends with our soul, allowing it to become expansive and fully fledged.

The security of home does not derive solely from being in a "nice neighborhood" or a beautiful environment; it comes in part from the innate sense of being at home with our soul. The safe circle of home is the expectation of every human being, the right of every child. Home is our microcosm, our little world, supplying comfort, warmth, nourishment, and a safe environment for learning about who we are.

Make a blessing of protection for all within your household.

Inauguration

There was a square stone . . . with a man's foot cut thereon, upon which he stood, denoting that he should walk in the footsteps and uprightness of his predecessors.

—Hugh MacDonald of Sleat, *On the Inauguration of Kings,*
quoted in Caitlín Matthews, *Arthur and the Sovereignty of Britain*

The ancient inauguration ceremonies of Gaelic rulers were far from the coronation rituals of modern monarchy. Instead of receiving a diadem or crown to mark the beginning of a reign, Celtic kings stood or were ceremonially ensconced upon a stone that conferred the rights of kingship. Many such ancient stones remain, including the famous stone at Dunadd in western Scotland; it has the impression of a footprint upon it in which rulers would stand—literally standing in the footsteps of their ancestors—to be acclaimed king.

From the swearing in of a new president or the chairing of a judge or the election of candidates to office, to the first day at a new job or the acceptance of great responsibility or the first moments as a parent or householder, we all need rites of inauguration to mark the special moment, making it a day to remember. Our ability to accept responsibility and maintain our obligations is invested in where and how we stand. For we make deep footprints upon the earth itself—footprints in which only those willing to share a like commitment will ever want to stand.

In whose footsteps do you aim to stand in a responsible and committed way? What kind of footprints will you leave? What are the oaths and promises that you have made to stand where you do?

Freedom

Ah! Freedom is a noble thing!
Freedom makes man to have liking;
Freedom all solace to man gives;
He lives at ease that freely lives!

—JOHN BARBOUR, "Freedom"

We take it for granted today that freedom should be possessed by all people, but there are still many places in the world where basic human rights are absent. There are many forms of freedom: national autonomy, individual liberties, spiritual and ideological freedom.

Individual freedom is composed of many things: the exercise of personal truth and integrity, freedom of spiritual belief, the ability to be educated and follow vocational urges, freedom of movement and of expression, and liberty to marry or not marry, among many other things. The measure to which we are free to exercise these elements of choice gives us our sense of liberty. When any of these are constrained, then the struggle for freedom is joined.

Regimes that scorn free states and countries often sneer at their permissiveness and inability to curb crime, disorder, and dissent—conditions that are generally stamped upon severely in totalitarian states. We live in a remarkably tolerant age in the Western world, an era when maintenance of the freedoms we enjoy is being pushed to its limits. But where tolerance spills over into permissiveness or disorder, totalitarian or restrictive legislation may be applied and freedoms lost.

The archetype of freedom recognizes and extends tolerance to all, but it stops short of allowing people the total freedom to behave as they will; it does not permit anarchy. The apportioning of freedom in a fair and ordered way has to be balanced to ensure that it does not become license to infringe on others' liberty.

Meditate upon the freedoms you enjoy in your life. What are the limits that demarcate your freedoms?

Negative Potential

There's no more savage beast stalks through Wales
Than the two-legged beast who talks.

—Welsh proverb

This grim little proverb sees humanity as the most savage beast that walks the earth, the top predator of the animal kingdom rather than the supreme species. The truth is known in our hearts: that every human being living is capable of acts of great cruelty. This capacity is not always acted upon, of course, but it remains as a kind of negative potential, a misuse of our human abilities that can bring about terrible violence and harm.

Acts of violence, harm, and coercive manipulation can stem from good intentions as well as from bad ones. There is no point in taking the moral high-ground against a particular trouble spot unless we each first understand our personal capacity for negative potential. Only a clear examination of motivation and intention and a mutual vigilance can keep us from walking the same road as the perpetrators of crimes against humanity.

Neither religions nor ideologies, however ideal, have the monopoly on the one correct way to behave. The only valid criteria for action are truth, compassion, and justice, together with a deep comprehension of the laws of cause and effect and a firm grasp upon the ethical pathways that lie under the feet of every human being alive.

Contemplate your own negative potential. What areas are potentially hazardous for you? Where do you have to be most careful in your actions? Clarify your motivations in order to place your life on an ethical pathway.

Our Given Name

Here's a riddle for you: it's not your hair, nor your curls; it's not the smallest part of your body; it's upon you but makes you no heavier. What is it? —Your name.

—Scots Gaelic riddle (trans. CM)

The naming of anyone or anything is a responsible task. Giving the right or apposite name clarifies a person's qualities as a beacon would, while giving the wrong name throws a blanket of obscurity over those qualities. The frivolous naming of children that some uncaring parents indulge in usually means a rash of legal name-changing later on. Even the family name has become problematic in our society, since many women no longer wish to be labeled by a patronymic or take their husband's family name, especially after a series of divorces.

In the Celtic world, babies were often known by an infant name until they were old enough to be counted as adults. As part of a child's rite of passage into adulthood, the community chose a name for the young person based on her personality and accomplishments. For example, the Irish hero Cuchulainn (Koo HULL'en) started out in life with the boyhood name Setanta. He gained his heroic name from a deed of defiance, when he fought with and overcame the dog of Culainn the Smith. In recompense for the smith's loss, the boy himself had to stand as watchdog. Thus he gained his new name, Cu Chulainn, or Hound of Culainn. Sometimes a given name would receive an additional epithet due to significant deeds or actions, as in Conn Cét Chathach (Konn KET KHATH'ech), or Conn of a Hundred Battles.

Sometimes our name changes as if by a process of osmosis, as we discover the person we truly are. If name-changing is done sensitively, it can reveal new facets of our nature that have been trying to get out.

What do you like or dislike about your name? Does it suit you? If you are not sure, ask friends. If you could have a different name, what would it be?

Tides and Seasons

*Five things a wise person should know: the day of the solar month,
the age of the moon, the tides of the sea, the day of the week, the
calendar of holy days.*

—*Saltair na Rann*, anon. Irish text (trans. CM)

In ancient times, knowledge of the tides and seasons was vital, sacred
knowledge that kept the tribe in harmony with the laws of nature. The
mysteries of sun, moon, and stars that collectively describe the intri-
cate dance of the day, the month, and the year were so important that a
whole new class of society sprang up: the sacred clan who, under a
variety of names, maintained watchful vigil over these movements that
governed the sowing and reaping of crops, the movement of animals,
the run of fish. These people were those who had an aptitude for
minute and careful observation. They also had an infinite patience that
we now find hard to comprehend.

They would watch and record the patterns and cycles every day,
every month, every year, over a whole lifetime. Their work was continued by their offspring into many generations, until eventually the vast
workings of the cosmos formed meaningful shapes and patterns. Over
the centuries, their observations would result in the erection of stone
circles and megaliths, each stone sited according to their observations.
It was said of St. Columba that he could understand the harmonious
dance of the moon and sun, read the tides of the sea, and enumerate
the stars of heaven. This alone is proof that as late as the sixth century,
the foundation lore of the sacred clan was being passed down.

Today, though we possess tide tables, calendars, and ephemerides
with which to track the seas, the days, and the movements of the heavens, the sacred knowledge of their mysteries is our own special heritage.

*Plan to observe one particular element of the cosmic rhythm over a set
period. What stories, lore, and traditions arise in your understanding
as you track your subject?*

～ 29 MAY ～
The Green Man

Every man marvelled mightily what it should mean
That a man and his horse should be such colour green.
　　—*Sir Gawain and the Green Knight,* anon. Irish poem (trans. CM)

Throughout northern and western Britain, this day is the focus of many May-time customs. These customs, banned by Parliament under the Commonwealth in the seventeenth century, were reinstated at the Restoration of the monarchy, when King Charles II made his triumphal entry into London. Known thereafter as Oak Apple Day, it is celebrated in Britain by the wearing of sprigs of green oak leaves.

An earlier veneration was restimulated by an incident that befell Charles II when he was but a prince. Fleeing from the parliamentarian soldiers, Charles was forced to hide in an oak tree. But the face peering out from among the green leaves, originally in the primeval forest but now also in contemporary May-time celebrations, is a much earlier one: that of the Green Man.

This Evergreen God is one of the earliest deities. He is represented in many summertime customs by mummers and disguisers who wear garlands of leaves and flowers or cover their bodies in greenery to ceremonially show the Green Man to the people. He comes out of the primal, all-encompassing forest that once covered the earth, dynamic and vigorous, with pulsing sap of summer in his veins.

The Green Man is the irrepressible wildness of the world of vegetation. He bides in the stillness of the deep forest or dances in the sun-filled arcs of leaf-green light that filter through the branches of the tree canopy. His name is delight, and his meaning is mysterious—a potent sexual force that invigorates the earth at this time. As the Evergreen God, he is likewise potent in the wintertime when he plays a riddling game at the thresholds of the year with such daring ones as Sir Gawain.

Ask your spiritual allies to take you to meet the Green Man in meditation or soul-flight.

Merlin of the Woods

He became a silvan man just as though devoted to the woods. For a whole summer after this, hidden like a wild animal, he remained buried in the woods, found by no-one and forgetful of himself and his kindred.

—GEOFFREY OF MONMOUTH, *Vita Merlini*

When Merlin views the terrible battle of Arfderwydd (Arv-DAIR'with), he becomes mad and runs into the depths of the forest. Within the forest's embrace, he becomes one with the trees and seasons and puts aside the terrible sights he has seen to focus upon the gifts of the wild world, becoming rusticated and "uncivilized."

Ever pertinent and prophetic, he sees through the pretexts and pretensions of those who come to lure him back to civilization with the sure instinct of an animal, with the abiding perception of a long-lived tree. Rather than look into the book of human nature, he prefers to consult the almanac of the seasons and discover his center within their compass.

But no human being, however gifted, can remain forever in the wild.

The displacement of our lives by difficult events may not be as severe as in Merlin's experience, but we each go through periods when the flow of events swirls past us too swiftly for us to cope. It is then that the indwelling presences of nature, the little unregarded things that surround us, reveal their own life and wisdom. These become precious handholds along the precipitous rock-face of our lives. Their innate familiarity makes them an ally capable of leading us on the pathway home to our soul.

Recall a time of personal disorientation. What factors were most important to your return to health and confidence?

Spontaneity

When he sees the subject—a person or thing—before him, the poet makes a verse at once upon his finger ends, or in his mind without studying: composing and repeating simultaneously.

—*Cormac's Glossary*, ed. Kuno Meyer

The ability to be spontaneous is granted when we touch something deeply important: a moment of clarity in which we see an eternal truth. We give our truest reactions and utterances when we stand at the moment in question, all previously prepared words and actions suddenly voided in the face of the moment. A spontaneous response results, if only we can trust it. Spontaneity requires us to let go of fear and of continual self-observation, to let pass the deeper truths that we have perceived or that have touched a cord in our soul.

Spontaneity is a great gift, and it grows stronger in us the more we attend to the present moment rather than living forever in the past or in the future: both memory and expectation can get in its way and expunge the upflowing revelation. Spontaneity occurs when all our senses are attuned to the present moment, when we see through the veil that usually separates us from the otherworld and see its bridging connections coming through to our side of reality.

Spontaneity lifts the ordinary dull rote of existence into life of another order; it is a sparkling touch of revelation that responds to whatever is true, beautiful, and harmonious, giving energy to the living moment.

Meditate upon the dull and unyielding areas of your life. Now temporarily remove the rules, limits, and proscriptions that surround these areas. Allow truthful realizations about the connection between your controlling or limiting behavior and the flow of your life to spontaneously arise, even though these realizations might initially seem frivolous or irrelevant.

JUNE

Month of June—beautiful are the fields;
Smooth the sea, pleasing the strand;
Beautifully long the day, playful the ladies.
—anon. Welsh poem

June sees the beauty of summer unfolding. The month's meditation themes include clarity and clearing away, times of light in darkness, turnings and returnings, changing and shape-shifting, divine and mortal gifts, the enduring soul, and shields and defenders.

Examinations

They would not take him among them till he had made a leap over
a stick the height of himself, and till he had stooped under one the
height of his knee, and till he had taken a thorn out of his foot with
his nail, and he running his fastest. But if he had done all these
things, he was of Fionn's people.

—Lady Augusta Gregory, *Gods and Fighting Men*

These fearsome tests that all men were set who wanted to join the
Fianna, the war band of the Irish hero Fionn mac Cumhail, were
designed to select only the best and strongest candidates. But the Fianna was made up not just of muscle-men or tiny-brained superheroes;
all candidates also had to have culture and knowledge.

At this time of year many students must take examinations in order
to try for places at a university or to gain certification for suitable
employment that will use and stretch their gifts. Examinations test
competency and reveal fitness for certain tasks and professions; these
days, exam results often involve students in a competitive lottery.
Only the most qualified take the plum places and jobs. Some educational experts would like this competitive element to be removed and
to have instead some kind of cooperative system where all candidates
are treated equally. If we look at the extensive variety of habitats in the
world, we find that there are animals who have adapted themselves
perfectly to the environmental challenges of the most barren and
remote terrains. Similarly, we human beings take the opportunities
best suited to our abilities and then find ways to adapt ourselves to
the challenges that stretch us.

Make your own blessing for students sitting their exams.

The Power of Story

The king asked the storyteller to recount the titles of those tales that he remembered. And so he recounted the titles of all the prime tales of Ireland that he was able to narrate.

—fifteenth-century Gaelic manuscript (trans. CM)

When Jeremiah Curtain collected stories in Ireland at the end of the nineteenth century, he met an old woman who fell ill and had to be taken to the hospital in Munster. She told him that she attributed her illness to the fact that she had told stories in the daytime. There is something magical and mythical about the power of story within many traditions worldwide that can be discussed only when it is dark or when it is wintertime. This tradition implies that the recitation of a story causes its power to be released, and that this power has to be carefully controlled if one reality is not to invade another.

The magic of story is everywhere acclaimed as healing and transforming. The power of story to change us and bring us to the brink of self-forgetfulness and wonder is a gift beyond measure. However, if we truly believe in the power of story, it is important that we find appropriate stories for our condition and that they are told at times when we are most receptive to (and therefore most respectful of) their power. We each participate in a greater story than appears in any book, film, or recording: the story that *is telling us* is more important than the story we are telling. It is unwritten and sometimes unheard by us, but it runs throughout our lives with an authoritative voice that we need to listen for. It is in periods of receptive silence and listening that this story becomes apparent.

Meditate upon your own story. What themes, protagonists, patterns, and cycles can you perceive?

~ 3 June ~

A New House

A blessing upon your new home,
A blessing upon your new hearth,
A blessing upon your new dwelling,
Upon your newly kindled fire.

—Scots Gaelic blessing (trans. CM)

When we move to a new house or apartment, it is always good to give a blessing to the place. Most of us move into houses or apartments that have just been vacated by other occupants. Before we can move in and settle down, we need to cleanse the house of old influences and unhappinesses, just as much as we need to clean off the previous occupants' layers of grime and dust. Open doors and windows, let in light and air, and take the broom and mop to floors, walls, and ceilings. All the elements can be included in this process. If there are rooms that feel particularly unhappy or disturbed after a simple cleansing, then we need to pray that these influences be lifted by the help of our spiritual allies, and we may want to light some incense to permeate the room.

Then we greet the spirit of the land upon which our residence is built—even if we have a fifth-floor apartment. Every region of the earth has its own indwelling spirit, and it is good manners to greet it and tell it who we are and why we have come to live there, offering the peace of our heart and a small gift of food or a song. (See 18 May.) Then, starting at the hearth, we give blessing to the structure, going sunwise through the house, through each room, with a verbal or sung blessing, taking light or incense into every corner until we arrive back at the hearth again. (See 5 October.) At the hearth, we can bless the occupants of the house and the activities that will take place within it.

Lastly, we can have a housewarming party at which everyone is asked to make a blessing for the future happiness and blessedness of the dwelling. (See also 23 December.)

Make a blessing for your own home, whether it be old or new.

Soul-Leading

Now is the soul set free,
Rising from the soul-shrine.
O Holy Eternal Ones from the Realms of Bliss,
Encircle the one we love in your own compassion.
 —CAITLÍN MATTHEWS, *The Celtic Book of the Dead*

When it strikes us suddenly, death usually finds us totally unprepared to leave our lives. There is often a great deal of unfinished business, and an uncertainty on the part of family or dependents as to what our intentions were for the appropriate disposal of our body. Ideally, we would have already made arrangements for these things before the moment of our death, but unconsciousness or grave illness may have prevented us from conveying our wishes. Although the sun shines upon us this summer and thoughts of death may be far distant, it is always good to have our death arrangements in hand.

Apart from practical considerations, there is the matter of our own route beyond death into the ever-living otherworld. We may not know what awaits us, or whether we will pass on to other existences, but we can at least cultivate those spiritual allies who accompany our soul's circuit so that we do not remain earthbound due to lack of orientation. If we have a close friend with whom we can share our soul's concerns, it is good to let her know what our dying needs will be. A soul-friend can act in a more independent way than immediate relatives. Our soul-friend may have no idea what route our soul will take, but she can implore our spiritual allies to give us good guidance to the realms of peace.

Meditate upon what matters need resolution before you die. Leave clear written instructions with family, lawyer, and doctor about your wishes concerning your death. Your dear ones will thank you for being so prepared at a time when they can least cope with important decisions on your behalf.

Weather Lore

Everything in time becomes . . . a sort of weather-gauge. The sun,
the moon, the stars, the clouds, the winds, the mists, the trees, the
flowers, the herbs and almost every animal. All these become . . .
instruments of real knowledge.

—The Shepherd of Banbury's Rules

Before long-range weather forecasts and satellite information became available, people relied upon their own observation of nature to discover weather trends. These often infinitesimal signs provided good guides to planting, growth, and reaping. People who rely upon the land for their living still have knowledge of these signs and watch animal movements, cloud shapes, and rain patterns with an eye that is more receptive than most. For our ancestors, good weather observation was often all that stood between plenty and dearth.

What we once took for granted as ready information has become increasingly mysterious or magical to those who do not order their lives by such observation. The wisdom and rhythm of the sun and moon are seldom noted by us now, except to the extent that we are timekeepers of the celestial continuum; yet solar and lunar weather lore—whether the flaming dawn or sunset that portends foul or fair weather, or the ring round the moon that speaks of frost—contributes to our most significant understanding of patterns. Such close observations may be needed by us again as weather patterns change, bringing rains, winds, and droughts at times and in places we do not expect them. We are going to have to find new—and possibly old—ways of realigning ourselves with the elements of weather wisdom.

Learn more about the weather patterns and lore of your district. Take
the gauge of the weather throughout the day and learn its patterns for
yourself.

~ 6 June ~
Soundboards of Truth

We who walk in white are but soundboards
Of a truth, frequencies of a faith, augurers
Of a song more mighty than this island can ever hold.
—Caitlín Matthews, "Stonehenge Ceremony"

We live in a time when more and more people are beginning to reappreciate the wisdom of their ancestral traditions. This is a very beautiful and needful thing for those who have been without spiritual direction or who have tried without avail to apply to their lives ways and practices of foreign cultures. There is nothing wrong with returning to our source and looking for living water. As long as we leave the stagnant, brackish waters of practices and beliefs that will not give life in our own age strictly alone, we can serve our own land and communities by applying timeless wisdom to our needs today.

There are many who decry what they see as the unwisdom of stirring up old, forgotten beliefs. For them, the revealed and written traditions of later centuries alone have primacy, and everything that is out of their compass is automatically demonized. Yet there can have been no time in which the eternal song of the sacred truth has not sounded. In different places, at different times, people have responded passionately to this song, expressing its meaning through myth, ritual, and humane behavior.

The song of sacred truth is not a tuneless lay on one unvarying note; rather, it is a call sounding at all times for living beings to respond to its challenge in ways appropriate to the time and circumstances. Sacred truth resides in every living moment that we draw breath. We can only be soundboards of this truth, receiving its vibration and absorbing and reflecting its tonality. If we insist that ours is the only authorized song, then we cut across the frequencies of others.

What are the notes of the song of sacred truth that you receive?

Violence

*The four things which a violent life brings: it shrinks borders, it
increases enmity, it destroys life and prolongs pains.*
—COLMÁN MAC BRÉOGNAE, *Agiptír Chábaid*, Irish poem (trans. CM)

In every generation, commentators state that there is more violence
than at any previous time. If we look through history, this is hard to
substantiate, however. Violence is part of the human condition, and its
effect fluctuates from time to time. Because we have a media system
now that connects the whole world, we certainly hear about violent
occurrences more often these days, making us believe that violence is
on the rise. This emphasis on violence makes listening to the news
very depressing; some days, we witness on the five-o'clock news a vir-
tual catalogue of violence that soils the whole day for us. Awareness of
violence is something that we would just rather not have.

What is the root of violence? How can we prevent its terrible force
from surfacing in our own lives (for we are all capable of acts of violence)? Violence initially stems from the thwarting of our will or desire;
it is an instinctive lashing out against things we do not like. Its contain-
ment is made possible by mature self-control and patience. Sudden
outbursts of domestic violence are usually triggered by a succession of
irritations that have built up until they are unbearable. In such circumstances, the way to defuse the situation is to attempt communication or
to leave the home (if provocation is continual and unsparing).

The narrow ways of violence circumscribe our lives and cause
anguish in many homes. But the levels of violence in our society are
not the responsibility of governments or the police: they stem from
every member in society, from each individual's attitude to life.

*What things trigger violent reactions in yourself? What strategies can
you use to restrain them? How can you channel your feelings into positive areas?*

Cernunnos

The suppression of Cernunnos was and is one of [the] greatest psychological calamities. Had we continued to be religiously hospitable to him, he might have evolved into a gracious, theranthropic, divine Patron of integration.

—John Moriarty, *Turtle Was Gone a Long Time*

Cernunnos (Ker-NUN'nos) is an antlered god surrounded by beasts and vibrant summer leaves like a shamanic, Celtic Orpheus, lord of the animals and master of life. Neither quite deer nor entirely man, his theranthropic animal-human nature crosses a bridge that few divine manifestations achieve in our own time. Because he is horned and holds a snake, he was expressly demonized by early Christianity, although medieval Europe could not entirely shake off his abiding image and often depicted Christ as the hoofed and horned unicorn, a figure who also mediates between the two natures.

In many depictions, Cernunnos holds the torc or neck-ring of human achievement in his right (or conscious) hand; he grasps the ram-headed serpent of animal wisdom in his left (or unconscious) hand. His eyes are closed in an inward-looking attitude of meditation or ecstasy. For the Celtic world, this was the image of the guardian of life: not a macho or retributive deity, but one of quiet strength, an icon who protected the vital power of all living beings and mediated the powers of spiritual insight and enlightened knowledge. Cernunnos may have been excluded from mainstream religion, but he remains a wellspring of dynamic mediation among those who follow the old ways. He enables us to appreciate and be obedient to our dual nature: as human beings with the power of the mind, and as evolved animals with the power of the body. He stands between the worlds, visible at forest's edge and twilight, tide-turn and dawn, as a patient and protective figure in the borderlands of consciousness.

Meditate upon your human and animal powers.

~ 9 JUNE ~

Metaphor as Life

My eye is my verse,
My art is my whole vision.
—DALLÁN FORGAILL, "Amra Senán" (trans. CM)

When spiritual darkness falls and we lose our sense of place or progress in life, the ability to see our way through our lives by way of metaphor can come to the rescue and give us a sense of restoration. We do not have to be poets to accomplish this. As living human beings, we all have the ability to tune in to our inner guidance system and gain perspective on our present circumstances, by asking the following questions:

- How do I describe myself in my present circumstances? What do I feel like? (For example, "powerless, like a car with a dead battery"; "unheard, like someone singing in a hail storm"; "overburdened, like a head of state.")
- How would I describe my normal sense of spiritual connection? (For example, "like receiving Morse code in a foreign language"; "nurturing and strong, like bathing in a hot pool.")
- What is the nature of help that my spiritual allies can bring to me now? What do I need? (For example, "space and time"; "a beautiful and deserted beach in the sun.")
- How do I envisage my return to a place of clear understanding? (Draw upon the images and metaphors that you graphically described in your earlier responses. Meditate upon the help you need right now. Let your own metaphors give you guidance and support.)

Diagnose your present condition by using the inner guidance system of metaphor, as suggested above.

Tasting the Ground

The druid Bicne bequeathed to his successor the duty that, when-ever he was unable to decide upon some obscure question . . . that he should first consume some of Ireland's fruit, corn, fish, milk or chestnuts.

—*The Metrical Dindshenchas*, ed. Edward Gwynn (trans. CM)

In ancient Celtic tradition, the druids are often shown literally tasting the ground in a practical sense, seeking an augury from the land and its fruits before uttering a judgment or answer. In all earth traditions there is an understanding that the land is a witness to truth, that its very molecules do not lie, that its constituent fabric and all life forms that naturally grow upon it are wise in ways that humans rarely match. The blind druid Bicne is able to divine answers to uncertain matters by eating the produce of the earth—a skill that he teaches to his successors.

Keeping a sense of deep discernment and taste is very difficult when there are so many different criteria to consider. In multicultural and pluralist societies, both our physical and subtle senses of taste are under pressure to determine issues and things in ways that are right for us, our families, and our communities. One thing is certain: whoever lives upon a land with respect is welcomed by that land in ways deeper than we can imagine—a fact that we should bear in mind when issues of race and culture are raised. For those who are true to the land shall find that the land also keeps faith with them. With our ability to move about the earth and settle at will, we do well to first consult the region where we are thinking of living, going straight to the land and speaking with its spirit, so that we can live with discrimination, truth, and respect.

Wherever you are living, go and stand on bare, unconcreted earth and commune with the spirit of the land. Return to your home and in soul-flight go back to the site you visited and ask for a better sense of discrimination.

～ 11 June ～

The Circuit of Births

Tuirigin is a successive birth that passes from every nature into
another . . . flowing through all time from beginning to end.
— *Cormac's Glossary* (trans. CM) .

Tuirigin (TOOR'ghin) is a very precise word for which there is no English equivalent; the nearest we can get to a translation is "a circuit of
births." One might assume, from that definition, that *tuirigin* is the
same as reincarnation, but this is not so. In *tuirigin,* the soul moves
between the otherworld and this world in a series of journeys.

This understanding and remembrance of past lives was acknowledged within the didactic stories told by the Celtic church, which saw
the ancient legends as vehicles of wisdom. Among these is the story of
the legendary Fintan, who passed from human to animal shape, finally
being reborn from a human mother. From his living memory, the
whole history of Ireland can be reconstructed. In conversation with
learned men of Ireland, he admitted, "A continuity of existence
remained in me, which I do not deny." This is significant, when we
consider that any notion of rebirth has been uncanonical within the
Roman Church since the Council of Lyons in 1274. Despite that offi-
cial condemnation, adherence to early druidic and similar classical
understandings of metempsychosis—the migration of soul from one
body to another—seems to have survived. (See 23 June.)

Tuirigin is nothing less than the birth of the true nature, for it is not
until the soul has been fused with everything else that it assumes its
true nature; the soul's many turnings bring about its wisdom. The
Celtic *tuirigin* is about fusion—not the refining of the soul till it reaches
nirvana, but a profound communion with everything that brings
authenticity to the soul.

Meditate upon your true nature and authenticity of soul.

Apocalyptic Imaginings

Something is happening to the whole human race at this dreadful hour. . . . [S]omething is happening down under the ground, and yet not so very far down underground.

—JOHN COWPER POWYS, *Obstinate Cymric*

As we approach the turn of the millennium, there arise opposing opinions as to its meaning and import. On the one hand are ranged those who see this as an opportunity to herald a new age of mature and practical spirituality; on the other stand those who perceive this millennial turning with dread, as the threshold of the world's ending. Somewhere in between stand those for whom none of this is of any significance whatever, and peoples whose cultures number the passing of years by other than Christian criteria. As our own century's millennial clock ticks towards 2000, the predominant fear of our era is that microchips and computers will not be able to cope and that electrical equipment the world over will grind to a halt.

The ends of centuries and millennia are always charged with fears and expectations—that ancient prophecies will be fulfilled or that the blank and unimaginable period of time to come will harbor dangers that we cannot protect ourselves from. The mythographer Joseph Campbell, when interviewed before his death, spoke tellingly of the end of the world as we know it. He said, "The world as the centre of the universe, the world divided from the heavens, the world bound by horizons in which love is reserved for members of the in-group: that is the world that is passing away. Apocalypse does not point to a fiery Armageddon but to the fact that our ignorance and complacency are coming to an end."

What are your fears and hopes around the millennium? Meditate upon the possibilities.

~ 13 JUNE ~

Divine Powers

Three things possible to none but God: to penetrate the eternal without loss of truth; to recreate the new from the old without destruction; to be able to change every shape but remain changeless.

—Welsh triad (trans. CM)

The ability to penetrate the eternal without loss of truth contrasts with our own patchy perception and understanding of the unseen realms. Even though imagination is a faculty of the soul, and it blends the information received by our inner and outer senses together, it can give us only partial understanding. (See 16 July.)

Science can now breed other life forms, DNA, or tissue, but not without the death of the donor or loss of integrity to the tissue in question. The issue of genetic research is surrounded by fear and desire. The ability to change every shape and yet remain changeless can be imputed only to those able to live through time and its many evolutions. Only the Divine does this. Although it is believed by many cultures, including the Celtic tradition, that the soul passes into many shapes, subtle changes do occur over the flow of time and nature of place. (See 11 and 23 June.) The unchanging nature of the Divine is only *reflected* in our world, never fully *revealed*. We truly apprehend only a few potent images suggesting a totality that is forever hidden from us while we live on this side of the worlds.

How do you perceive divine powers from your own spiritual experience?

The Right to Be Happy and Sad

Man was made for joy and woe;
And when this we rightly know,
Safely through the world we go.

—William Blake, "Auguries of Innocence"

Joy and sorrow do not perform according to logical rules and laws; they come unbidden like the clouds, the rain, the sunshine. If we assume that happiness is our sacred right, we tend to warp the all-covering garment of the universal bounty into a selfish cloak of self-appeasement. This cult of happiness can devolve into a pleasure-seeking pilgrimage that excludes all difficulty and awkwardness. Our dissatisfaction, grief, or disillusion is then projected upon less-fortunate others.

The gifts of sadness, like the gifts of happiness, come to all conditions and types of people. They provide moments of self-clarification that keep our lives on course. Sadness stems nearly always from some form of exclusion, separation, or rejection. When we are disconnected from life, we yearn for union. Joy connects us strongly with life; like people who plunge into the stream, we enter the swim of life in ecstatic connection. Our going safely through the world is based upon a true regard of both conditions. When we value the gifts both of joy and of sorrow, our taste for life increases. When we accept both happiness and sadness as our mortal bequest, we grow as human beings.

What have you learned from your own sad and happy times?

Remarriage and Mourning

I charge you not to take a new wife until you see a briar with two blossoms upon my grave.
—Culhwch and Olwen, from *The Mabinogion*

We live in a era when divorce and remarriage are more and more customary. At the demise of any relationship, whether because of a partner's death or his decision to move off and out, there is always a period of mourning. Even in the most violent and unhappy of relationships, a breakup is followed by a time of disbelief and reorientation, a time wherein we have to rediscover our own identity and self-esteem.

This time of self-rediscovery is essential to keep us from remarrying or forming unsuitable relationships on the rebound, out of grief, loneliness, or depression. Without a period of mourning, a lacuna of time and space to let the dust settle, we tend to choose a partner who imperfectly echoes the last partner or a person who temporarily compensates us for the hollowness left by our severed relationship.

This does not mean that we should not meet other people or potential partners, only that we should be careful not to make too sudden a commitment after a relationship has ended. When love flowers in us, rather than need or longing, we will be fully aware that the time is right to enter into a new partnership.

Meditate upon your own experience of loss in partnership and observe the signs and circumstances that taught you timeliness and new love.

Mother and Child

Despite the bitterness of every sickness,
The strife that's the gift of each living soul;
The child born of one's fair body,
That is what lives in the mind.

—GORMLAITH, "Trum Anocht Mh'Osnadh," in
Osborn Bergin, *Irish Bardic Poetry* (trans. CM)

The bond between mother and child, between child and mother, is regarded as a sacred one in most cultures—a bond that is upheld by most legal systems, at least while the child is young. In cultures where women are less respected than men, motherhood can be a potent tool of repression, however. Motherhood has become a sacred cow over which politicians argue and bicker, alternately nodding respectfully and pulling it off the highway as a massive obstruction. Our society is ambivalent about the rights of mothers and their children, especially as the strain on the nuclear family to earn a decent living cuts across child-rearing and child-support issues.

The child-mother bond goes through a series of different phases. After the intimate nurture of babyhood and infancy, the mother becomes the watchdog vigilante—often sharp-voiced and forthright—determined to ensure the safety and well-being of her child. After the child leaves home, the role of mother as caregiver evolves into a variety of different areas, depending on the mother's adaptability. The distance of age and maturity on both sides of the relationship can bring a mutual appreciation of great beauty. Every human being comes from a woman's body, and though mother and child may be unknown to each other after birth, nothing can rend the sacred bond that lies umbilically between them.

Meditate about the mother-child bond in your own experience.

The Golden Age

The sleeping place of the Age of Gold is in the depths of every human heart.

—JOHN COWPER POWYS, *Morwyn*

Within Celtic belief, the Golden Age is a paradigm of the living otherworld, where there is no winter, no death, no disease, no want, no work. In every age, we look back to times that we judge to be less imperfect than our own. Grandparents remember better times than they see ahead for their grandchildren; traditional craftspeople remember times when their craft was truly valued, before mass-produced goods; soldiers envy troops who could fight on horseback or hand to hand without facing mass annihilation. The grass is always greener and the times always more rosy in retrospect.

The Edenic principle of Paradise has replaced the picture of the classical Golden Age within our own times, growing out of a story of disobedience that bruises the human heart and echoes after us, becoming the pretext for ideological brutality to all living beings, animals, and people. The reaction against this has created other Golden Ages: the Matriarchal Golden Age, when women were supreme and the Divine was predominantly seen as goddessly; the Pagan Golden Age, when all ancestral doings were good, wise, and true. Our longing for a Golden Age is not a fantasy or a historical reality; rather, it is a real remembrance of something profoundly, mythically, true. Its images shimmer upon our inner sight like a mirage—a recognition of the eternal, living otherworld whose lands we travel to when we dream, meditate, or make soul-flight to its regions, a realm to which we instinctively belong.

What is your vision of the Golden Age? How does it sustain hope in you?

The Sacred Lore of Tradition

The songs of our ancestors are also the songs of our children.
—PHILIP CARR-GOMM, *The Druid Way*

The true meaning of tradition entails the handing over by one generation to another the sacred lore by which life can be lived. The sacred lore of tradition is a living, moving thing, flowing like water from one age to another, reforming itself from one generation to the next, adapting to the needs of the new. Each one of us is a tradition-bearer, though we may not think of ourselves as such. But when we need the sacred lore of tradition—when a family reunion comes along, when death hovers close, when the community gathers together—a sense of unworthiness, a suspicion of fraudulence, a foreboding of inauthenticity shadows our steps. We reach for the ancient song of our ancestors and falter because we have not personally rewoven the sacred theme into our own time, place, and living. We are often driven to borrow the traditions of other people because our own have been mislaid or forgotten.

Without us, the children will have no songs. Without our humble efforts to grasp and transmute the sacred lore that descends to us, there will be no tradition. Before that fate comes upon us, let us silently ask the ancestors for help. Pray that the song of the sacred lore may be sung, that we may catch its echoes and, through the understanding of our hearts, find the melody that harmonizes with our times.

What beneficial traditions have you inherited? How do they work best now?

Cause and Effect

A stone thrown into water measures its own depth.
—Welsh proverb

When people live their lives as though there were no cause and effect within it, great harm comes. When they believe that this world is the only world there is, they live less carefully in respect to cause and effect. Unaware of the correspondence of the apparent with the unseen world, they perform actions and harbor intentions that have a ripple effect. When a stone is thrown into water, we are aware only of the rippling on the surface of the pool; however, when the stone lands at the bottom, it displaces something else.

A careless word, uttered without proper intention, lodges somewhere. A thoughtless deed, performed however secretly, leaves its impression somewhere. When our actions and intentions measure their depth in the otherworld, we may not be immediately aware of what has happened, but the sonic resonance of their falling returns to the world in a variety of ways, as a fresh set of ripples in another part of our world. Unchecked anger, spiraling fear, the theft or manipulation of the rights of other beings—these are but a few causes that have terrible effects. Anger directed at another is like an actual weapon that impacts upon its target. By ignoring the subtle messages of the unseen realms that lie about us and interact with us at every moment, we cut ourselves off from sources of spiritual joy and alignment. The result is a dispirited or stubborn self-dependency whose boundary of responsibility stops at the egocentric limits of the self. The universe is larger than we have conceived it: it encompasses not only the explored physical cosmos of our kindred beings but the unexplored cosmos of our otherworldly family.

Consider the wider cause-and-effect patterns that interweave you with both worlds. What effects have you noticed?

Defending the Territory

Peredur saw a chess-board in the hall, and the chess-men were
playing against each other, by themselves. Now the side that he
supported lost the game, while the other side set up a shout, as
though they had been living men.

—Peredur, from *The Mabinogion* (trans. CM)

In Celtic tradition, gaming boards represent the land itself, and the
pieces represent the people who fight over the rulership of the land.
Games of this kind teach players to defend their territory and to hazard
their pieces in defense of the king. In an age that expects us to be
open, pleasant, and friendly, we could perhaps learn some salutary
lessons from the "wood-cunning" of the gaming board and rediscover
how to better protect the territory of our soul. We do not want to live
our lives on the defensive or on the attack, but by being always open
and welcoming to everyone we meet, unaware of the need to protect
our own very necessary boundaries, we expose ourselves to the danger
that our soul will be encroached upon by people whose smiles hide
manipulative or malign intentions, people interested (perhaps unconsciously) in coercing us to render our services without any reciprocation whatever.

Those who live as if the world and its contents were set there for
their personal convenience have no notion of boundaries, and they will
steadily encroach upon the territory of others unless they are checked
or challenged.

Meditate upon where your personal boundaries are and set up checks
and challenges to those who attempt to come across them without your
express permission. Where are you encroaching upon the territory of
others?

The Prayer of Midsummer

Sun-stone's kiss, midsummer pleasure,
Welcome all and some.
At the hele-stone sing and gather,
Every blesséd one.

—CAITLÍN MATTHEWS, "Midsummer Blessing"

On this, the longest day of the year, an annual miracle occurs. At dawn, the first rays of the sun touch the hele-stone, the solitary sighting stone that stands outside the great circle of Stonehenge. The miracle of the longest day is celebrated by peoples all over the world as the time of greatest light and blessedness. Tonight we will have the shortest night, the least darkness of the year, as the sun climbs to its zenith in the heavens.

At midday, stand in the sunlight, which (unless you are very far north or very far south of the equator) will be directly overhead. Check to see where, if anywhere, your shadow is. Most people will find that there is scant shadow at all. All living creatures cast shadows; it is only spirits who have none. This is the nearest we can come to resembling spirits in this reality. Become attuned to the midsummer sun. Absorb the warmth and blessedness, and in return hold in your heart those who lack the blessing of light. Do not make any prayer for things to be changed one way or another; just hold these places and beings in your heart and let the sun shine upon them. Come back to awareness of your own time and place, and give thanks for the longest day.

It is traditional to make a bonfire at twilight and stay up late dancing, singing, and making merry with the community. If you cannot do this, light a candle and make your own blessing for all beings on this happy day.

Commune with the longest day and shortest night, adapting the suggestions above to your own needs and those of your community.

Care of the Soul

There's little wisdom,
owner of the sap-laden tree,
to watch the growth of your frail apples,
yet to be careless of your own soul.

—anon. Irish poem (trans. CM)

As with the care of trees and plants, care of the soul cannot be left up to nature if we wish to have the best results. The fruits of spirit never ripen upon an unfrequented soul. Care of the soul is at least as important as care of the body. Listen to the soul's needs carefully—though these may not be easy to hear if we have been in the habit of ignoring them. The soul feeds on beauty, harmony, recreation, creativity, and connectedness with all that nourishes its core.

Look closely at what we have been put on earth to achieve. Pursuing our vision and putting ourselves upon the path of our vocation can help bring us into greater alignment with the soul's powers. From this alignment will come a living, connective bridge between ourselves, our world, and the otherworld.

If your understanding of spirit has been envisioned in unhelpful images or metaphors, use your soul's intrinsic sensitivity to change those metaphors and images and find ones with which you can be fully responsive. The soul is wiser than we.

Listen to your soul. Ask your spiritual allies to show you what it most needs.

～ 23 JUNE ～

Past Existences

I have been in many shapes
Before I assumed a constant form.
—TALIESIN, "Câd Goddeu" (trans. J. Matthews)

The Welsh poet Taliesin (Tal-ee-ESS'in) remembers all his past existences on the circuit of births after he has achieved the gift of knowledge. His existences include being a drop in the air, a star, a bridge, an eagle, a sword in battle, a string in a harp, and a tree in a grove. He concludes that "there is nothing of which I have not been a part." Few of us alive today can speak with any kind of accuracy about the past existences that we have experienced. Human beings do not usually remember their incarnations. It is perhaps fortunate that this is so: if we had memory of everything and everyone that we have been, the burden would be intolerable. It is given to few people to know their full past, because there are indeed few with the maturity of soul to understand and bear the burden with neutrality, without anguish.

Unfortunately, inquiry into past lives is now a common pursuit, taught at weekend seminars. Within the bardic initiation, such knowledge was taught not to the beginner, nor to the curious, nor to those who wished to discount the faults of their present life by casting responsibility onto another era, place, or person; it was taught only to those with the maturity not to misuse the knowledge. The poet's fusion with the myriad life forms of nature is thereafter never just a memory, but a potent, living understanding of life as it is lived in the present moment. Let us be grateful for the often salutary glimpses that we are given of our own *tuirigin* and learn all we can from them.

Review the disharmonious recurrent patterns in your present life if you
want to learn more of past lives. These patterns reveal things you need
to deal with or assimilate.

The Strong Protectors

Each day and night
That I recite the genealogy of Brighid
I shall not be killed nor despoiled,
I shall not be imprisoned nor wounded.

—Scots Gaelic blessing (trans. CM)

There is a strong tradition throughout the Celtic realms of special protectors who stand between our world and the otherworld. These are the "greater dead," the ancestors who do not pass into the next phase of their *tuirigin* (see 11 June) but stand ready to intercede, facilitate, and assist us. In early times, these figures behaved as protectors against attack and invasion. One such protector is Eoghan Bel, a sixth-century Irish king of Connacht, who insisted on being interred standing, with a spear in his hand. Similarly, King Arthur did not die but is held to be ready to come again from Avalon to Britain's defense.

These early traditions were not overthrown but were supplemented by other strong protectors. The saints who had power to stand between mortals and the dangers of the natural world, for example, would also intercede to the Divine on behalf of beseechers. This guardianship could be invoked by pilgrimage: visiting the tomb of St. David in Pembrokeshire, Wales, was said to ensure that you would not go to hell, as was the annual barefoot climbing of Croagh Patrick Mountain in County Mayo, Ireland. The recitation of Brigit's genealogy not only protected the speaker but made him part of the saint's family in a special way. The strong protectors are not superbeings, gods or spirits in their initial appearance; they are mortals who become endowed with supernatural power after their death, vehicles of special grace. They form an ancestral hotline that stretches directly between ourselves and the sacred, unseen world, ever ready to assist us.

Who are the strong ancestral protectors to whom you appeal?

The Shield and Sword of Music

Be valiant, princely,
Be active, exceedingly bold,
Be ready, fresh and comely!
—LACHLANN MOR MACMHUIRICH,
"Battle Exhortation to Clan Donald"

Before armies set forth on expeditions, and on the eve of battle, bardic poets sang to encourage warriors and to give heart to the fearful. Armies also went into battle with their musicians to encourage them. Music is still very much a shield and sword in our own age. Though few of us go into conflict with sharp-edged weapons, we still go into danger with better heart when music accompanies us. The songs that come unconsciously to our lips when we are in need of comfort, courage, or new heart are always very significant. Their words and themes are often either akin to our own situation in that very moment or able to shield us from the danger ahead.

Recognizing and seeking out the songs and music that support us in such times is a wonderful way of being prepared. We can gather our own repertoire of music, ready to serve us in need: the battle songs that arm us with courage as we go toward challenge, the soothing songs that restrain our fears, the shielding songs that speak of our deep resourcefulness and that set danger at naught, the songs of spiritual exhortation that urge our sacred allies to accompany us. All these songs can go with us wherever we are. The music that is our own sword and shield derives from strong sources of inspiration—from the deep core of meaning that moves us to joy and new heart.

Begin to recognize and gather your own repertoire of soul-strengthen-ing music. Which songs do you use for different occasions?

Treasures of Experience

And O! when from life's transient cup
Thy lips have drunk their nectar up,
And left it empty, frail as this,
May the last golden drops be bliss,
And like this gem beneath the wine,
The glorious deathless jewel thine.

—JOHN SOBIESKI STUART, "With an
Antique Crystal Cup and Ring"

Our cup of life is forever filling and emptying as the tides of life ebb and flow. To appreciate the rewards of life as we are living it gives flavor to the draught that we drink as well as shape and luster to the soul that accompanies us in all our existences. Like a jewel dropped into a glass, so does our soul adorn our body. The body, like the wine, will be consumed; but the soul, like the jewel, will endure.

The treasures of experience well lived and appreciated are brightly reflected in the facets of the soul, making our jewel yet more precious. The work of polishing the soul takes a lifetime, but at the end of this life there is a special urgency to "make our soul" before we leave this incarnation. Those who have ignored their soul do not know what lies in the treasury of experience. Whatever is left in the cup of life looks to them like the lees of the wine, because the jewel is obscured to their vision. Sometimes we need days off to enter our own treasury and spend time reviewing our experience, both in the long and short term, paying attention to the patterns and spirals that have unfolded. Such times are never wasted, for they enable our soul's luster to brighten the wine of our life.

What stories and experiences brighten your own soul's jewel?

Color

What is it?—
Near and far, its shape I see
Twelve miles from me over the sea:
The man of the little green boat
And his shirt sewn with red thread.
[A rainbow.]

—Scots Gaelic riddle (trans. CM)

In the rainbow we see the beam from the eye of the sun, the spectrum of colors that pervade our world from end to end. Those who learn their own codes of color and its meaning discover ways of regulating their mood and appearance. For different people and cultures, these meanings and gifts can vary considerably. The whole rainbow spectrum of colors can be derived from ingredients in the natural world to create dyes: from the bold statement of red that grants courage, through the protective hue of orange, to the brightness of yellow that gives energy, the calming or harmonious shades of green, the joyful and sorrowful blues, the dutiful and responsible service of indigo, and the rare holiness of purple.

Color is an essential nourishment to our senses. If we are starved of color for any length of time, or our surroundings have tints that depress our spirits, we begin to feel very strange indeed. Color is an unappreciated joy that offers itself freely to all sighted people. The rainbow bids us remember and reacquaint ourselves with the beauty and gifts of its rich spectrum.

Which are your favorite colors? Which ones do you not care for? What kinds of feelings and qualities do you associate with the rainbow's spectrum of color?

The Painted People

They tattoo their bodies not only with likenesses of animals of all kinds, but with all sorts of drawings.

—HERODIAN, *Commentaries*

The use for body-painting of native plants such as woad, whose leaves yield a bright-blue dye, is attested by many writers. Isidore of Seville, writing in the sixth century, tells how the Picts—another name for the Caledonians of Scotland—"have a name derived from the appearance of their bodies. These are played upon by a needle working with small pricks and by the squeezed out sap of a native plant, so that they bear the resultant marks according to the personal rank of the individual, their painted limbs being tattooed to show their high birth." One seventeenth-century Scots writer asserted that many a Pict took on "the forms of beasts, birds and fishes on his face; and not on it only, but on his whole body." These totemic shapes remain on the Pictish standing stones of eastern Scotland: the eagle, salmon, bull, stag, seahorse, seal, and many others. Were these their tribal or personal totems? We have no means of knowing, as they left no written documents. In fact, the Pictish language remains unknown, though historians know that they used ogham, the Celtic tree script employed only in inscriptions.

In our own time, the tattoo, long seen as the fashion statement of green youths and hardened workmen, is fast becoming a mature statement of personal identity and belonging among a remarkable number of people—women as well as men. As we seek the shapes that our soul has touched, as we quest for the circuits of birth and the meaning of our life's weaving, potent images and symbols arise. Although we may not wish to have them lastingly engraved upon our bodies, they are nevertheless etched upon our souls.

Meditate upon the totemic symbols and images that typify your life's journey.

The Soul-Protecting Shield

I seek a mantle that cannot be folded,
That neither holly spike nor tree branch will catch upon;
That guards me as a brooch guards a cloak;
A powerful cloak of beetle-green.
—*The Metrical Dindshenchas,* ed. Edward Gwynn (trans. CM)

The shield that is desired here is a *lorica,* or breastplate for the soul. The *lorica,* a spell or charm that invokes the different powers of the universe to keep the reciter free from harm, was used by the ancient Celts and by their Christian descendants alike. The soul-protecting invocation calls out to the universe, to every place and shape that the soul has been in, to come and weave help around the reciter in time of need.

The nature of the *lorica* depends very much upon the one who makes it. Traditional invocations have been passed down, but it is always better to create our own, for our own needs. Those whom we invoke may include the powers of nature with which we feel attuned, the beings and creatures who are our spiritual allies, and heroes, gods, and ancestors. The *lorica* protects the mantle of our soul, the soul's shrine of our body, from harm. Without intention, the words of the *lorica* have little effect. But when our heart is aligned with our words and our intention, our utterance can go forth; and with the help of the *lorica,* the connection and weaving together of the assisting powers can surround us in a sure mantle.

Create your own lorica *to help shield you against whatever you are fearful of. Weave into your litany of assistance all your soul-friends and spiritual allies, the powers of the natural world that are meaningfully protective to you.*

～ 30 JUNE ～

The Spirits of Trees

Working with the spirit of the tree can bring us renewed energy, powerful inspiration and deep communion.
—PHILIP CARR-GOMM, *The Druid Tradition*

The Celts saw trees as sacred powers, mediators between the worlds, with their roots penetrating the depths of the Underworld and their branches straining at the ceiling of the apparent world. Druids congregated within *nemetons,* or sacred groves that were open to the sky, so that they might be ringed by the protective wisdom of the trees. Certain very ancient trees were virtually accorded the status of tribal ancestors, standing as sacred protectors at the center of the tribal region and venerated by everyone in the district. The laws against laying blade against these trees were particularly severe.

We may also be able to work with the powers of the trees, if we approach them cooperatively. Some people take their troubles to a particular tree and gain refreshment and solace from its company; others derive inspiration from sitting at its foot or in its branches; still others have discovered that trees are truly mediators between the worlds, living bridges between our apparent world and the unseen realms of the otherworld. When we approach a tree, we need to slow down our breathing, slow down our rapid pace, our mental busyness, in order to be attuned to the spirit of the tree itself. Without touching it, we slow down and then put out our intentions, greeting the tree and then sitting down by it, or—with its permission—standing against its trunk. Then we sing or croon quietly to it, leaving speech alone. With our heart, we ask the tree to show us part of its nature. (It will take many visits to know its full nature.) We listen and give thanks. Even when we are just passing a tree, not visiting, we can still send out a greeting to it.

Begin to make the acquaintance of a chosen tree near you.

JULY

Month of July—the hay is apt to smoke.
Ardent the heat; dissolved the snow;
The vagrant does not love a long confederacy
                              —anon. Welsh poem

July brings us to the height of summer. This month's meditational themes include opening the ways, the goddess and the feminine, holidays and wider horizons, the world as lover, recommitment to promises and vows, and secrecy and privacy.

Pillars of Society

The three ruinations of a tribe: a lying chief, a false judge, and a lecherous priest.

—ancient Irish triad

In Celtic society, the chief was known by his truth and generosity, the judge by his equity, and the priest by his sexual continence. When state, legislature, and church fail, then the land and its people are at risk. The condemnations cited in the above triad do not strike us as old-fashioned, since our newspapers are still full of stories of the failure and falsehood of our own leaders. The corrupt politician, the bribed judge, and the abusive priest are still common characters in our society.

Corruptions of office may have become more commonplace throughout the world, but there are still many who uphold the dignity and honor of the oaths befitting their positions.

Nothing less than the overhaul of all public institutions is now needed if suitable candidates for office are to be inspired and called forth to act on our behalf. If we hope to continue to find leaders worthy of their calling who will not fall under the burdens of the office or fall into the temptations of the office, we all must pay serious attention to the need for change.

The oaths of public servants and ministers represent sacred, binding contracts between a people and their gods. The chief or the politician is contracted to the spirits of the land; the judge is contracted to the spirit of truth; the priest is contracted to the guiding spirits of the universe. The breaking of such contracts brings great unhappiness to all.

What are your personal criteria for those whom you elect to public office? What changes do you feel are necessary to public institutions?

Reinaugurating the Grail Quest

I sometimes think that now, in our day, the Grail Quest has been reinaugurated. . . . This time the difference is, it isn't only men who will ride out.

—John Moriarty, *Turtle Was Gone a Long Time*

In an era when the Wasteland spoken of in the Grail legends seems an ever-present possibility, the time is dawning when all beings who are attuned to the well-being of life must step forward to be the questers of this generation: to go seek and find the Grail, to bring its gifts of restoration to our sickened world. The Grail represents whatever is spiritually restorative: for different people, this may be different things.

What is the quest today, and who becomes a quester? The quest is for solutions that embrace all levels of existence—not the material world only, but also the otherworld whose spiritual impulse beats beneath the pulse of the manifest world. The questers are drawn from all walks of life, men and women of all generations who long with all their hearts for the world and all that is in it to be healed, whole, and in harmony. They are not idealists who simply meditate and dream; they are strivers who long for this restoration more than they love their own lives, who are willing to endanger themselves. They are rising up now, in every land, working in a variety of ways, but always keenly aware of how important is the reconnection of our own world with the other. The Grail itself is a bridge that links both worlds and that, by the agency of the questers, is able to dispense its healing to those places that need it most. This healing is the living currency of the otherworld, streaming between the worlds in a flood of creative ideas, technological solutions, and more mature ways of living. This quest awaits all who feel the world's pain as their own.

What is the Grail in your own spiritual quest?

Protecting the Animals

Keep them from harm,
Keep them from jealousy,
Keep them from spell,
From North to South.

—Scots Gaelic blessing (trans. CM)

The protection of domesticated animals was an important concern to our ancestors, who relied upon the strength and life-giving nurture of animals in the daily round. In our own time, the protection of animals takes on other connotations, involves other responsibilities.

The ancient prayer above was uttered to protect beasts from straying, from theft, from natural dangers; it was never intended to protect them from imprisonment in factory-farms, from circumscribed lives of great misery, from live transportation in long-distance trucks, or from fearful mass slaughter. The protection of domesticated animals today is something that everyone can be practically involved in by their choice of food, by their active campaigning, and by their boycotting of methods that are cruel and unnecessary.

Regarding those animals that are used as guinea pigs in laboratory testing of chemicals, pharmaceuticals, and diseases, we have less justification for their ill-treatment and more responsibility for their care. The torture of any living creature is abhorrent; one does not have to be a bleeding heart to witness to the pain involved in this work. Finding other alternatives to the laboratory testing of animals will perhaps remove the onus of cruelty from their human kindred in the near future, but not until more humans use their voices to protect the animals who have no voice.

Make your own prayer and blessing for animals and for those who are involved in their welfare.

Inalienable Rights

*Three indispensables of a nobleman are: his harp, his blanket and
his cauldron.*

—triad from *Laws of Hywel Dda*

Under most modern laws of distraint—whereby goods are removed
from a household in compensation for debts unpaid—there are certain
articles that cannot be removed. These usually include the items by
which the householder earns her living, the tools of a worker's trade,
the bed, and the means to make food. In the triad above, from the
Welsh legal code formulated by King Hywel Dda (HOO'wel THA) in
the ninth century, we discover that the three indispensable objects of
the nobleman are the harp by which his bard entertained him, the blanket that kept his body warm in bed, and the cauldron that heated his
food. Today, these items would probably be equivalent to the television
set, the bed, and the stove: means of entertainment, sleep, and food.

We have become used to the possession of certain inalienable rights:
life, liberty, the pursuit of happiness, among others, in our modern
world. These are rights that we take for granted, that are enshrined in
constitutions and maintained by the law of the land; and yet even
within civilized societies there are many who do not enjoy these rights.
The poor, the disadvantaged, and others who live on the margins of
society need the actions and voices of those who honor the commitment to the inalienable rights that we should all enjoy.

*If you could take only three things from your house right now, which
would they be? Of all your basic, inalienable rights, which do you most
cherish?*

Goddess of the Door

Dark is the night, far is the dawning.
Sing for the shining of light on the way!
Hearken, be ready, attend to my calling,
Sing all you guardians who wait at the door.
—CAITLÍN MATTHEWS, "Midsummer Song"

One of the ancient names for the island of Britain is the Island of the Strong Door, a title that is associated with Merlin's magical defense of the land. Another guardian, the Goddess of the Door, is discernible within the story of Merlin as a distinct archetype who works in association with her prophet. When he is still a little boy, he prophesies the history of Britain, ending with the appearance of the goddess who comes to close the door of the aeon. At the end of his life, Merlin's sister, Ganeida, takes over his prophetic role. She builds an observatory with seventy doors and windows into which he retires.

The ancient Goddess of the Door turns the key of prophetic inspiration in those whom she appoints to the spiritual guardianship of her land. The task of prophet of the land passes from man to woman to man to woman down the ages, every time the Goddess of the Door turns her key. These prophets successively enter her service as guardians of the door, becoming the timeless singers at the threshold between the worlds.

The Goddess of the Door stands at this nexus point between the worlds for all people, regulating the flow of sequential time in our world and rejoicing in the timeless knowledge in the otherworld. She gives us each prophetic insight that enables us to guard our own boundaries and thresholds.

Visualize and visit the place between the worlds where understanding and insight come to you. Greet the guardians there, and find one who will instruct you to guard your thresholds.

The Familiar Road

Mony an ane speers the road he kens weel. [Many a one inquires about the road he knows well.]

—Scots proverb

Our anxiety to know that we are on the right road and performing life's actions in the correct manner often leaves us a long way from our destination. This syndrome is found in perpetual students, who are always taking courses, and in those who take every known therapeutic aid even though their health is good. It can be caused by an excessive perfectionism, by a longing for approval, or by sheer blind doggedness. A lack of confidence or validation often prevents us from realizing the obvious: if we perpetually seek some outer approval for our actions, we will never consciously walk our own road.

A Welsh proverb that complements this Scots one tells us that "he travels fastest who takes the road that he knows"; in other words, the path of least resistance yields speedier results. Swimming against the tide is hard work, requiring more energy than we may have to give out, exhausting us before we arrive. If we can recognize the tides of our own life, we will begin to move with their flow with grace and ease.

Of course, it is not always of benefit to only and always take the road that we know best. Choosing the predictable path, never exploring the byways or parallel tracks that could enrich our journey, may lead to complacency and a dull demeanor. But it is good, on that predictable path, to get in touch with our own power and purpose, to not always be seeking the approval of someone else.

What destination have you already reached (and yet are still struggling to attain)? Where are you swimming upstream in your life?

The Divine Feminine

There was an Old Woman lived under the hill
And if she's not gone, she lives there still.
—traditional British rhyme

Feminine and masculine are the left and right hands of God. We have only recently begun to remember the divine feminine and to respect her again, but she has never been far from us. Earth herself reminds us of the living presence of the feminine principle as she unfolds her many faces through the cycle of the year. The Old Woman who lives under the hill is the oldest grandmother of us all: our very substance derives from her; and as we trace her many aspects through the seasons, we appreciate the different gifts with which we are endowed.

As a young girl in spring, she is innocent; playful and delightful, she responds to beauty with joy. When our hearts are in springtime mode, we are filled with clarity and truth, in touch with our integrity. In Maytime, when blossom's heady scent of desire is in the air, she reaches the borders of womanhood and looks with desire upon the beloved of her heart, rejoicing in the song of summer's freedom. When our hearts are in summer mode, we have power and self-confidence.

In autumn, she becomes mother, fierce protector of all that she loves. In autumn, we reflect this face as our creative vision is fulfilled. When winter comes, she strips bare the bough, clarifying each soul. But many do not choose to know her now, for she grows thin and gray. Yet she is ever stronger, as ice and snow cover her with a new mantle.

Those who fear the Old Woman's features never kiss her or call upon her wisdom. But she welcomes all, calling us to look again and find in ourselves the reflection of her wisdom. She calls us to realize that she is in every part of the universe, that the earth is but our most immediate mirror of her features. Her truth, beauty, compassion, and wisdom are in every place, in every face.

Meditate upon the divine feminine.

Irritations

I went to the hill and I got it.
I sat on a knoll and I sought it.
And if I would get it I would leave it.
Since I did not get it, I took it with me.
[A thorn in the foot.]

—Scots Gaelic riddle

There is no surefire way to avoid irritations, no magic formula that will ease them out of our way. They arrive without warning to plague us, and we have to get on and deal with them. Some of the tiresomeness can be alleviated, however, if we see many of our irritations as reminders of neglected areas of our life. The laws of cause and effect set in train a whole series of actions; similarly, undone actions have effects upon our lives. The things we neglect return to plague us: from the overdue car service, to the dental examination we keep meaning to have; from our failure to reply to an important letter, to the long silence we have meted out to a close relative. Breakdowns, aching jaws, lost opportunities, aggrieved friends, and irate family members suddenly loom large in our schedule, neatly overturning everything we had planned.

The universe has its own way of getting our attention and making us attend to what is important. Sometimes little irritations that go untended become larger ones. A thorn in the foot can be removed, but if gangrene sets in, the whole leg may have to be removed. The little irritations may bite and worry us, but they certainly do not take kindly to compromise or neglect.

Review the irritations that you have currently; trace back their root cause, where possible, and find any connections between your negligence and their arrival. Act swiftly and appropriately if particular irritations seem to recur frequently.

Following Our Path

"Whence do you come and whither do you journey?"
"I journey on my own errand."

—Pwyll, Prince of Dyfed, from *The Mabinogion*

When Pwyll (POO'ilh) first encounters and is questioned by his future wife, Rhiannon (Hree-ANN'on), he gives her a polite but noncommittal answer as to his identity and purpose.

It is not wise, after all, to disclose too much about yourself upon any first meeting, unless you have a clear idea of the other person's intentions. As it turns out, Pwyll and Rhiannon are traveling the same road, for she has come from the underworld with the express purpose of marrying him. Discovering and following our own path is something that is our personal business; it is not something that one person can do for another. We each have to make our own contract with Spirit, rather than existing as an unwitting signatory to someone else's previously drawn-up contract. We have to read all the fine print before we sign, learning everything we can about the obligations and commitments before showing our hand. Spontaneous response and heartfelt enthusiasm are not good bases for decision making.

When we search for our spiritual path, we need to reassess, consolidate, and recommit our spiritual focus—and check contractual details. It is all right to change course as we seek the best way to Spirit; it is equally all right to stay where we are—as long as we realize that compromising our truth is dangerous.

If you are oriented on your path by a set of rules not of your making, or coasting along with a contract you have not fully consented to, ask yourself what strongly held beliefs that course is ignoring or causing you to change or diminish.

Ancestral Bequests

Alienated ancestors gather, drawing close
To our bicker and complaint, to knock at aggrieved hearts.
Their plaint to our ears is "restore, restore."
—CAITLÍN MATTHEWS, "Avebury Easter"

We have many ancestral inheritances that contribute to our condition. Some are genetic and highly visible; others are not so obvious but are still part of the ancestral bequest—the unfinished business that members of our ancestral family have put off and put off until it comes seeping out in our own lives.

Many deep, atavistic, or unwelcome urges that have lain dormant within our family line are activated when we reach a certain age or condition of maturity—when we are trying hard to put our life on the right track, to purposefully avoid legacies of failure, fear, anger, or control. There often comes a point when we have to consciously decide not to buy into the negativity of past scenarios and expectations but to turn towards the illumination of the heart.

The ancestral bequest can be cleared when we stand back and look into the issues that have been haunting our family line. The ability to recognize ancestral failures and expectations for what they are is exceedingly helpful. With that ability, we can acknowledge that our ancestors, like us, were vulnerable, frightened, and attached to their unfinished business. It is not our part to blame them, but rather, in our amending, to leave out hatred and revenge; it is not our part to recreate spirals of exclusion, but rather to pray for the ancestors to be released and to attend to our own lives with the help of our spiritual allies.

Looking into your recent family history, what issues show signs of being ancestral bequests rather than personal problems?

Conspiring with the Descendants

Thou shalt be in league with the beings of the future, and the generations to come after shall be at peace with thee.

—JOANNA MACY, *World as Lover, World as Self*

In what way can we be in league with the beings of the future, or conspire with them? Meditate upon your parents, sense them as though they stood behind you. Now visualize their parents behind them, and theirs behind them. Go back as far as you can from knowledge, and beyond that imagine the lines going back as far as you like. Be aware of all the good things you have inherited from your ancestors. Now come forward from past times to your own time, aware of the tributaries of blood that flow into the river of your own veins. Now visualize your descendants in front of you, and their children and their children. Go as far forward in time as you like, imagining future generations. Be aware of all that you will bequeath them. Extend your meditation to include all the beings of the future—the many different species of life forms. What is their expectation of you? What can you do to bring peace between you?

Many people live their lives in fear of an all-powerful deity who they believe will zap them for bad behavior; they are like children who tiptoe around a cranky parent for fear of arousing his temper. How would it be if instead we lived our lives envisioning our descendants, the beings (of every species) of the future? How would it be if we regulated our decisions and life-style with *them* in mind? Instead of living fearfully or distrustfully, instead of trying to cut corners and steal a march on our forebears, how about living with our *descendants* in mind?

What most practical wisdom from your own life would you bequeath to your descendants? Try the meditation suggested above.

Making Love with Life

How can we make love?
It is making us—
Every second,
Every minute,
Every hour.
—CAROLE BRUCE, "The Beloved Sequence"

Life embraces living in a playful, creative process in which we are not the controlling agency, but rather a beloved partner. Once we glimpse the action of love in our lives, we can never again live with disrespect, complaint, or displeasure. The yeast of love bubbles up through our hardening crust, leaving little holes filled with life-giving air, escape routes to the heart of ecstasy.

The British mystic and poet Thomas Traherne wrote, "Place yourself in the midst of the world as if you were alone, and meditate upon all the services which it doth unto you." This is a good place from which to experience the world as lover. It helps us turn round our self-centered view of life and shows us receptive areas wherein we engage most deeply with life. If we make a practice of coming from this place— from the sense of world as lover—our core instincts will be kindled and we will know how to respond to our lover without rehearsal or preparation.

Making love with life is a revolutionary way of living, because it involves our loving reciprocation rather than our defensive, self-shielding mechanisms. We must abandon those mechanisms, letting go of our personal control and defensiveness when we are with the lover so that love's creative and liberating influence can be free to work. Although this is a playful way of living, it is also seriously intent, insightful, and intuitive.

How does life make love with you? How do you make love with life?

Appropriate Prayer

Hear my faith-cry for them who are more thine than mine. Give each of them what is best for each. I cannot tell what it is. But thou knowest.

—ALISTAIR MACLEAN, *Hebridean Altars*

This carefully worded prayer by a Scots minister is a good all-purpose appeal that does not overbalance the scales one way or the other; it neither neglects to remember those in need nor sets out to bring satisfaction to the pray-er. All too often our prayers are tipped in favor of our own envisioned goals for others, rather than merely bringing their needs to divine attention.

When our words are combined with strong intentions, we make a magic that we cannot begin to realize. Intentions are the pathways of desire, and when words travel along them, they go as spirit messengers to their source. If we frame closely worded requests with a particular end in sight, we cease to be pray-ers and become sorcerers instead.

If someone is indeed dying, for example, it is not helpful to him to offer prayers for his full recovery to health. This might only lengthen a life that he is ready to leave. We might more appropriately pray for his general well-being and comfort. And prayers for someone's harm— appeals such as, "I wish she'd drop dead" or "I hope he chokes on it"— follow the same pathways as our other prayers (and just as effectively, as many have found to their cost).

Our prayers should not harm the world; nor should they attempt to tie up the threads of other beings and their soul-circuits for our own solace or satisfaction.

Examine for harmful content any prayers, words, and intentions that you have uttered this day. Ask your spiritual allies to neutralize or defuse any inappropriate prayers that have passed your lips. Create a general (and harmless) prayer for common needs.

The Language of the Birds

Birds . . . now represent the continued presence of the past . . .
[which is] evoked by the singing, whistling and calling that fell into
millions of ancestral ears and there left images that we all inherit.
—JACQUETTA HAWKES, *A Land*

The Celtic peoples held birds in high esteem, as the mouthpieces of Spirit. Their flight and calls were widely used in divination. The term "language of the birds" is used to mean the secret knowledge that runs beneath the web of words; it implies an almost magical intelligence that does not depend upon the help of any kind of human communication system. It is innate, subtle, coded knowledge that we can somehow understand.

The idea of the unchanging song of the birds singing in our ears as well as the ears of our ancestors conjures a potent image of the continuation of life—an inheritance so subtle that we must immerse ourselves in the sound of birdcall in order to enter into its richness. The oracular calling of birds speaks directly to our hearts, bypassing our minds; it is a mode of divination that both we and our ancestors had to learn—an unchanging language of meaning.

The little songbirds who make the sweetest song, the crows and ravens whose raucous call is most vocal, the estuary and marsh birds with their lonesome sound, the hawks and owls shrieking and signaling—all have their own language and special symbolism, essential elements of our living world.

If we wish to understand the flight and calling of birds, we must listen, near dawn or in the late afternoon, to their song; and listening, enter a place of stillness within in order to comprehend their message to us.

Listen to the singing of birds today, at dawn or twilight. Meditate with a clear mind and listen to what you are told.

Surveillance and Privacy

Then Llefelys ordered a long horn of copper to be made, and they talked through it together. But whatever each said to the other through the horn, nothing but hateful hostility came to the ears of the other.

—*Lludd and Llefelys* (trans. CM)

In this humorous incident from a Welsh story about the legendary King Lludd (HLITH), the king's realm has been overrun by the Coriannied (Kor-ANN'y-ed), an otherwordly people so omniscient that no secret can be spoken without their hearing of it. Lludd takes to sea to meet up in private with his wise brother, Llefelys, king of France.

After cleansing the speaking trumpet of obstructing spirits, Llefelys proposes the sprinkling of the crushed bodies of certain insects into the drinking water, which will be poisonous to the Corannied but harmless to the people of Britain. Lludd returns home and follows this suggestion, destroying the ubiquitous Corannied without harming his own folk.

We live in a society where surveillance is becoming total: in most public places, security cameras pursue and record us. With more aspects of our lives open to scrutiny, there is precious little sense of privacy left. A growing sense of irksome invasion is beginning to characterize our streets, as the new Corannied dog our every step, recording our every move. We no longer feel like private individuals.

There is no magic insect that will rid us of this ubiquitous plague; indeed, the bugging is all on the other side, as telephones are bugged to record private conversations. There are still wild, open spaces, of course, but even those are monitored by satellite these days. This problem of lost privacy can be combated by forceful representation by human rights organizations to world governments. If we value our liberty, we need to defend our privacy in more vigorous ways.

How does surveillance bug your life? Is it really necessary?

Imagination

Imagination is the faculty of the soul.
—Caitlín Matthews, *Singing the Soul Back Home*

Our imagination is the eye of our soul, the retina of the psyche whereon are reflected the truths that our soul experiences. To be without contact with our imagination is to be truly blind.

The imagination perceives the *imaginal realm,* the reflected image of the otherworld that we cannot see with our physical eyes. Our imagination is commonly stimulated when we make connections based upon this perception: like a ready needle that pierces one piece of fabric and emerges through the other side of another piece of fabric, pulling them together, so does our imagination penetrate the veil between the worlds and show us likenesses of what is eternally true. For some people, these perceptions are very vivid and accurate; for others, they are misty or short-sighted, though they provide a glimpse of something very important.

If we begin to honor the imagination as a faculty of the soul by taking our problems and dilemmas (as well as our visions and desires) to its threshold, we will be asking the soul for a wider view, a solution that we cannot personally envision but that will enrich our lives.

Meditate upon a dilemma or creative project, actively allowing the imagination to provide perspectives, solutions, and answers. These may come as visual images or nonvisually (in sudden insights and intuitions) provided immediately or over the next few days. Record your findings and test them for truth and helpfulness, without discounting what you experience.

The Prince's Truth

Being without truth, without law, defeat in battle, famine during his reign, dryness of cows, ruination of fruit, dearth of crops.
——Audacht Moraind in Caitlín and John Matthews,
The Encyclopedia of Celtic Wisdom (trans. CM)

These seven proofs of unworthy kingship rest upon the understanding that the land resonates sympathetically with the qualities of the ruler. A good ruler is known by "winters fine and frosty, springs dry and windy, summers warm with showers, autumn dewy and fruitful. . . . A bad ruler brings perverse weather upon a wicked people and dries up the fruits of the earth."

At this time of year, when crops are nearly fully ripe and the preparation for harvest begins, we do not look at the land with ancestral eyes and see written there the testimony of our rulers' administration. For us, the land is the land; the weather merely the weather; and the governmental upsets and lack of integrity just part of the old, old story. And yet, for us, the messages of the earth are auguries of a wider issue, of a truth that is not being upheld worldwide.

Without integrity and the observance of natural laws to maintain good order, conflicts and other evils manifest across the planet. Greed, opportunism, mass production, consumerism, and other factors that satisfy personal needs have replaced the promises that rulers and their followers once made directly to the land beneath their feet. Yet to some degree, each of us shares in those promises to serve and uphold the natural laws of life that our elected representatives make on our behalf.

What commitments and responsibilities do we have to the natural world? How can our life-style support and maintain its good order? To what degree do we contribute to its decline?

The Perfect Partner

I demanded a strange bride-gift such as no woman before me had asked of a man . . . a husband without meanness, without jealousy, without fear.

—*Táin Bó Cuailnge*, Irish text

In this quote Queen Maeve of Connacht enumerates the qualities she seeks in a husband. She cannot choose a mean husband, she says, because of her own generous nature; as long as a man is without fear, she is satisfied. She concludes that a jealous husband would not be of service to her either, since she is known for never being "without one man in the shadow of another"—meaning that her successive lovers might be seen as an encumbrance to a jealous man!

What are the qualities of a perfect partner? These will vary from person to person. The qualities that most people seek are loving trust, faithfulness, and commitment. But in any relationship, we must determine the nature of the contract from the outset, so as to avoid disappointment. If we later learn that our unspoken expectations are beyond the prospective partner's ability to fulfill, then we have only ourselves to blame for not making them clear enough earlier.

The perfect partner is generally the one who complements our own qualities, not the one who is the exact equivalent of ourselves. To have an exact counterpart would become very boring after a few weeks. The differences in a relationship often prove to be its strengths, while the similarities can become bones of contention, especially if the competitive element enters the relationship. In the presence of unhealthy competition, mutual respect soon falls by the wayside.

What are the qualities of a perfect partner according to your personal criteria?

Off Days

Many a time I wish I were other than I am. I'm weary of the solemn tide; of the little fields; of this brooding isle.
—ALISTAIR MACLEAN, *Hebridean Altars*

Some days the very thought of having to go to work, having to go about our accustomed duties, having to process our tasks and meet our commitments conscientiously just makes us want to scream. It is especially hard to continue working when everyone around us is enjoying vacation. The sense of dissatisfaction can become almost intolerable. Sometimes we just wish we could be somewhere else, far enough away that we would not even glimpse the furniture anymore. When things get this bad, it is time to have a free day or two, time to do something uncharacteristic and spontaneous.

But sometimes these feelings of dissatisfaction are a symptom of something more important than the need for a temporary break or holiday. When divine discontent strikes, this feeling often will not go away until we have taken radical action. When we ignore our spiritual mainspring, when our power is neglected, minor illnesses and depressions serve as the body's escape route.

Being in an intolerable position—whether in our job or in a relationship—can also drain our power. Depression, involving an involuntary loss of vitality and appetite for life, is often a strong symptom of power loss. When power is waning or absent, it is essential to discover what is draining the battery and deal with it quickly, before our vital energy is gone. Continued powerlessness leads to low self-esteem, which in turn leads to diminished physical and spiritual nurture. (See 22 June.)

Are you just needing a break, or are your feelings of dissatisfaction symptomatic of a more profound need for change? Reconnect with the things, places, and people that give you energy and rekindle your appetite for life.

Overthrowing Illusions

Each man is in his spectre's power
Until the arrival of that hour
When his humanity awake
And cast his own spectre into the lake.
—WILLIAM BLAKE, "Each Man Is in His Spectre's Power"

Long before Freud and Jung, William Blake coined the word *specter* to signify the illusory self that, by its appetites and desires, overrules and dictates to the true self. The illusory self becomes our personal image, the projected likeness we want others to see.

The specter is fed by our patterns of appeasement, by our fear of authority, by our need to be perfect. Lest it take hold of our lives, we have to return to our essential humanity, to the core of our being, to the soul within us, and clarify by the soul's mirror what constitutes self and illusory self. In everything we do, we need to determine whether we are acting out of the core of our integrity or at the dictates of the specter.

Where mind and heart, reason and compassion are separated, there Blake's specter roams hungry and unchecked through our life. Casting off our illusory self is an act of maturity that strengthens the light of the soul. Acting out of our own heart, rather than out of projected self, we come once more to the true likeness with which we have been endowed.

Where is the specter raging through your life? What false projections of your soul are showing on your screen this week? Meditate upon what life would be like without the support of those projections. Search for your true, authentic self.

Mother-Right

They bound themselves by the sun and moon that the possession of the [Pictish kingdom] . . . should be held by right of the female rather than that of the male progeny to the end of the world.
—GEOFFREY KEATING, *Forus Feasa ar Eirinn*

In our times, a reconsideration of the role and status of women has brought us into new relationship with mother-right, with a proper acknowledgment of the gifts of the feminine. For men and women this has been a rediscovery of a secret inheritance, for our connection with the mother-country of the soul has been fractured. Our society has been (and for the most part still is) patriarchal: things are ordered from the masculine point of view, generally for the benefit and enhancement of masculine privileges. That which partakes of the feminine has been marginalized and neglected—including not only the lives of women but also the feminine side of male nature.

A whole new way of living and valuing things comes into focus when we consider the mother-right. The hidden side of our nature, the side that intuits rather than reasons, the part that views things from the inside out rather than from the outside in, can come into play when mother-right is allowed to function normally. This does not mean switching a patriarchy for a matriarchy, for each of these extremes is as unbalanced as the other. Rather, it means allowing the side of our society and individuality that has been recessive to take its rightful place. This recognition of the feminine quietly acknowledges the intrinsically royal nature of mother-right, which speaks as sovereign from the depths of the mother-country—a land that still waits to be fully rediscovered and restored.

Meditate upon the feminine within your life. Revisit the mother-country of the soul where the feminine's holy and regal nature is recognized.

Journey to the Heart of the Labyrinth

Spiralling towards the centre,
We know that we have come to the centre of who we are.
—Philip Carr-Gomm, *The Druid Tradition*

The old Cornish midwives of the southwest tip of Britain used to have a flat stone into whose depths a spiral labyrinth was carved. Expectant mothers about to give birth would be encouraged to trace this spiral pathway in order to help the birth. By tracing it over and over with their fingers and reciting certain secret prayers, they could help the long gestation of the child draw to its close. It was believed that this practice would clear any obstacles standing in the way of an easy birth and bring the child forth from its long months in the dark.

The correlations between the birth process and our own spiral circuit with the labyrinth become clearest when we trace the route of our life to date. (See 11 June.) In order to begin our spiritual journey, we must first be born from the heart of the labyrinth: the mysterious womb. As children we know our origins; as adults we begin to forget, so we have to painfully take the path home in unknowing, coil by coil. For many of us, the heart of the labyrinth, the goal of the spiritual journey, is anticipated as a place of horror: a stalking place for Minotaurs and other beasts. But though we may expect to find all kinds of alien and external influences lurking there, we find, on arrival, nothing more than ourselves.

Only by treading the turning, spiraling coils of the labyrinth of our lives can we come to perfect understanding of what lies at the center. It is as familiar to us, as dear and memorable, as the road that leads homeward.

Meditate upon the different phases of your life in roughly seven-year intervals. Write down the qualities, discoveries, and themes of each phase. Arrange each of these phases around the paths of a labyrinth, noticing which paths and themes come close to each other.

Fierce Defenders

*I thank you, Andraste, and call out to you as one woman to
another. . . . I implore and pray to you for victory, and for the
maintenance of life and freedom against arrogant, unjust,
insatiable and profane men.*

—Dio Cassius, *Roman History*

This speech is attributed to the British Queen Boudicca (BOO'dik-a),
known to later generations as Boudicea, queen of the Iceni. When she
assumed the rulership of the tribe after her husband's death, the
Romans did not recognize her queenship. She was given a punitive
lashing for her defiance, and her two virgin daughters were raped.

Before going into battle against the Romans, Boudicca released a hare
from the fold of her cloak, in order to make a battle augury: the direction and nature of its running would determine her chances of victory.
She also called upon the Goddess of Victory, Andraste—She who is
Unconquerable—in order to uphold the Icenian cause against the
Romans. With her troops, this mighty queen killed an estimated eighty
thousand before she was defeated. Rather than risk capture and the dis-
honor of being paraded in a Roman triumph, she committed suicide.

There are many who will applaud Boudicca's forceful action against
Roman barbarity to herself and her daughters. Her shock tactics and
powers of leadership certainly confounded and weakened the Romans
for a significant period—long enough at least to have avenged the
insult to her royal person and her daughters' honor.

When men encounter the fierce defender who lies within women,
they are frequently dismayed or even terrified. Let a child be harmed
or an animal mistreated, a beautiful place polluted or human rights
diminished, and we see that the warrior queens are not dead and forgotten; they still stride among us, calling out to the Unconquered Goddess for help in times of need.

What causes your warrior instincts to surge to the surface?

Exile

Exile, like memory, may be a place of hope and delusion. But there
are rules of light there and principles of darkness. . . . The expatri-
ate is in search of a country, the exile in search of a self.

—Eavan Boland, *Object Lessons*

One of the strongest sorrows of the Celtic world was exile from one's
own country. To be banished beyond the ninth wave of the shore was
to lose touch with the integrity, power, and belongingness of the land.
Another form of exile came to the Celtic peoples in the Christian era:
the self-chosen exile of Christian service in foreign lands. This was
known as "white martyrdom" to those who endured the pain of exile.

Unwilling exiles need the completion of their native land to make
them whole. They are always longing for it—indeed, they will repro-
duce it, living within a ghetto created by memory and regret—and are
ever suspicious of anything the new land has to offer. When the darkness of exile's night passes, the light of expatriate dawn can arrive. The
new land and the immigrant can begin a fresh relationship in partnership, and (though the old country is never forgotten) the new homeland can begin to bring nurture, support, and joy in all possible ways
to the welcome guest.

From what are you exiled (for example, home, customs, people,
places)? What new opportunities surround you now?

The Elements

*If I break faith, may the skies fall upon me, may the seas drown
me, may the earth rise up and swallow me.*

—ancient Gaulish oath of the elements

This mighty oath binds the swearer's existence to that of the ancient
Celtic elements themselves. We take the elements' gifts for granted: we
do not think for even a minute about the air we breathe, the water we
wash with, or the earth that sustains our every step.

But this ancient oath has more ominous and immediate connotations in our age. We have taken the elements so much for granted, disrespected their gifts so absolutely, that we have made it more than possible for the skies to fall on us, for the earth to swallow us, for the seas
to overwhelm us. As heavy industry pollutes the air, the air quality
grows poorer; as the earth heats up from the greenhouse effect, the ice
caps begin to melt and the seas rise; as we fill the earth with our unre-
cyclable waste, the soil itself becomes poisonous and infertile. We for-
got the meaning of this oath long ago, and now we are reminded.

The broad and beautiful gifts of the elements are so willing, able,
and bounteous. They clothe, nurture, and irrigate the planet and all its
inhabitants freely and blessedly. To keep faith with the elements, we
need to make an intentioned effort to sustain the life-flow of our planet
by putting our minds and hearts and actions to the uplifting of life.
These precious elements of air, water, and earth are the triad of powers
that maintain the life of the world. Preserved by the warmth of the sun
and these three mighty powers, our earth has heat, light, and life.
Without them, it is cold, dark, dry, and barren.

*Consider each of the elements as you use them. When washing your
hands, lighting a fire or stove, taking your first breath of fresh air,
walking to work, stop and be thankful for their gifts. Bless them and
pray that they be preserved in peace, so that human hubris may not
invoke the ancient oath upon our dear planet.*

Insults

Curcog and her ladies . . . went to swim in the Boyne. When they had had enough swimming and diving they returned to their garments and left. But Eithne did not notice the maidens' departure and it so happened that the magic mist left her.

—*The Fosterage in the House of the Two Pails,* from
Caitlín and John Matthews, *The Encyclopedia of Celtic Wisdom*

The earthly maiden Eithne (EN'ya) served the faery woman Curcog. She was brought up with her mistress and other maidens and lived happily within the *feth fiadha* (FAY FEE'a), or cordon of invisibility, that surrounded the faery dwelling-place of Newgrange. All was well until a guest, Finbarr, from a neighboring faery hill, came to visit their home. Noticing that Eithne was the most beautiful of the maidens, but disturbed that she was of a different race than he—a human rather than a faery—he purposely insulted her. Eithne began to lose her health and confidence from that time forward, and so it was that eventually she began to find life within the faery hill insupportable. She slipped beyond the reach of the magic mist that shrouded faeryland into the realm of mortals. Unable to get back, she died.

The exclusion that we feel when we are insulted may similarly cause us to become separated from the things that normally support and inspire us, to become depressed or antagonized beyond bearing. Insults, whether they bear a grain of truth or not, cause us to reexamine and sometimes doubt just who and what we are. We can become adrift from our soul's center and slip into a state of uncertainty and destabilization. How can we reestablish ourselves after so severe a knock? We can call upon our spiritual allies to pull out the barb that has lodged in our being and neutralize its effect on our system, so that we can be restored to ourselves again.

What insulting barbs still lodge in your being? Call upon your spiritual allies to help dislodge them and restore you again.

Incubatory Divination

"What is your name?" asked Maeve.
"I am Fedelm, poetess of Connacht," she replied. "I have come from
Albion after learning the art of divination."
"Have you the power of prophecy called imbas forosna?" *asked*
the queen.
"I have indeed," said Fedelm.

—*Táin Bó Cuailgne* (trans. CM)

Here Queen Maeve of Connacht interviews a prophetic female poet in order to determine the outcome of the battle. Only poets who had trained in the highest divinatory techniques could illumine dark matters that could not be solved by normal means. *Imbas forosna* (IM'bas for-OS'na)—literally, "the inspiration of the great sigh"—was one of the "Three Illuminations" or prophetic techniques of divination. Fedelm tells Maeve, "I see it bloody, I see it red." She then prophesies accurately, and in some detail, the valor of the hero Cuchulainn, who will be responsible for laying waste Maeve's champions.

Imbas forosna is a form of Celtic incubatory divination that can be employed when we need to get more information about things that are unclear to us. By using the technique with modifications, we can attempt to "dream true." *Imbas forosna* requires well-framed intentions and an ability to remember our dreams. Before sleeping, create an invocation that addresses your spiritual allies and asks for help about the matter in hand; include the instruction that you wish to wake up when the answer has been revealed. Immediately write down any remembrances on waking, bearing in mind that the "answer" may be in riddling or hidden form. In order to unlock the answer, keep asking yourself how your dream experiences relate to your question. Try this for not more than three nights in succession, as continual attempts to "work" instead of rest during the night can disrupt sleep patterns.

Make your own incubatory divination, as outlined above.

The Mound of Wonders

Whoever sits upon this mound cannot go hence without either
receiving blows or else seeing a great wonder.

—Pwyll, Prince of Dyfed, from *The Mabinogion*

Ascending to mounds and high places in order to look out over the land in a divinatory way was a common practice among the Celts. It was especially customary in the days leading up to Lughnasa, when the harvest was in its last week of ripening. It was a method of auguring what the year would bring, as well as an honoring of the land.

The Mound of Wonders is a place where the veil between the worlds is thin. Prince Pwyll decides to ascend this sacred seat of wonder in order to take an augury of his reign, and while there he sees a great wonder indeed: a woman in a golden dress riding upon a horse. He learns that she is Rhiannon, a woman from the Underworld, and that she has come thither in order to marry him. Pwyll believes himself to be in receipt of the wonders promised by the Mound, but his subsequent story has enough heavy blows in it to render his prophetic expectations low.

Pwyll's experience on the Mound of Wonders demonstrates the double nature of seership and prophecy: the thing that is shown often bears an unsuspected barb in its tail. Our expectations of divinatory methods lead us to accept the best and to reject the worst findings of our augury, to embrace the prophesied end but to ignore the rather irksome human means to its achievement. But once we have called out in question to the otherworld, we have to bear the burden of the answer.

Go out into the countryside and climb to a high place where you can
look out over the land. Ask for an augury of the land for the coming
season.

Holy Day or Holiday?

The sharp division of work from play and the natural from the supernatural has turned holy days into holidays.

—Jacquetta Hawkes, *A Land*

For most people, holy days are now just holidays, periods when they do not work, perhaps enjoying themselves in a recreative way. There is little or no sacred element left in holidays anymore; they have become one-way streets, days to be spent solely in gratifying our own needs. In centuries past, holy days were two-way streets: time was spent not only in recreation but also in honoring the Holy Ones to whom the day was dedicated, with some part of the time set aside for spiritual communion, remembrance, and veneration.

Holy days are days outside mundane time and business, days when we give ourselves time to be present, soul to spirit, with our spiritual helpers. It is important that we celebrate the days that are holy to us, whether they be religious festivals, personal remembrances, memorials for friends and family no longer alive, the two equinoxes and two solstices, the four Celtic festivals, or days dedicated to inspirers and teachers who have changed our lives.

When spiritual and recreative observances each inform and delight the other, holy days and holidays take their rightful balance in our lives.

Which holy days do you celebrate? If you could create a special holy day in the calendar, what would it be in aid of, what activities and celebrations would honor it, and on which day would you hold it?

Voyage to the Summer Stars

Come let us build the ship of the future
In an ancient pattern that journeys far.
Come let us set sail for the always islands,
Through seas of leaving to the Summer Stars.
—Robin Williamson, "Seasons They Change"

The sense of being visited by our spiritual allies is strong in many people. The beautiful, potent ones who are our spiritual friends and whose inspiration and encouragement keep us company come to us in moments of solitude and insight, speaking to us of the unseen world that lies on the other side of the veil from our own. This sense of visitation is not alien, unfriendly, or extraterrestrial; it is common, ordinary, and familiar, giving us hope, not fear.

Our awareness of the region of the "Summer Stars"—that area just within the boundaries of the otherworld—is often very powerful. We may feel, when we enter into communion with our spiritual friends, that we have indeed slipped over the horizon of our world and entered into a new blessedness. The vessel that "journeys far" is indeed the vessel of the living imagination that exists beyond time and space. As a vessel, it is very ancient indeed, and in its bows have stood many a voyager to the other shore. (See 16 July.)

The two-way traffic between ourselves and our spiritual allies is purposeful and creative, The communion between the spiritual voyager and her otherworldly friends is profound, respectful, and reciprocal. Our own voyage to the Summer Stars is taken in company with thousands of human beings who enjoy their lives and who have responsibilities that they are not going to throw over just because they are spiritually inclined. They voyage in order to enhance life, not in order to leave it, returning to speak with soul-friends of the wonders and joys that have been the secret of all mystics.

Make your own voyage to the Summer Stars to meet your allies.

Lughnasa

About the Calends of August Taltiu died, on a Monday, on the feast
of Lughnasad of Lug; around her grave from that Monday forth is
held the chief fair of noble Erin.
　　—*The Metrical Dindshenchas,* ed. Edward Gwynn (trans. CM)

This feast is often understood to be a celebration of the Irish god Lugh
(LOO'kh), but this is not the case. The festival is celebrated primarily
in honor of Lugh's foster-mother, Taltiu (TAWL'too), who single-hand-
edly cleared the plains of Ireland of trees in order that agriculture and
the grazing of cattle might take place. This necessary work is remembered and honored in the myth of Taltiu. The word *Lughnasa* (LOO'-
nas-ah) comes from the old Irish *Lugh nasad,* or "the binding promise
or duty of Lugh." On the death of his foster-mother, Lugh caused
funeral games to be held in her honor. Over time, these games
devolved into a fair, held annually at Telltown in County Meath. On
this eve, the sacred time of harvest is celebrated—a time for harvest
suppers and for enjoying all the varieties of food that have been in
short supply.

At another level, Lugh's honoring of Taltiu acknowledges the bounty
of harvest and the contract that exists between all living beings and the
earth. It is in that acknowledgment that the last sheaf of grain is har-
vested and honored, to be bound about the churn-dash in the form of
a woman of sprouting hair and spreading stalks, or to be woven into
complex shapes as a corn-dolly.

Make your own promise to the land this evening, as the sun strikes the
harvesting earth with its last rays. Meditate upon how you can keep
this time sacred in your personal spiritual practice.

Lughnasa

Season of Autumn

AUGUST

Month of August—covered with foam is the beach;
Blithesome the bee, full the hive;
Better the work of the sickle than the bow.
                                        —anon. Welsh poem

The month of August sees the beginning of autumn, with the gathering in of harvest. This month's meditations explore the following themes: gifts, ancient wisdom, sharing and respect, changing and growth, getting to the heart of things, recognizing possibilities, spiritual ecstasy.

Lugh: The Many-Gifted One

"There is a man at the door," said the doorkeeper. "His match would be hard to find: every art answers his skill."
— Gofraidh Fionn O'Dálaigh, in Osborn Bergin,
Irish Bardic Poetry (trans. CM)

The nickname of the Irish god Lugh (LOO'kh) is *Samildanach,* or "The Many-Gifted One." He earns it when he comes to the court of King Nuada (NOO'a-ha) just as everyone is sitting down to feast. The door-keeper challenges Lugh for his name and skill, for no one without a special art or skill may enter Tara. Lugh tells him that he is a smith, a builder, a champion, a harper, a hero, a poet, a magician, a healer, a cup-bearer, and a fire-keeper. His boast is tested by everyone there, and he is ultimately admitted.

Lugh is what we now call a "Renaissance man," one whose many skills pass beyond narrow categories of accomplishment, spilling over into many fields of artistic skill. His boast at Nuadu's court causes as much skepticism as would that of a man attempting to enter Congress or Parliament who claimed to be a great politician, a military hero, a Nobel-winning scientist, a shaman, a pop musician, a film star, and a poet of international acclaim all rolled into one.

Lugh's many-gifted nature holds sway at this time of year, reflecting the rich variety of the harvest, heralding the beginning of the many-colored autumn months. For ourselves, the month of August enables us to pass beyond the narrow confines of our daily occupation and enjoy the full range of our own skills and abilities as we take our vacation.

On this day of festival, review your own many-gifted nature with appreciation. How does it serve your community? Which of your gifts are you hiding away? Which ones will you be enjoying this autumn?

The Unending Quest

I watch the star to guide me home,
I found my soul and spirit's rest,
I travelled far across the foam.
There is no ending to my quest.
—Caitlín Matthews, *The Celtic Book of the Dead*

Our spiritual quest leads us on many a long voyage, across unknown seas to distant and unguessed-at destinations. Like the heroic voyagers of Irish tradition who took ship to the furthest shores of the Blessed Isles, looking for the Land of Women and the Land of Heart's Desire, we too strike out into unknown seas.

To all spiritual quests there are two main features: the outward voyage, on which all is strange, new, and frightening; and the homeward passage, on which there is time to consider all that we have experienced and to make sense of it. It is in that context that the epic of Troy makes sense when that other wily mariner, Odysseus, makes his own epic journey home. The manner in which we make our own spiritual homecoming is very important, since the return is a critical stage of our progress. Whatever beckons us from home will surely lead us, as we return with our new spiritual luggage. Once home, we must unpack everything, retaining what is useful to us and freely giving away what does not serve.

The spiritual quest is unending. It may lead us to revisit old destinations, but we will disembark as different people at each stop as we progress on our meandering and fruitful voyage.

Chart the major island landfalls of your own spiritual quest to date. Note any recurring patterns and check the usefulness of the spiritual baggage you have acquired on the way.

Retracing the Animal Presences

In the infancy of culture ritual and art were one, and the hunters who drew the animals they desired and performed ritual dances in fissures deep in the rock must also have had poetry to evoke this physical and spiritual sympathy.

—Jacquetta Hawkes, *A Land*

The cave and rock paintings of the ancient world depict bison, mammoth, horse, and deer, all of which have a powerful presence not found in domesticated animals. These wild creatures who prefigure a primal world of nature are figurative of more than meat and hide: they hold and mediate spiritual powers greater than the present consumerist mentality can evoke. The spirits of animals open gateways to deeper worlds of understanding, shared worlds in which people and animals learned from each other.

We do not know what rituals attended the painting of these creatures in ancient times, but looking at comparable cultures extant today, we can see that among the aboriginal Australians, for example, the rock and cave paintings are retraced by subsequent generations. This is a method of honoring and reconnecting with spiritual presences drawn by ancestors.

The power to re-evoke the spirits of animals with whom we once shared our world more equitably is still with us, if we will set aside the time and space. Retreating to our own dark cave, lit only by the torch of our willing understanding, we come again to the ritual kindling of spiritual vision wherein the ancient animal powers speak to us, creature to creature, in the dance of life.

Meditate upon a species of animal now under threat of extinction. Listen to its wisdom with respect and thankfulness. Make a drawing of your experience.

Ancestral Wisdom

We who have no elders, come
To your strong knees for counsel.
—CAITLÍN MATTHEWS, "Avebury Easter"

Most of us are sufficiently distanced from our own ancestral wisdom to feel disoriented in a time when indigenous knowledge is being reevaluated. How do we rekindle the ancestral fires once again? Where is the wisdom that will help us through the night of ignorance and doubt? Instead of elders, we now have elected politicians who speak with corrupt and self-serving voices; instead of fragrant local wisdom, we have homogenous civil law and institutionalized religion to guide us.

Ancestral wisdom does not cease because the elders are no longer as important in our society. Indeed, the wisdom is retrievable and implementable now. Part of the solution lies with ourselves. By changing the way we think—extending our planning to include the next ten generations rather than just our own lifetime and vigorously upholding the rights and privileges of elders in our community—we shift from a basis of neglect to a more respectful and empowered position.

If we genuinely want to look to our recent or ancient past for wisdom, then we must give time, effort, and study to *our own* spiritual and indigenous traditions, or to the traditions of those lands whence our ancestors came. Whatever is useful, whatever is practical, whatever is wise will never be lost as long as one person is practicing it.

Ask one of your own wise ancestors—someone known or unknown to you—to come to your circle of meditation. Ask this wise one for help about some aspect of your own life that is problematic. Then implement the advice you are given and see what results.

Colonization

Until we have learned to stand Grand Canyon deep in the earth,
we shouldn't even think of setting foot on the moon or Mars.
—JOHN MORIARTY, *Turtle Was Gone a Long Time*

The bequest of colonization is a miserable one, and it stems entirely from selfishness and greed; from lack of respect for land, beast, and culture; from a superior attitude that leads to untold violence and abuse. Even where nations have extricated themselves and peoples have gained their independence, the legacy lives on. Colonists may leave, but colonization burrows ever deeper in the land and people, leaving crooked souls and wounded attitudes.

There are many who silently pray for a complete change in human behavior before the space program becomes much more advanced. It is one thing to live with animosity, selfishness, and greed upon our own planet; it is another to take those traits beyond our atmosphere to other planets and spread the plague of violence and disrespect there. But how can we learn to "stand Grand Canyon deep" in our own planet, in the good earth from which all life comes, before that moment arrives?

To love what we have is perhaps more important than to aspire to that which we do not possess. To respect and maintain the earth, to find resourceful ways of living, is actually a greater challenge than to find ways of propelling ourselves at ever-greater speeds to ever-further destinations. Let us hope that the immensity of space itself may teach humankind a better wisdom.

Meditate upon one of the uplifting places of the earth that you have visited. Go there in soul-flight now and learn from the spirit of the place what it is to live upon the earth with respect.

∽ 6 August ∽

The Courage to Try Again

I will rise, I will go back to the white and silver shore.
I will have courage, as the sun does, rising and setting.
I will go as the sea in its turning.
I will rise, I will go back, I will rise!

—CAITLÍN MATTHEWS, *Celtic Devotional*

The courage to return to places (emotional as well as physical) of trial or difficulty is often lacking in us. Sometimes the injury, offence, or experience we underwent in a place was so dreadful that we choose to avoid it altogether. Any mention of a person or place associated with that experience may cause disorientation or even nausea.

Sometimes we must summon up the courage to surmount our careful avoidances, to step back onto ground where we have been hurt or injured or mocked. How do we find the courage then? Only by surrendering our fear, only by transforming it into the ability and power to move again. By avoiding our fear, we give it more substance. By facing our fear, we transform it.

The truly courageous go into danger realizing and accepting the terrors ahead. Most importantly, they do not plumb the depths of courage by an act of will alone. They draw upon their spiritual helpers, upon the familiar strengths of their daily lives, upon the love and friendship of their kindred and their dear ones. With them, because of them, for them, the courage within grows and conquers fear, shame, and anger.

Consider a painful situation or experience that is causing you to avoid certain places or people. Pray to your strongest spiritual helpers for courage to return.

∼ 7 August ∼

Harvest

All among the barley,
Who would not be blithe,
While the ripe and bearded barley
Is smiling on the scythe?
—anon., "The Ripe and Bearded Barley"

Every year brings the miracle of the harvest. The grain has ripened beneath the great golden sun of summer, with the assistance of the sharp, lancing showers of spring, with the help of the germinating chill of winter's icy grasp upon the seed hidden within the earth. It is only in autumn that we can begin to enjoy the fruits of the earth.

The seasonal round is no longer part of our daily life, accustomed as we are to helping ourselves to the good things of the earth at any time of year. Food preservation methods are now so sophisticated that we can enjoy cherries in December or hazelnuts in March.

The mysteries of the grain were hallowed by our ancestors, because grain created two stable items of diet: bread and ale. The complex processes of flour refining and fermentation were discovered millennia ago, bringing their own special gladness to everyone's hearth.

Though the celebration of harvest no longer brings us together in communities to rejoice that the cycle of life can continue into another year, we can still be blithe and thankful that there is sufficient food for all to share. Every time we eat bread, every time we drink beverages brewed from grain, we also partake in the mysteries of harvest.

What is your own life-harvest this year? Consider the riches of the year's experiences and ponder how they will fuel the year to come.

Wisdom Teachers

The three teachers who impart wisdom: suffering, thought, and a truthful heart.

—Welsh triad (trans. CM)

It is often said that on the path to spiritual wisdom we must suffer in order to learn. Certainly whatever breaks us out of the path of ingrained habit leads us into a wider and deeper existence. Those who have endured great sufferings are indeed sometimes forged by their terrible experiences into wiser people; adrift from what is normal and familiar to them, perhaps even forced into the regions of pain and terror, they have experienced the full enormity of suffering and come out whole. There are also many people who feel that suffering is an overrated teacher, however.

It takes an active curiosity, in conjunction with the perseverance to research human motives and behavior, to reach new understandings about our experiential sufferings and how they can be altered or accepted. The exercise of thought can lead us, in turn, to the truthful heart within us—unless, of course, we remain bound in fetters of useless analysis and recrimination about our condition. A truthful heart has no room for blame or revenge. It maintains its own living watch on what life sends, transmuting the toxins of difficult experience into a regenerating draught, siphoning away whatever cannot be changed.

The way of freedom is to draw upon the compassion plumbed by our suffering, upon the clarity of our thought, and upon the essential truth of our whole human existence.

Select one difficult experience from your own life and—with compassion, clarity, and truth—consider what wisdom has been revealed to you.

The Moon

I give you praise, moon of guidance,
That I have seen you again,
That I have seen the New Moon,
The lovely leader of the way.
                    —Scots Gaelic prayer to the moon (trans. CM)

Few people today mark the moon's phases, unless they go out a lot at night or their work calls them to contemplate the mysteries of the moon. The tides and seasons of our own mood have their correspondence with the moon's phases, which we can use with benefit once we are aware of them. It is easy to live only a daytime life, obedient only to the sun's diurnal rhythm. The longer monthly pattern of the moon is less discernible to us, but much more profoundly connected with our unvoiced preoccupations, with the subtextual feelings, memories, and instincts that inform us with their subtle messages.

To be aware, as the writer of this invocation was, of the moon as "leader of the way" is a great gift. The inexorable daily rhythm of the sun can sometimes beat us upon the anvil of life as problems hassle us, and the sun's longer rhythm of the four seasons brings us through changes over a whole year. But the cycle of the moon sees our soul through the phases of birth, growth, achievement, and death in one month, giving us relief, change, and encouragement. Whatever the problem, no matter how heavy the burden, we can look up and see that the moon has renewed itself yet again—as we also can.

Go out and commune with the moon tonight, whether it is visible or not. Note your mood over a couple of months and see how its changes correspond to the moon's phases.

The Soul of the Land

How has Ireland been apportioned?—Knowledge in the west, battle in the north, prosperity in the east, music in the south, kingship in the centre.

—*The Settling of the Manor of Tara*, from Caitlín and John Matthews
The Encyclopedia of Celtic Wisdom

Beneath the physical form of hills and valleys, beneath the rivers and mountains, there is another appearance. It is not only in the minerals, nor in the folded rocks; it is not only in the soil, nor in the trees and plants. Yet somehow in and under and through all these things, the land has another nature: its living soul. Many people believe that there are no such things as souls in people or anywhere else, and yet we know that this cannot be so. As the soul of a person looks out of her eyes and makes her who she is, so too does the soul of the land shine out of its features and give it special qualities.

However small or large our own country is, certain regions have their own distinct nature. They are centers of administration, trade, learning, art, spiritual wisdom, and so on. All contribute to the land as a whole. Certain regions foster one quality more than another; they are like a garden in which certain skills flourish and grow strong.

In the Celtic lands of yesteryear, each region had its sacred center or assembly, as did each country—a center that was not necessarily central in mathematical terms. The sacred center of any land has a greater spiritual pull than any other part, so it is here that the major assemblies of national importance are debated or decided. As Tara is to Ireland, so too is our own country's sacred center to the land itself: a hallowed place where the soul of the land shows through in all its splendor.

Become closer acquainted with the different regions of your own country through travel, study, and meditation.

Imagining the Future

To imagine your future constantly and vividly is to create your future.

—JOHN COWPER POWYS, *Obstinate Cymric*

One of the best preparations for the future is to pay attention to the present moment. Not by being provident, cautious, and miserly with life's experiential wealth, but by attending to the unfolding of today's events and one's part within them.

For those who have places to go and tasks to accomplish, the active use of the imagination to shape their destiny should never be despised. There is no such thing as a "destined future"—one that is fixed and immovable—since every step we take toward the future, every action and intention, changes the dance of our life to some degree. By imagining our future in an active way, we become more sensitive to the influences and interests around us. This active imagining also helps break down our romantic or false expectations and sets up pathways of practice toward our life's purpose, as we grow ever more sensitive to the unfolding patterns. Furthermore, it helps sustain us when achievement seems far off or unendingly delayed.

The work of shaping the future consists not in the ruthless excision of everything and everyone standing in our way, but in the gentle retuning of ourselves and our abilities to the pitch of our innate life's purpose. This is a daily, intentional shaping whereby we become attuned to the song that is always singing us.

Use your own active imagination to create the pathway that leads toward a plan in the future.

Mapping the Secret Territory

*For some years my heart was proud, for as the beauty sank into
memory it seemed to become a personal possession, and I said "I
imagined this" when I should humbly have said, "The curtain was
a little lifted that I might see."*

—A. E. (George Russell), *The Candle of Vision*

Those who are trying to map the thresholds of vision, to pass beyond
them into the mysterious hinterland of the unexplored spiritual terrain, know that they have to heed the messages and visions that come.
The recording of such information can be very valuable as a reminder
and an encouragement in those times when the spiritual borders are
stubbornly out of reach. But such records should never become territorial claims, proofs of purchase or evidence of our spiritual prowess.
Exclusivism has no part in the work of mapping the terrain of vision.

The human failing of hubris, that spiritual pride which claims more
than it has a right to, follows us from birth to death. To lift the curtain
is not to claim what lies beyond it. Perhaps this is one of the reasons
that our spiritual explorations have never been commensurate with our
geographical discoveries. At heart, we realize that there is no monetary
profit to be gained from spiritual discovery and that those who indulge
in spiritual materialism are merely poseurs, not the spiritually enlightened. The fruit of our vision is not for hoarding but for sharing: only
when shared can it become a fruit that satisfies eternally.

*Where are the borders between you and the spiritual realms most
clearly discovered? What have you learned from your own visions and
experiences during your lifelong discovery?*

Dispositions of Character

Some are born to sweet delight;
Some are born to endless night.
—William Blake, "Auguries of Innocence"

We are blessed by the nature we were born with, and—optimist or pessimist—we must somehow find our way through life. Whichever way we are disposed, we must take our character into account when we make decisions or form opinions; our nature plays a big part when we form alliances, friendships, and associations; the way people interact with and react to us has much to do with their reading of our character.

Sunny temperaments have the ability to make friends easily. Those who make heavy weather of life, on the other hand, hunch their shoulders against inevitable disaster and trudge along without an encouraging word to anyone. Each person is born with certain characteristics, which are then modified by upbringing and circumstance. It is quite possible to meet sweet-tempered people who have had difficult lives, however, as well as ill-tempered people who have had every natural advantage.

To steer by "sweet delight" may be a joy in the right circumstances, but it probably is not a great help in times of crisis; to be bound in "endless night" may keep away unbidden guests, but it certainly attracts no friends. Natures, like plants, can be trained to reveal other traits and strengths. Such training is hard work and requires constant vigilance, but with humor and humility, even hardened natures can change.

What kind of temperament do you possess? What strategies can and do you use when tempted to give in to your standard reaction, your natural inclination?

Sovereignty

And Sovereignty said to Niall, "And as you saw me ugly at first but at last beautiful, even so is royal rule. The land cannot be won without battles, but in the end everyone finds sovereignty is both beautiful and glorious."

—*Echtra Mac Echach Muigmedoin*, early Irish text (trans. CM)

There are many Irish stories concerning the qualifications necessary for rulership—stories that reveal the true nature of sovereignty. In these similar tales, the candidates for kingship are sent out into a dangerous place to fend for themselves. In the dark of the night, they each seek for water; at the only ford or well, each encounters a fearsome hag who refuses access to water unless the seeker first kisses her. When the successful man embraces her, she turns into a beautiful woman who declares that she is the Sovereign Goddess of the Land. Only the spirit of the land can acclaim and accept the ruler who is humble enough to submit to her.

Sovereignty is not something that can be claimed with pride or with thought of self-aggrandizement or glory. Sovereignty exists only with the agreement of the land itself. Until, or unless, this is sought with understanding, territorial disputes will continue.

In our own sphere of life, we each seek the sovereignty of our profession or of our soul's depths. If it is sought for self-gain, or in order to disable another, sovereignty is never truly ours. If, however, we seek out the heart of our craft, of our soul—wherever we live our lives—the spirit of sovereignty will indeed come to us and we will have a true contract of understanding based on mutual respect and exchange.

What are the boundaries and duties of your soul's sovereignty? Consider how you serve, defend, and maintain personal sovereignty in your life.

Reproach

Reproach, however strong,
Redresses no wrong.

—Welsh proverb

The eternal motion of vitality, energy, and power is forever circulating in the universe; we are each part of its movement, receiving vitality, passing it through our lives and letting it pass on again. There are many ways in which we can (and do) arrest this natural motion by clutching parts of the flow to ourselves. One of these ways is when we become stuck in cycles of reproach—whether we blame ourselves or others for our predicament.

From the moment that a person tastes reproach, he ceases to live in the present moment. His whole life is caught in a web that spreads out and covers everything he touches. Not only does time cease to flow for him, but his relationships are all tainted: those who interact with him sense that their own lives are used as comparisons for the original reproach. There is no life or energy in the vicinity of a person who holds firm to that awful moment of betrayal and cannot let go.

The first means of returning from that time-held moment into the present is by a determined releasing of reproach, with its attendant anger, resentment, and guilt. This release has to be complete, without strings, unconditionally without revenge. Then can begin the gradual rebuilding of life, with its everyday expectations, hopes, and disappointments.

The release of reproach enables the universal motion of vitality to flow again. Like a long-dammed-up tide, vitality sweeps toward the arid shores of the soul with compassionate moisture, bringing life into perspective and rhythm once more. (See April 6.)

How is reproach clogging up your own life? Flush it out of your heart by letting it go with a blessing.

Divine Origins

The time has come for us to fully acknowledge that our Origins,
our source and our basis, are Divine.
                    —Philip Carr-Gomm, *The Druid Tradition*

Though the origins of human life are now tracked by paleontologists through the fossil records of the earth's millennial aeons in ever more surprising and enlightening ways, we seldom regard the origins of life itself as emanating from a divine source. Though we may have set aside the old biblical narratives as naive or mythological, we still have to consider our part within the sacred formation of matter.

The Celtic tradition has no creation narrative; rather, it tells stories of seas, rivers, and wells bursting their banks, and of cauldrons in which all the ingredients of life are mixed together and remade in many eras of time. The Divine does not have one central image or characterization. There is no story that explains the mystery of our origins, no scripture that regularizes our thoughts about the Divine.

Though human nature has many detractors, and though we fail our own best intentions sometimes, the treasury of the soul reflects its divine origins time and again in our life's track. True divinity of soul shines out in the most unexpected moments: when we are hard-pressed, when care and support must stretch just a little further than we think we can give, when the moment of danger comes unexpectedly, when a deeper and more farsighted action is required of us. The invisible mantle of the Divine is about our shoulders and can lend us help and strength in daily life. The divine ingredients within our making do not make us into gods, but they do sparkle through our human lives in ways that illumine the universe.

Just for today, regard intention in everything you do as a divine work
that respects the sacred nature of you and everyone, everything, and
every place around you.

Respect and Reciprocation

Comb me smooth and stroke my head,
And every hair a sheaf shall be,
And every sheaf a golden tree.
  —George Peele, "The Old Wives' Tale"

Many folk tales tell of spirits who, if they are granted respect, give generously, but who, if they are abused, give gifts that are less desirable. In Peele's play *The Old Wives' Tale*, a girl who comes to draw water from the well meets the spirit of the well—a floating head that has the power to grant wishes in return for respect. It has ears of corn growing on its head rather than hair, yet when the girl combs the head, the ears of corn turn to gold and she combs it into her lap.

The wisdom of folk tales still has much to teach us. Heroes have respect toward the beings they encounter on their adventures. They never rush on by without a greeting or take what belongs to someone else without permission. However strange or frightening the appearance of those whom they meet, the protagonists of folk tales have a duty to be polite.

This advice still holds good when we approach sacred beings, spirits of the land, or our own spiritual helpers and friends. While these beings are sources of benefit to us, they also deserve and require our interaction and respect. To always go knocking on the otherworldly doors to ask for spiritual gifts without recompense or friendly conversation is hardly good manners: such behavior in our own world would eventually cause even our friends and neighbors to grant us short shrift.

With those who are spiritually dear to us, we have a special duty of reciprocation. And even toward those spirits whom we do not know, we can extend a cautious respect, one that bridges the worlds between us but does not steal anything or incur any offence.

Meditate upon and go meet one of your spiritual helpers. Ask what service you can perform for that helper.

Trouble

The cheek cannot conceal the trouble of the heart.
—LLYWARCH HEN, "Gorwynion"

Whether trouble creeps up on us or takes us suddenly by surprise, our perspective on the world alters completely from that moment on. Whatever hopes or expectations we had, we know that trouble will halt or divert us from their achievement. The way that we deal with trouble makes a big difference. Finding resourceful help, rather than simply complaining to everyone and doing nothing, is a fruitful strategy in time of trial. But if the habit of self-sufficiency is deeply ingrained in us, we may find ourselves unable to ask for help. And even when we can ask, sometimes there is no easy or immediate solution.

We often complain that trouble is not of our own making. It is hard to tell, though, because the strands of cause and effect are generally woven too far into the unconscious for us to track points of intersection with any certainty. Sometimes we have indeed interfered in something that was not our business and been pulled into the vortex, but most times there seems to be no specific cause relating to our actions.

Trouble is the lot of human existence. Its challenges shake our sometimes complacent attitudes and force us to respond. Its tremors in our life, like the messages of pain in our body, are indicators of something out of balance, something that must be put right.

Look at the flash-points of potential trouble in your life now. Is there action you could take to avert trouble and bring balance? What coping strategies did you use when trouble last visited you?

Satisfaction

Abstinence sows sand all over
The ruddy limbs and flaming hair,
But desire gratified
Plants fruits of life and beauty there.
　　　　　—WILLIAM BLAKE, "Abstinence"

Abstaining or fasting from the things that we enjoy is not in itself a bad thing; indeed, it can restimulate our appreciation and give us a better balance in the way we use life's resources. When desires become bullies that have to be pacified, when our freedom is in thrall to those desires, we may well need to employ abstinence to bring ourselves back to normal.

Yet desires submerged or imprisoned can bring us to equally unbalanced regions. If we never allow the fulfillment of our desires, we doom ourselves to perpetual dissatisfaction, to lives that are neither enhanced nor enchanted with delight. It may be that we learned such abstinence in times of hardship, difficulty, or illness and are still living under the sway of impossibility. It may be that we were injured by rejection or lack of love—an experience that often consigns all forms of fulfillment to a foreign territory. Let us also recognize, however, that the subtle forms of abstinence that we all practice may spring from laziness or from fear of loss of control as much as from any other cause.

Enjoyment, pleasure, and the satisfaction of our desires are legitimate human duties, as long as they harm no other being. The pursuit of our desires can lead us deeper into life and toward the fulfillment of our life's purpose.

Today, really enjoy doing something you love but have not done for a long time.

Communion of Hearts

We swear by peace and love to stand
Heart to heart and hand in hand.
Mark, O Spirit, and hear us now,
Confirming this our Sacred Vow.

—Druidic prayer of unity

The "Sacred Vow" of unity in this prayer is sworn "by peace and love"—the two requisites without which any spiritual communion is invalidated. In every assembly of human beings, there is a wide variety of different opinions, beliefs, and perspectives; each unique viewpoint is essential to prevent abnormal homogenization, wherein people suppress their personal views and maintain a phony unity. A communion of hearts is focalized by an act of intention that includes each unique opinion but goes beyond personal boundaries, entering the circle of Spirit.

The mantle of unity is conferred—can only be conferred—by Spirit, which manifests in many different forms to those who are gathered together. Even to those with a formal religious upbringing, Spirit will be present to each person in the most immediate metaphors and appearances. Like a mountain, Spirit may be approached by many routes, and each route will influence the ways we see the mountain. Spirit offers us each a vision of unity if we will accept what we are uniquely shown: that the circle of life in which we stand encircles and includes everything and everyone we have ever known.

Stand in meditation, visualizing those with whom you share the circle of life most intimately. Be aware of the rippling out of your circle in all directions. Be also aware of the many forms in which Spirit manifests to each of those in your circle. Make your own prayer of commitment to this circle, or use the one above.

Sharing Our Dreams

But I, being poor, have only my dreams:
I have spread my dreams under your feet;
Tread softly because you tread on my dreams.
—W. B. Yeats, "Had I the Heaven's Embroidered Cloths"

In what circumstances is it safe to share our hopes and dreams? Something so personal cannot always have meaning or relevance to another. Like someone else's holiday photos, our dreams may bore or alienate. With a soul-friend, however—a friend with whom we can reveal our soul—we can share not only our night-dreams but also our daydreams, the deep desires we wish to fulfill. Our soul-friend can be trusted not to laugh, mock, or abuse, and can act as a witness of the heart's desires.

We can also share our dreams through the work that we do, through the creative endeavors of our hands and hearts, with other creative dreamers. Though we live in a society that has forgotten how dreams can be shared in order to heal the community, there are still many who yearn to meet and dream together and whose collective dreaming can bring wonder and joy to the world.

Those night-dreams that arrive in often overwhelming or frightening power often need incubation in a journal, where their complex metaphors can be scanned for significance. The dreams that will give hope or insight can be selectively shared with those whom we meet: the confused, the doubtful, the fearful, the undecided. Not all dreams are ours to own. Sometimes their message is intended for greater sharing, so that the dream may be manifest in our world.

Share one of your own dreams, your deepest desires, with a soul-friend.

Studying with Intention

It is not sufficient for us to study the most excellent things unless we do it in the most excellent of manners . . . and that is impossible to find till we are guided thereunto by the most excellent end.
—Thomas Traherne, *Centuries*

It is no good expecting that we will be improved by our researches unless our subject is near to our hearts. If study is motivated by anything except the heart, a good deal of resentment and impatience will enter into our work. Each field of knowledge has its own pathways and natural growths. If we approach an unknown field with respect and set ourselves to discover where those paths lead us, we may discover some interesting things. Study is not a one-way street, however: as we direct our attention toward the object of our study, so too will something come back toward us, meeting and melding with knowledge that we already have, creating a new synthesis of understanding.

Our "most excellent end"—that is, the intentions that underlie our study—is critical. Most of us study to improve our condition in some way: to find a more remunerative job, to extend our horizons, to train in a skill or interest that we already enjoy, to catch up with education that we failed to receive when we were younger. Whatever our intention, the most important factor is how our soul and integrity are involved.

What part does your study or work play in the greater continuum of life? What does it contribute? What do you receive in exchange?

Spiral Tower

I have been three times in the prison of Arianrhod.
—TALIESIN, Primary Chief Bard

Caer Sidi (Kire SID'y), the Glass Castle or Spiral Tower of the British goddess Arianrhod (Ar-ee-ANN'hrode), is traditionally the place wherein poets serve their apprenticeship. The terms of apprenticeship are strict, which is why the great poet Taliesin speaks of Arianrhod's tower as a place of imprisonment. Of his own poetic initiation, we know that he was chased by the Goddess of Inspiration, Ceridwen, and assimilated by her as her own child. Taliesin was one of those who descended into the Underworld of Annwfn (AN'oon) to help the battle leader, Arthur, steal the cauldron of heroes. Like all poets, he is constant in his service of his poetic mistress, who is both muse and inspiratrix.

However many lifetimes our soul may have inhabited, we are compelled to seek the spiraling tower in which our soul is refined. Arianrhod is the mistress who hones the soul, by helping it recognize the configurations and resonances of our soul-track through the stars. This search is not confined to one lifetime or to waking hours; within the long spiraling of the soul and within the cavern of dreaming, we come to a deeper understanding of our true living metaphor. By whatever image, metaphor, story, sign, or symbol we steer, we will find the clues as we pass through the otherworldly, mystical, and subtextual life of our spiritual quest; within the mystery of Caer Arianrhod's labyrinthine turnings, we may discover the very reason for our existence. (See 11 June.)

Visualize the spiraling tower of Caer Sidi, the place of initiation and clarity. Ask to be shown the important patterns of your soul-track in your dreams and your reflective moments—those times when you are most truly yourself.

Visiting the Countryside

It is always wise to avoid show-places and choose for your excursions into the country the simplest and most natural scenery you can find.

—JOHN COWPER POWYS, *The Meaning of Culture*

The countryside takes on the burden of our needs for refreshment, especially at the end of the summer when we take to the roads on the last few days of holiday to seek recreation.

Ironically, the very places that are solitary and full of sacred power are now becoming the most exhausted places of all. Even sites of natural beauty that offer wide-open spaces of forest, water, and hill are choked with holiday-makers seeking the wilderness and the refreshment of nature. Instead of wildlife, vista, and peace, they find only each other—and in increasingly large bands.

The burden of expectation upon the countryside is something that we can help redress, with a little consideration. This redress may involve finding other, less popular countryside places to visit, or finding places within or near the city. But chiefly we should consider what we can give when we make our country visits. To leave the countryside as we found it, without traces of our passing, is a duty we can teach to our families, so that the beauty may be preserved for future generations.

Our pilgrimage to the country, whether it be for spiritual refreshment or physical recreation, can be a purposeful and beautiful excursion that restores us in soul and body. Our thank-you gift to the country and the beings who live within it is our respect and the gratitude of our heart.

Meditate upon your favorite place in the country and visit it in soul-flight. Consult the spirit of the place and ask its advice and permission about your next visit. Ask what gift (a song or a blessing, perhaps—something that will not harm the land) would be acceptable. Do this whenever a visit is planned.

Guarding the Tongue

Curses, like chickens, come hame ta roost.

—Scots proverb

One of the great curses of Celtic tradition is that of the faery woman Macha (MAK'ha), who comes from the hollow hills to live with an earthly husband. The conditions of their partnership include that he shall never speak about her to others. One day, hearing the king boast about the speed of his horses, Macha's husband remarks that his wife would easily beat them in a race, so fast does she run. The king then demands that Macha be brought forthwith and prove her wretched husband's claim. The heavily pregnant Macha is brought before the king and pleads exemption, as her time is near. Nevertheless, she is forced to run the race against the king's horses. She wins outright, but at the finishing post gives birth to twin children before dying of exhaustion. Her last breath is a curse upon the men of Ulster, that they shall suffer the weakness of a woman in her confinement at their time of greatest need. This curse descends to the ninth generation, striking always in the time of Ulster's need. Some say the force of that curse still runs.

Curses wound deeply, whether they be thoughtless words spoken in a moment of anger or intentioned ill-wishing. They also have a habit of rebounding upon the curser in ways that are unexpected. The words that we weave can become a web in which we also are bound. Once uttered, these words cannot be called back; they fly out on the winds until they find their target. In a tradition that recognizes the power of words, we also maintain a watch upon our tongue, lest it speak words that we will regret.

Call to mind an occasion when you have wished someone or something ill through anger or exasperation. Recall your words and offer a blessing that will rescind your curse.

Shape-Shifting

I will go in the name of God,
in the likeness of deer, in likeness of horse,
in likeness of serpent, in likeness of king.
More victorious am I than all others.

—Scots Gaelic invocation for justice

The Gaelic practice of the *fith-fath* (FEE'faw), dating back to ancient days, is a kind of shape-shifting spell; it is uttered when people feel themselves to be endangered or vulnerable, needing a measure of invisibility or better confidence in difficult situations.

Sometimes the *fith-fath* is said, as in the example above, for the purposes of endowing oneself with helpful qualities in difficult circumstances: when seeking justice in a court of law, for example, or when entering a strange place. The magic of the *fith-fath* does not lie in the words that are recited, but rather in the intentions with which the words are said. The words, most often spontaneously chosen, are generally apposite to the circumstances and the moment's need. The intentions of the speaker are everything, drawing upon real alliances between the self and spiritual helpers whose friendship is already strongly established.

Fith-fath shape-shifting is undertaken in moments of great need. The spell itself—the first phase—is uttered privately, even secretly, certainly not in a crowd; in the second phase, the shape-shifter, now prepared, goes into the situation or place and does whatever is necessary; finally, in private again, the *fith-fath* is dropped and the original shape resumed.

Whether we go into challenging interviews, venture into dangerous places, or attempt to pass through a crowd unnoticed and unscathed, the old custom of shape-shifting can serve us well if we use it with respect.

Make your own fith-fath *invocation, to recite at times when you need a little more confidence or when you would like to be less noticeable.*

Appreciation

The three supporters of inspiration: success, acquaintance, praise.
—Welsh triad (trans. CM)

This triad is written with prestigious bardic poets in mind, the Celtic *glitterati*, equivalent to our pop stars and film idols. It speaks to their insecurity, to reputations based on noble patronage and local adulation.

Building on our own success is a way to foster inspiration and confidence in our lives. There is little impetus to further effort without some sense of achievement, whether our successes are large or small. To become dependent upon success alone, however, is the road to egomania, disillusionment, or even suicide. (See February 10.)

Our special connections in our chosen field of work are very important to our confidence and success. It is not just the contacts who can pull the strings for us, putting us in touch with the right person at the right time, but the colleagues who work with us, our family, and well-disposed friends. We cannot depend on our connections alone, however; we must also prove ourselves worthy.

The cordial of praise is more intoxicating than any other. Although we may seldom drink of its draught, when we receive compliments or praise, our confidence soars. While it is good to receive praise, it is even better to bestow it. Praise offered from the heart is the greatest inspiration of all.

It is by steadily building on our successes; valuing our connection with friends, family, and those we serve; and noting what people are truly appreciating that we set our inspirational work in its true context.

How often do you encourage your friends and family? Make a point of sincerely appreciating someone's achievement today.

The Return of Mabon

"When will I see you, Mabon, my son?
When will I kiss you, my pretty one?"
"When the ages turn round at the brink of the sun,
When the birds at the wellhead have ended their song."
—Caitlín Matthews, "Mabon's Journey"

This song is a dialogue between Modron and Mabon, respectively, the divine Mother and Son of British tradition. Mabon is eternally lost, taken from Modron's side when he was a baby—and just as eternally rediscovered and released. (See February 10.)

Human need and sacred response are the two voices of their dialogue—a dialogue mirrored in our own. There is locked within us something so deep and sacred that we often feel we have lost or mislaid the key to the treasure. If we could see it, it would look like a child: simple, innocent, powerful as a shaft of light.

We may have ceased to search for this lost child long years ago; we may feel unworthy to call up the deep, sacred appearance of our own soul, believing that it will no longer answer so soiled a need as our own. And yet that part of us which is Modron, an urgent mother in search of her child, still rises when the need is strongest, descending to the darkest places, rousing any who will aid her quest for her child, the soul.

At the sharpest edge of need, Mabon still returns, down every age of the world, bearing a bright sword to defend the right. The integral innocence of the soul that lives within us cannot help but shine like a mirror, like a child whose innocence turns away harm.

Commune with the innocence of your own soul. Visualize what your soul might look like.

The Heavens Within Us

Draw into thy Centre-deep . . . thy Heavens within. . . . Take
present care of the Heavens of your Mind. . . . Dive into your own
Celestiality, and see with what manner of spirits you are endued:
for in them the Powers do entirely lie for Transformation.
— Jane Leade, *A Fountain of Gardens*

How do we find our center-deep? We have hid from it all our days,
though it beams upon us like a lighthouse and continually shows us
the path to the center. This path of light can be discovered in times of
quietness and solitude, when we withdraw from the bustle of life and
contemplate who and where we are in the great web of existence, when
we still our minds from the spindle of anxiety and redefine our being
as a partaker in the vast macrocosm.

In the stilling of our body, mind, and soul, we discover the special
spirits who are our guides and helpers on the spiritual path. These
spirits are not fantasies or psychological archetypes; they are real, living beings.

Finding out which spiritual helpers we are gifted with is the primary
task for those who would seek out their center-deep. All of us have our
own spiritual friends—those beings who do not have a human or
earthly existence but who nevertheless exist and accompany us. We do
not choose them; they and we are drawn to each other according to the
gifts we share. They cooperate with us in the work of transformation;
for, by our encounters with the spirits of our center-deep, we grow and
change as we are accompanied and taught.

Sitting in silence, become aware of your own center-deep. What kind of
landscape does it have? Who is there with you? What has drawn you
both there?

The Ecstasy of the Word

Hwyl . . . is a curious Welsh word that expresses the sing-song cadence, the rhythmic auto-hypnotic transport evoked by musical syllables, in which both poets and orators . . . have the power of losing themselves.

—John Cowper Powys, *Obstinate Cymric*

Hwyl (HOIL) is the untranslatable Welsh term for the ecstasy which grips the priest, orator, poet, or actor and which, in ancient times, would have been the clear sign that the Goddess of *Awen* (inspiration) attended the speaker.

In our day we tend to be suspicious of charismatic speakers who have the power to sway the crowd. Oratory, like all other arts, must have integrity or it can lead to such horrors as the Nuremberg Rally. *Hwyl* comes when the speaker accesses the way between the worlds, when he clearly envisages his subject in a true, living sense. When the voice is flooded with superhuman power like a singer's, when the words appear in strength like a host of soldiers, when the listeners lose all sense of time and place and their emotions are loosened—that is when the inspirational power of *hwyl* is present.

The ecstasy of the word still has power to change and encourage listeners. We hear its tones in the voices of Martin Luther King, Jr., Nelson Mandela, and other great speakers of this century—men and women who give their voices, hopes, and hearts to their people as a free gift and to whom is granted the gift of prophetic and inspired speech.

Make it your practice today to honor the ecstasy of the word by speaking from your heart rather than making small talk. Listen with attention to what is said and meant.

Apprehending the Possible

If you escape the narrowness of dimensions
and create a space for all things
to become what they desire to be
you will see the time which is placeless
you will hear what has never been heard
and you will see what has never been seen.

—Dei Hughes, "The Rose and the Atom"

One of the disciplines used by the bardic schools was to enclose the student poet in a darkened room, there to pursue a set subject through the spirals of metaphor until a poem resulted. This custom was the last remnant of druidic meditational practice, whereby darkness became the womb of light. (See 27 July.)

In our own spiritual practice, there must be some similar way of creating space, of allowing the unseen to be perceptible, of putting our little world into the context of the greater universe. Whatever method of meditation we employ, the results of our contemplative experience cannot be compared or shared with anyone else's. When we have stretched time, defied the boundaries of space, walked where the planet was fashioned, and heard the song the sirens sang, then have we passed beyond the limitations of everyday speech and understanding.

We become part of the larger universe as we allow our fixed grasp to loosen. The power of imagining the possible is great, but how much greater the power of perceiving the possible unfolding in its own myriad, unimagined way! The space where this can happen exists within and around each one of us each time we enter into the discipline of spiritual attention.

Sitting in darkness and silence, be attentive to the mystery of the universe rather than to yourself. Record your findings in words, music, or pictures.

SEPTEMBER

Month of September—benign are the planets;
Tending to please, the sea and the hamlet;
Common it is for steeds and men to be fatigued.
                              —anon. Welsh poem

The month of September sees the fruit and berry harvest, and the turning of the trees to their many colors. The meditation themes for this month include appreciating the harvest, home, wandering, belonging, boundaries, nationhood, music, beauty, and ceremony.

Landmarks

We can have inherited no single syllable from the names given by Paleolithic hunters, but never since their day have our landmarks been without them, without some sound to enrich and confirm their personality.

—Jacquetta Hawkes, *A Land*

The abiding landmarks of our country have personality, quality, and emotive properties. Landmarks—features of the land that speak to us of the ancient sculpting of the earth in distant eras—recall the coming of humankind, who raised and shaped the land in new ways; and they embody the myths, deeds, and actions that have happened there.

The process of naming places in the land began in ancestral eras too distant to imagine, but we can guess that our ancestors, like us, saw the broad outlines of gigantic figures—the jut of a giant's knee, the rocky profile of a noble face, the upturned breasts of a goddess, the vast cauldron of a river-filled canyon or valley.

Every natural landmark is redolent of the myths and legends of the land. Even in seemingly featureless places, those stories still run like veins of golden song beneath the sleeping earth. The utterance of the landmark's name can be a magical evocation of its stories and remembrances.

Recall the features of the landscape around your own home. What would they be like without manmade structures upon them? What stories, traditions, and songs abide in your land? If your land was once occupied by other peoples, what was its name in that time, and how does it preserve that meaning?

When you next walk in your locality, be sensitive to the spirit of the place. Name the area; get to know it; let its story be told again.

Kinship of Nature

One touch of nature makes the whole world kin.
—WILLIAM SHAKESPEARE, *As You Like It*

As we walk through the countryside at this time of year, it is easy to feel our symbiotic connection with nature. The rich profusion of colors and the abundant seeding and fruiting of the land in preparation for autumn all beckon us into a wider family circle. We return home after such a walk, perhaps to the city, brimming with a sense of belonging, but this feeling fades sooner or later as we are immersed once more in the daily running of our lives.

We place reminders of nature's beauty about our home. Driven by recognition that our kinship with nature is slipping, we surround ourselves with "natural" or "organic" things. While such things may remind us of our wider relationship, they do not truly connect us, since kinship must pass beyond strictly visual reminders if it is to be authentic.

It is in the touch of nature that connection is most strongly made, for it is at the most physical levels that recognition of kinship is triggered. We engage with our kindred when we are in physical contact: whether we tend our garden, groom our dog, or receive the kiss of rain upon our skin. These moments of precious contact are opportunities for loving thankfulness, in recognition of the fact that we are wholly akin to a greater family. When we live our lives open to such moments, we enter a wider embrace that includes us all.

What relationships do you have with your natural kin, apart from other human beings? What trees, animals, rocks, and places call out to you as kindred? Become more aware of these precious kindred and the way in which you yourself are included in the relationship.

The Service of Beauty

The concern of the Primary Imagination, its only concern, is with sacred beings and sacred events. The sacred is that to which it is obliged to respond; the profane is that to which it cannot respond and therefore does not know.

—W. H. AUDEN, *The Dyer's Hand*

We each have an instinct that informs us when something is aesthetically pleasing; we are aware of the interplay of order, balance, and harmony. When a house or an object is ill-conceived, when a garment or a plan does not sit well, we have a strong sense of physical discomfort or agitation.

The "primary imagination" reveals to us the hidden beauty and order of the universe, giving us a sense of the sacred. Unfortunately, our society now seems to foster a stronger instinct to acclaim the profane, to deviate from the sacred simplicity of harmony and beauty as a "fashion statement."

The difference between sacred and profane is this: the sacred includes all that can be conceived of in the history of existence, while the profane excludes everything except what serves our present craving. The profane can be easily spotted because it lacks beauty and harmony. The primary imagination will not dance to the profane; it is a servant only of the sacred.

The sacred is often narrowly defined as pertaining only to religious institutions, but the service of the primary imagination runs in every aspect of our lives. We ourselves are not exempt from the service of beauty. The way we furnish our homes, the objects we buy, the kinds of theories we buy into—all these are subject to this sacred service.

Look around your home with the eye of the primary imagination. What grates upon your sense of harmony and beauty? How can your home better reflect the service of beauty?

The Tune of the Cosmic Dust

Human beings, vegetables, cosmic dust, we all dance to a mysterious tune, intoned in the distance by an invisible player.

—ALBERT EINSTEIN, interview

Those who, like Einstein, come daily into contact with the physical laws that order the universe cannot help but catch the strains of that great dance in which we are all whirling. Whether it be in the intricacy of cellular formation, or in the flow of currents, or in the vast patterning of the stellar orbits that illuminate the heavens, scientists are privileged to see into the structure of that dance.

The inapprehensible motion of life escapes our daily awareness, as does the tune of the cosmic dust that orders us all in one great dance of life. We do not hear it playing until we come to a point where our ordinary and subtle senses are aligned together. Then we come into harmony and awareness of both worlds at once, the apparent and the unseen worlds in conscious communion within us. These privileged moments cannot be sought; they come unbidden, surprising us into mystical vision. It may be that when we interrupt a walk on a high place at evening to admire the view, we apprehend the revolution of the earth as a physical motion beneath our feet; it may be that we become aware of a rhythm that weaves about the steady beating of our own heart, as if it were a partner in the dance.

The resonances to which we respond and the relationship between ourselves and the music of life give us the only clues available about the nature of the invisible partner—clues reassuring enough that we can trust the source of our music.

Attune to the cosmic tune and rhythm of life; stand and dance.

Ceremony

How else but in custom and ceremony are innocence and beauty born?
—W. B. YEATS, "A Prayer for My Daughter"

Ceremony enables transition. Rituals of initiation, such as baptism and graduation; seasonal rituals; rituals of prayer and remembrance; dedication rituals, such as marriage; protective rituals in which we invoke our guardian spirits—all these help create a sacred link between us and Spirit, conferring special grace. Ceremony does not have to be dramatic or wordy, and it need not involve a cast of thousands. The constituents of a ceremony are simple:

- The need or impulse for ritual
- Space and time dedicated to the ceremony
- The intentioned, sacred use of objects, elements, and expressive and apposite means of music/speech/silence/meditation
- A role for everyone participating, if appropriate
- A space of silence or emptiness in which divine interaction can happen
- A clear statement of the purpose at the beginning and a thank-you afterward
- A point at which celebrants remember and include the rest of the universe, especially those who share their needs

Ceremony can happen in any suitable place: our own home is our hearth and shrine, and as such is quite suitable for personal ceremonies. In times of transition, new ceremonies that meet the needs of a society are urgently needed, so that innocence and beauty—the currency of Spirit—can flow into our lives.

Choose a real need in your life. Devise a short and simple ceremony that will address that need practically. (Examples of needs include beginning a new job, preparing for retirement, cleansing the home after a burglary, adjusting to children leaving home, and entering the hospital.)

The Unquiet Mind

Oh the mind, mind has mountains, cliffs of fall
Frightful, sheer, no-man-fathomed. Hold them cheap
may who ne'er hung there.

—GERARD MANLEY HOPKINS, "No Worst, There Is None"

As social pressures to be all things to all people increase, so does the prevalence of mental illness. It has been customary to think of such illness as an unfortunate heredity problem suffered by others, but it becomes clearer every day that it is common to all of us.

Signs of mental disquiet are not usually apparent to others and do not impinge upon others' lives until the person's behavior is affected. Behavioral changes do not have to be labeled as madness to draw our attention, however. We may realize that our partner's failure to make good decisions results from his inability to shift his received expectations, for example, or that our friend's addictive behavior is based upon terrible insecurity. We may even notice signs of creeping paranoia in our own lives: a fear so great that we avoid any occasion to notice it, a truth so frightful that we spend our lives projecting it upon everyone but ourselves.

The ability of soul-friends to recognize the early stages of such states of mind is often acute. With our own friends, we can keep a watchful eye out for signs of disquiet, offering reality checks, asking questions, and giving opportunities for help to be requested. It is not generally our place to treat the early signs of mental disquiet, but it is always our task to encourage, support, and befriend in times of turmoil.

What are your own current "cliffs of fall"? How did you get there? What help is available (or could you seek) to help you down?

Healing the Violation of Theft

The children of the wicked
In storm and in wind
Lie in the heather,
Their blood on the field,
Their shafts by their sides,
And their quivers full.
—Scots Gaelic song (trans. CM)

In our society, theft, robbery, and burglary are very real threats, causing us to take many arcane precautions. Theft—even if it happens when we are out of our house—is a terrible violation of our space and causes great insecurity. The fact that someone has taken our things is almost swallowed up by the thought that a stranger has been in our space and touched our surroundings with his malice.

It is clear that of thieves there will be no lack till the world's end. Whether theft arises as a result of envy, greed, or need, the one who suffers theft will be just as shocked and violated in the end. So how do we restore a sense of safety or security afterward?

The healing of such violation as theft requires a ceremony that reconsecrates ourselves or our surroundings. Such a ceremony involves a statement of facts, an expression of anger or frustration at those facts, an actual and a symbolic cleansing of the violation, a restatement and marking of our own or our home's boundaries, and a reconsecration affirming our home's sacredness. All these aspects can help reweave the violation after theft.

Create your own simple ceremony to reconsecrate your home, your car, or yourself after a robbery.

Fall

Autumn is a good time for visiting;
During its short days there is work for all. . . .
There are sweet acorns in the high woods,
Cornstalks are kind over the brown earth.

—ancient Irish poem of the seasons (trans. CM)

After the labor of the grain harvest, the people of the Celtic world looked forward to a more sociable time together, although they by no means stopped work. This autumnal time is full of the bustling preparation for winter, a task to which animals and birds still pay serious heed. Without their intensive harvesting and harboring in the storehouses of tree and earth, there would be little to sustain life in a very few weeks.

As the garden begins to look straggly and unkempt, the work is to uproot, to collect seeds from the clustering seed-heads, and to dig up the ground in preparation for the winter ahead. Autumn's many-colored intensity begins to deepen and wrap us round as this season makes its royal progress, shouts its long goodbye to the growing time. Trees lean together in more contemplative coteries, their summer dancing stilled until the strong winds begin, when their leaves will tear loose to be blown about the world in wild jigs and solitary war dances.

There are those who find autumn a time of melancholy reflection, a reminder of death and decay; but the world is a wiser place if we attend closely to its turning. The cycle of our years is annually enriched by the lessons of the fall: as students return to school and college, so we can turn to this expansive tutorial of the year's new term in search of maturity, heart's sharing, and the work of our dedicated living.

Take a walk where you can best appreciate the turning season. As you walk, commune with the spirits of the plants, trees, and animals that you encounter and learn from them the message of fall.

The Blessing of Story

If poet's verses be but stories,
So are food and raiment stories:
So is all the world a story:
So is man of dust a story.
　　　　　　　—*Amra Columcille*, early Irish text

There are many traditional Celtic texts and stories that have their own blessing upon the reciter or listener. At the end of the Irish story called "The Fosterage in the House of the Two Pails," the reciter blesses the people about to embark on a long voyage with safety, those about to be wed with fertility, those about to open an ale-house with peaceful business, and kings who are threatened by destruction with a peaceful reign; it further promises to bless prisoners with freedom!

Here we see the therapeutic blessing of story as a healing agent to certain conditions of life. The receipt of story by eyes or ears was regarded as a vital pathway of blessing, if the reader or listener were in a state of proper attention and respect. Those who merely siphoned the words off the page like a vacuum cleaner, those who sat inattentively, mentally wool-gathering, did not receive the blessing. Our own saturation with printed materials sometimes renders us insensible to the sacred blessing of story and its many gifts. That blessing flows past our eyes and ears without impact.

But when we memorize a story, its blessing works at a deeper level within us. It is then that we enter fully into its workings; it is then that we *become* the story. When we become garments of story, we are able to clothe others with blessing.

What is the story to which you turn again and again for nurture?
What kind of blessing do you derive from it? How is that story akin to
your own life? Write a blessing that seems to derive from this story for
other readers or listeners to benefit from.

Homecoming

Come you in and sit you down,
What you lost shall here be found.
Bowl and cup shall slake your lack,
Cast the bundle from your back.
No more wandering, no more war,
Come you in and close the door.

—CAITLÍN MATTHEWS,
"The Wanderer's Welcome Home"

The annual sense of settling down to things as the year turns toward winter makes us appreciate our home at this time. Home supplies us with roots, it nourishes us and makes possible all that we do, holding and cradling us when our activities are concluded for the day.

Yet there are many for whom the family house is no home: young people who yearn to fly the nest and who are dissatisfied with their parents' way of running things, for example, and relatives who have to live with their family as dependents because of age or infirmity. And there are many who are without a home of their own, who lodge uneasily in inconvenient, noisy apartments, in temporary accommodations, in dirty alleyways or on draughty doorsteps. For wanderers and travelers, the home is wherever they lay their heads.

The home that lives in our hearts and minds forever calls out to us to come and be where we are most true to ourselves. It is a strong spiritual calling to our soul to inhabit our body in the fullest sense. When the spiritual concept of the soul's home and our desire for a place to live become confused, there is remarkable upheaval, even war.

People move from one land to another, seeking a home of their own. When we acknowledge and welcome the soul within, we come home in truth: we can jettison the burden of expectation that we have been carrying this long while and, for the first time, come home, *really* home.

What or where is home for you?

Cutting Through the Celtic Twilight

Facks are chiels that winna ding. [Facts are things that cannot be shifted.]

—Scots proverb

The reappreciation of the Celtic tradition in the nineteenth century led to an overly romantic view known as the "Celtic twilight." Professor J.R.R. Tolkien once remarked that "anything is possible in the fabulous Celtic twilight, which is not so much a twilight of the gods as of the reason." It is a very dangerous place to inhabit, this twilight, as the poet W. B. Yeats discovered; he, who had himself been instrumental in the formation of that twilight, hit the hard iron of reality during the savage Irish civil war, writing in "The Stare's Nest by My Window":

> *We had fed the heart on fantasies,*
> *The heart's grown brutal from the fare;*
> *More substance in our enmities*
> *Than in our love.*

Many of the popular myths and fantasies that have been woven around the Celts—some self-fabricated—have been designed largely to mantle the unpalatable facts of conquest, colonization, and cultural diminishment. Romantic traditions are tales that both colonizers and the colonized have spun after the event. The living, transformative myths are those that speak to us in all eras and conditions. But the minute we listen to romantic traditions, with their victimhood and inadequacy thinly veiled by bombast and boast, we mire in a quicksand that will suck us out of reality into a jealous cauldron where bitter nationalism and retributive terrorism can be brewed.

Take a hard look at the romantic traditions concerning your own people. What enemies to the common good are lurking behind them?

Protecting the Boundaries

Cuchulainn's geasa were that no woman should leave his land without his knowing of it; that no birds should feed upon his land without leaving something for him; that no fish should leave his waters unless he had caught it; that no warrior from another tribe should be upon his land without his challenging them.

—*The Adventures of Nera,* early Irish text (trans. CM)

The untranslatable Irish word *geis* (GEE-YES—the plural form is *geasa*) means a binding obligation that has to be upheld at all costs; it is sometimes also used in the sense of "taboo," something forbidden. The concept of *geis,* in the ancient world, was very much tied up with one's honor, and the obligations or prohibitions it entailed were often pronounced by seers directly after a child's birth or at her initiation into adulthood. We each have things we must observe and actively do, as well as things we must strictly avoid. Our *geasa* are our boundary-protectors. If we observe them, they will ensure our own survival and integrity; they will keep us from harm.

Our *geasa* increase or evolve as we ourselves grow. Self-chosen *geasa*—"I will always dye my hair red" or "I will never eat meat"—are joined by *geasa* that are laid upon us—"My employer requires me to wear a black suit" or "My religion enjoins me never to make war on others." These may be followed by stronger and more binding *geasa*— "I pledge to keep faith with my country" or "As an addict, I must never use alcohol." Our identity, talents, and integrity all have their own special obligations and prohibitions.

We do not *choose* all our *geasa;* those that are laid upon us are often highly inconvenient, restricting our freedom. Yet they protect us and remind us of the boundaries of our honor; and, as the contracts of life itself, they maintain the boundaries of the universe in a special way.

What are the geasa *of your life? What obligations are you bound to perform? What prohibitions must you observe in order to be safe?*

Conversation

What is sweeter than mead?—Intimate conversation.
—"The Wooing of Ailbe," early Irish story

The kindling of mind upon mind, the flame of word upon word, is the essential fire that brings hearts gladly to the hearth of friendship. In the charmed circle of intimacy, friends lean together just as stars in their loneliness seem to draw closer together at nightfall. In our separate revolutions in time and space, we sometimes become like planets, solitary and aloof from all others, unable to bring ourselves into the fold of intimacy, able only to preach portentously from a high pulpit, uninitiated into the vulnerability of the truly human.

But in our special relationships, we can enjoy a wonderful exchange when we take time to draw together, to share and to listen, to quicken to the ideas and viewpoints of another. In intimate conversation, our thoughts and opinions find a yoke-fellow who will help draw them nearer to manifestation. In deep converse, our uncertainties and anxieties can be uttered fearlessly, and just as trustfully received and allayed.

An intimate friendship passes beyond the intimacy of lovers; the shared currency is not physically sexual, although it can prove just as intoxicating. As ideas cascade and themes are tracked to their very source, a heady ferment fills the cup of friendship. It is in the quiet times of intimate talk that we really come to know each other and realize how much we share.

Make an opportunity in the next month to have a really good, deep, and intimate conversation with a close friend.

~ 14 September ~
The Seasonal Thresholds

This has been our way: Spring for plowing and for sowing;
Summer for strengthening the crop; Autumn for grain's ripeness
and for reaping; Winter for consuming its goodness.

—*Cath Maige Tuired*, from Caitlín Matthews,
The Celtic Book of Days (trans. CM)

The gifts of each season create thresholds and doorways of opportunity for us as the year turns. The circuit of the earth about the sun is like the *turas* (TU'ras), or revolving walk of a pilgrim about a sacred site: at each point of the circumambulation, there arises a different symbology in the changing weather and in the correspondences of the growing world. As we become more sensitive to the annual *turas* of these changes, we can become attuned. (See 28 November.)

When the first spring flowers emerge, the winter may still hold sway, but we sense the time of beginning; we struggle, like the young plants, to bring ourselves over the threshold of emergence. When summer's heat encourages us to leave off our warm clothing, we pass through the threshold of confidence and action. When autumn leaves drift from the trees, we look for the threshold of gathering. When winter fastens its grip on the world, we cross the threshold toward reflection and stillness.

Through every station of the earth's revolution, we pass through a kaleidoscopic variety of moods, expectations, and opportunities. Everyone has preferred seasons, accepting their gifts with pleasure. Those seasons that we actively dislike may be offering us opportunities to come to terms with aspects of our own annual distress—with depression, impatience, anger, or fear. If we can live each moment of the year as it is happening, with attention to the seasonal thresholds and their gifts, we may discover a new resourcefulness that will enrich our lives with special joy.

Consider the gifts and opportunities that you receive from each season.

The Song of Recovery

And there came three birds who began singing such a song that all the songs they had previously heard were without harmony compared to this.

—Branwen, Daughter of Llyr, from *The Mabinogion*

When the remnant of a British host returned from a disastrous war against the Irish, bringing with them the remains of their great leader Bran, they entered into an otherworldly sequestration. Rhiannon (Hree-ANN'on), the British goddess who eases the burdened soul, sent her three birds to sing their melodious song.

This period of temporary forgetfulness of all that had passed was a wonderful recreation for Bran's followers after their dreadful defeat. Their leader was able to speak with them, easing their sense of loss and anxiety. They remained in the otherworld until one of the men opened a door that had been forbidden to them when it opened, serial time began again for the survivors, and they continued their journey in full remembrance of all that had happened.

The birds of Rhiannon still sing to us in times of loss, illness, or crisis, bringing their three gifts of tears, forgetfulness, and laughter. These three gifts are central to any recovery or restoration. Tears help us discharge our pain and sorrow, so that there is room for healing to enter in. A period of forgetfulness or sleep enables the fraught soul to cease its mental turmoil and find rest. Without such a period of respite, the anguish could become overwhelming. The gift of joy and laughter reconnects us with the everyday world once again and is a real sign of life.

The resumption of everyday life often seems to us as sudden as the opening of the door in the otherworldly island of Gwales. Time runs, life is lived, and past events take their place in the treasury of memory once again.

Ask your spiritual allies to remove from memory some burden of your remembrance.

Authentic Spiritual Traditions

The Druid system forbade learning from books . . . and insisted
on oral and meditational communication with other people and
Nature . . . sustaining spiritual Traditions through individual rela-
tionship with the Infinite, rather than by ready-made recitations
from previous people's findings.
— W. G. GRAY, *Patterns of Western Magic,* in
R. J. STEWART, *Psychology and the Spiritual Traditions*

Genuine, living spiritual traditions arise from our own life-context, not from our adoption of other people's experiences and teachings. This rather startling revelation is the received tradition of the Celtic realms and of traditional societies worldwide that rely upon oral rather than written sources.

Today, when so many people are seeking to appreciate their ancestral spirituality, there is a hunger for "authentic sources." Unfortunately, many seekers gravitate to poorly researched or speculative commercial works that have no basis in any kind of practical spirituality.

Our individual relationship with Spirit has to be personal and immediate for it to have authenticity. It cannot be gained by reading books. In every place, in every time, with every person, Spirit communicates in its own ways. Those who advance their spiritual lives by spending time in nature, in meditation, and in practice learn the eternal knowledge which is the heritage of mystics in every tradition. To simply make repetition or to blindly accept the findings of others, without personal perception and understanding, invalidates our spiritual path.

The truly authentic spiritual tradition is the one we are actively practicing: while it may indeed correspond with that of many other people, there will always be features within it that arise uniquely from our own living context, which we know to be authentic to the very core.

Recognize at least three principles discovered from your own life-context
by which you spiritually steer.

Wanderers, Nomads, and Outcasts

Alone in the greenwood must I roam,
Hollin, green hollin [holly],
A shade of green leaves is my home,
Birk [birch] and green hollin.

—"Green Hollin," anon. Scots ballad

Among the Celtic peoples, young warriors were temporarily outcast from their tribe as part of their rite of passage into adulthood, under the guardianship of elders and teachers. Some of our young people today purposely choose to enter a period of nomadism during which they can learn the freedoms and hardships, learn the self-sufficiency, practical wisdom, and unfettered vision of the "uncivilized."

The choice of the wanderer to live a nomadic and unsettled life is often bewildering to those who are settled. Before civilization, many lived in encampments, while others followed the movements of animals. Settled folk have often denounced nomads as low-class, uneducated, and suspect—easy scapegoats upon whom accusations of murder, theft, and black magic might be lodged.

In our own era, we see new patterns of nomadism emerging as civilization begins to swell and become unwieldy. Those who no longer "fit" either become exiled from settled existence as outcasts or choose to "drop out." The outcasts of civilization roam the streets in homeless vagrancy. Some have merely fallen through the cracks, others have chosen to scavenge the society in which they cannot succeed, and still others are natural nomads or solitary hermits who need a concrete wasteland or a natural wilderness to encompass them.

We who are settled do well to consider the strengths of the nomad, to honor the wisdom and freedom of having no roots, to respect another way of living that we may one day need to learn.

Monitor your own attitudes toward nomads and wanderers. What part of your own being and beliefs is nomadic in character?

National Self-Esteem

When a country is out of love with itself the whole of life conspires against it.

—Jacquetta Hawkes, *A Land*

When a people is out of touch with its nation, it is usually also out of touch with the mythic being and consciousness of its land. The self-esteem of any nation stems from the relationship of its group-soul to the soul of the land. Tradition, custom, and memory all play their part as touchstones and thresholds of meeting in this relationship. But when we no longer come to those thresholds, instead sealing ourselves off from deep mythic meaning by engaging in shallow living, the group-soul no longer receives its nurture. When there is no meaningful correspondence between the land and its people, a strange and undefinable malaise springs up.

When a land is out of love with itself, many people want to leave it and live elsewhere, sensing that something dynamic has gone out of the relationship. But, just as in marriage, the first signs of fracture require deeper attention and better communication, not just a parting of the ways. This is the time to remain and work hard at the brightening of the relationship between ourselves and the land.

The contract of nationhood is not drafted in bigoted, nationalistic displays of patriotism; rather, it arises from the deep, mythic engagement of lives lived in the context of a land. This requires an ongoing communication with the archetypes and love affairs that preoccupy the spirit of the land. By becoming active lovers of our land ourselves, we learn to sense and see the things that injure our beloved's good, as well as perceiving the things that make it glad. When enough people engage in this way, the self-esteem of the nation will rise.

Test the pulse of your own country's self-esteem by going to the threshold between nation and land in meditation. What is the nature of the contract between your people and its land? Where is it failing?

Truth, Lies, and Videotape

There are few who know
Where the magic wand of Mathonwy
Grows in the grove.

—"Daronwy," medieval Welsh poem

The magic wand of the wise, druidic Math (MAHth), king of Gwynedd in northern Wales, had the property of causing things to appear as they truly were. This was demonstrated when Math was interviewing his niece Arianrhod (Ar-ee-ANN'hrode) for the post of royal foot-holder.

The most important qualification for this post was virginity. When Arianrhod came to court, Math stretched out his magic wand and asked her to step over it. Unfortunately, as Arianrhod did so, she gave birth to a child in full view of the court. Math's wand had the effect of accelerating his niece's secret pregnancy to full term, to her great embarrassment (since she was thought by all to be a virgin).

We may each be glad that none of our secrets can be so exposed to public scrutiny. There is fortunately no Math's wand, that can spill the beans to our embarrassment. But whatever faults we gloss over in the inner grove of our spiritual allies, there can be no concealment of our intentions and actions, however easily we deceive our fellow humans.

Our allies do not throw such things in our faces, though; they do not rewind the surveillance videotape to embarrass us. There is no judgment or condemnation from them. Rather, like good friends, they suggest other ways of behaving that might serve us better; they stand by the truth which is the mirror of our soul and invite us to look within and change what we do not like. If we attend to them, they compassionately enable us to make manifest our true selves without the need for lies and deception, so that our outer life and our hidden intentions are aligned and balanced.

What areas of your own hidden life would be revealed by Math's wand?

The Flitting of the Faeries

The Faeries remove to other lodgings at the beginning of each
quarter of the year . . . being impatient of staying in one place and
finding some ease by sojourning and changing habitations.
—ROBERT KIRK, *The Secret Commonwealth*

The removal of the faery folk from one place to another is traditionally called "flitting" in Scotland. The faeries of any region—and every region has its faeries—have a variety of homes that they use at different times of year. In Irish tradition, this movement was usually observed at Beltane and Samhain, when the doors of the *sí* (SHE), the faery realms, were opened. Among humans, the spring and autumn equinoxes and the winter and summer solstices were times when the quarterly rent on property was paid to the landlord. Those who could not pay their dues also flitted.

Cleaning and cleansing through movement is the pattern of earth's nomadic peoples. They do not remain long in one place for many reasons, but chief of these is that the land on which they have rested becomes "worn out" or "dirty." The act of moving on, then, is for them an act of renewal and care, allowing the earth to rest and recover from their occupation.

The spring and autumn cleaning of the house that many people favor is but one side of an orderly life. The visible clutter in our homes reflects a corresponding clutter in our internal lives. The wise lesson of the faeries and of nomadic peoples is to leave little trace of our passage upon the earth, to leave no mark that mars the wider world. By cleaning up after ourselves, we help lift the impress of our presence upon the earth.

With attention and intention, clean at least one room of your house
this week. As you restore cleanliness and order, be aware of the corre-
sponding spaciousness within yourself, so that your autumn cleaning
becomes a meditation in itself.

The Prayer of the Autumn Equinox

We should pray before sunrise and after sunset, pray prayers that have for their purposes no personal advantage, but are as native as are the vesper cries of pairing partridges, and as full of natural gratitude as is the heart of a lover.

—LLEWELYN POWYS, *Earth Memories*

The sun is at its midway mark, halfway between the golden glory of midsummer and the silver secret of midwinter. This is a time of appraisal and thankfulness, a time when we can be glad of the harvest of work behind us. It is also a time of application and expectation as we look forward to the work ahead.

The prayer of the quarter days is not one of personal request or self-regarding ceremony; it is our special offering of space and opportunity for and on behalf of the whole quarter and all that is happening within it and inhabiting it at this very moment. Set this day aside as one of meditation, undertaking only necessary and undemanding tasks.

At midday, stand facing the sunlight. Notice that the fall of your shadow is already longer than it was at the same time on midsummer day. Turn and face your shadow on the ground; feel the sun upon your back. The shadow that falls before you is the only mark of your presence that you should leave upon the earth. Meditate upon your shadow; then turn toward the sun again, eyes closed, and bathe in the light. Meditate upon the *turas* of the sun at this season. Become aware of the fusion of your body and your soul within you, and open your eyes, becoming present to where and who you are.

At sunset, tune your heart again to the season: feel within your body the sense of your own *turas* from midsummer toward midwinter and give thanks for the light and darkness. As you prepare to sleep, be aware of your body's rest and the readiness of your soul's shadow to go forth on its nightly round.

Make your prayer as suggested above.

Enemies of Wisdom

There are three things that spoil wisdom: ignorance, inaccurate knowledge, and forgetfulness.

—ancient Irish triad

Wisdom supports and maintains the universe in every place. Although we now feel that ignorance is largely conquered in our world by better education, it still holds sway in many areas, especially where people are purposely kept away from sources of spiritual wisdom by experts and professionals who prefer to keep them ignorant.

We live in a world of easily coined and readily accessible facts, a world where true wisdom is contaminated by or mingled with wild supposition, doubtful hearsay, and poor research. Inaccurate knowledge arises when people are keen to get the meat but lack the patience to capture, kill, or cook it. A remarkable number of books appear yearly, for example, claiming to teach the reader everything about a subject in a month or even a week! It is hard to know where most censure should be heaped: on the hubris of the writer and publisher or on the credulity of the reader. Inaccurate knowledge will not connect us with the living roots of wisdom; only precise knowledge wedded to practical experience can do that.

But a far greater enemy of wisdom than either ignorance or inaccurate knowledge is forgetfulness. Wisdom has been warped by forgetfulness, because we have lost both wisdom's context and its application as our traditional guardians have virtually died off. Few alive now have access to anything more than the theoretical structures of spiritual wisdom. Now we must urgently bring wisdom out of its academic closet, putting theory and practice into harness together so that the living power of wisdom may be restored to our world once again.

What are the characteristics of wisdom by which you steer your life? How are they manifest in your actual practice?

The Fruit of the Otherworld

Every high and lonely thought that thrills my spirit through
Is but a shining berry dropped down through the purple air,
And from the magic tree of life the fruit falls everywhere.
—A. E. (George Russell), "Connla's Well"

Over Connla's Well grow the nine hazelnut trees of wisdom that drop their nuts into the water. The salmon of knowledge eats of the nuts and is found by Fionn mac Cumhail (FINN mak KOOL), who, like Taliesin (Tal-eeESSin), becomes omniscient. (See 9 April.) This experience changes the very nature of perception, retuning the ordinary senses to perceive in more subtle ways.

This story, in its various permutations, stands as an explanation of how the fruit of the otherworld comes to ripen in our world. The fall of the hazelnuts into the waters of Connla's Well is an image of the abundant generosity of the otherworld to our world. The ideas that come to us in moments of inspiration arrive in our heads so instantaneously that we may be tempted to give credit for their arrival to ourselves. The generosity of inspiration is frequently seen percolating throughout the world. When the nuts of the nine hazels fall into our world, they fall in many places simultaneously, ensuring that the fruiting wisdom will germinate in at least one location in our world. This explains the seemingly coincidental discovery of inventions or the realization of ideas in several places at the same time: the same idea is in the air, ready to be pulled out of the ether. Only the most promising, dedicated, and attentive become the stock upon which the otherworldly fruit is grafted, for the benefit of all.

Give thanks for the fruits of the otherworld that you have received and helped ripen. Be aware when the nuts of wisdom are falling into your lap: run with the inspiration!

The Continuity of Society

Society is a partnership not only between those who are living but between those who are living, those who are dead and those who are to be born.

—Edmund Burke

At every moment, several generations are simultaneously alive: those just born, children, and students; young, middle-aged, and elderly adults; those about to die. As the older generation dies, new opinions and customs replace the old ones. But at one time, there are simultaneously many different generational viewpoints jostling together for attention. The sense of society as a partnership is not always apparent to us as we pass through life. The way to reconnect our society is to keep before us the partnership between those now living and our ancestors and our descendants.

The ancestral viewpoint is formative to the way society subtly changes over the generations. It helps codify the protocols, procedures, and customs that the present establishment upholds; it also forms a norm against which reactionary and reforming spirits can rebel. These two notions of conformity and rebellion, like two intertwining shoots about a sapling, define the growth of the trunk. The influence of our descendants is a more subtle one. We need inheritors to guard what we have established, but we cannot entirely dictate and mold them to our desires. Our descendants will modify and change what we leave them. The continuity of society is woven from many generational needs and influences. Only when we stand at the hub of time, as ancestor, self, and descendant concurrently, do we become fully aware of the contract that our partnership involves.

What are the terms of your contract with the partnership of society? Do these change as you consider them from the standpoint of ancestor, self, and descendant?

～ 25 September ～

Spiritual Nomadism

The Holy One is near to all who call: we have no need to cross the sea to find God.

—Saying of St. Samthann (trans. CM)

Spiritual nomadism is a phase that everyone goes through at some time. It appeals to us at those times when everything in our spiritual practice seems barren and stale. At those times, we seek the stimulus of fresh fields and foreign shores; we want out, now! This may take our steps into other fields of spirituality where we can graze at will, tasting and appreciating the differences, taking what is useful for us at one spiritual oasis before wandering on to the next. This phase can take many forms, and it can strike at any time, especially if we have lived within the strict restraints of a religious upbringing; it is not undergone only by the young and unsettled.

Our wandering often brings us to a fresh appreciation of our own spirituality; from a different perspective, we can see what we have been missing or how we can practice in more intentional ways. When spiritual nomadism goes unchecked, however, we do not learn from what we wander through; we begin to fall into a kind of spiritual tourism wherein we travel too fast and too frequently to learn anything.

In whatever place we find ourselves, we must make sure that our spiritual path is under our feet. It may spiral wildly or meander across different kinds of terrain, but it will bring us to the place just right if we engage continually with Spirit. We cannot separate ourselves from inclusion in the sacred, whatever we do and wherever we go.

What useful and encouraging factors have you gained from your own spiritual nomadism? What do you look for in your spiritual expression and practice that is not currently officially on offer? It may be that your spiritual practice has no name or label, but it is still a valid path to Spirit.

The Morrighan's Signs of the Times

Summer without flowers,
Cows without milk,
women without modesty,
men without courage . . .
—*Second Battle of Mag Tuiread,* early Irish text

The current signs of the times are there to be read by anyone with an ounce of perception. We notice signs of decay and disorder, thoughtlessness toward the environment, urban chaos and breakdown, famine, and senseless wars. To the Irish Goddess, the Morrighan—a being who often takes the form of a raven overflying the field of carnage—these are all areas of potential scavenging out of which new energy can be born. In her creative aspect, she is one of the holy ones who gave birth to mountains and rivers in her ecstatic union with the Dagda, the God of Virile Knowledge. Like the Hindu Goddess Kali, the Morrighan acts as challenger and remembrancer of the totality of time: she bids us look not only at the end-times but also at what leads up to them. By allowing the Morrighan into our lives, we value each living being for itself, enabling it to find its own place, to see the interrelationships between all life forms.

The Morrighan keeps her ancient place and role in our society, however much we try to deny her. She speaks the end; she utters the beginning; she announces the victory and defeat of our life's struggles. With her far-seeing eye, she comprehends the germination of the acorn and the felling of the oak.

What is at its ending in your life? What is struggling to be born? What is growing, and how can you help it to grow?

Envy

From the swift arrows of the slender banshee,
From the envious heart and the eye of evil,
May the herd be encircled!
—Scots Gaelic herding charm (trans. CM)

In many lands, envy is known as "the evil eye," whereby someone looks possessively or jealously at something of his neighbor's. The Celtic peoples had their charms against the evil eye—or "overlooking," as it was often known. The herding charm above is concerned not only with the envy of neighbors or strangers, but also with the retribution of the *bean sí* (BAN SHE), or "the faery woman." Because the Celtic world did not see itself as separate from the otherworld, faery and spirit inhabitants might also be considered sources of envy. It is for this reason that many people, then and now, put out offerings for the faerykind, that they might share our resources, feel included, and consider us to be good neighbors.

When we envy today, our eyes and desires are led from our own sphere into that of others; we subtly penetrate the boundaries of other people and commit an intentional theft—not by physically stealing something away, of course, but by undermining another person's essential soul. Envy is not seen as dangerous in our society; indeed, advertising companies do business by inculcating envious yearnings everywhere, vaunting beautiful people with lovely possessions, well-appointed houses, and brilliant skills. Good-natured people of special skills and abilities are often devastated to learn how little their friends think of them, horrified to realize how envied they are. Let us appreciate and admire, by all means; but every time envy surges up within us, let us call back the impulse to possess.

Make your own prayer against the kinds of envy most often directed against you. Meditate upon the brand of envy that arises within you and pay closer attention to what it indicates about you.

The Air We Breathe

World-mothering air, air wild,
Wound with thee, in thee isled,
Fast home, fast fold thy child.

—GERARD MANLEY HOPKINS, "The Blessed Virgin
Compared to the Air We Breathe"

The breath of life has always had a special, sacred meaning for people worldwide, since it is the mark of our mortality. The first and last breaths are marked with particular attention: as air is drawn into a baby's lungs for the first time, the soul is considered to be truly incarnate; as the death rattle heralds the last exhalation of air, we know that the soul is unhoused, free to return to the unseen world. Our continual breathing in and out is a reminder of these two moments wherein we are recreated anew.

The air that we take for granted is now polluted by industrial production, petroleum fumes, and other unpleasant exhalations. The immensity of this desecration of our atmosphere leaves us feeling powerless, since its cure depends on the whole world cooperatively using wiser strategies to protect the environment from damage. It may mean using our cars less, or switching off the motor when we are waiting; it may involve us in influencing governments and industries to use environmental-friendly solutions, remembering that politicians are in power because they represent the people. But the task that we can each engage in on a daily basis is a respectful acknowledgment of the sacred breath of life. The Irish expression for taking one's time translates literally as "drawing one's breath." If we make it our practice to spend a short time each day remembering the holy element of air, we restore the original blessedness with our prayerful in-and-out breathing: "Blessed be the precious and preserving air that sustains our life!"

Meditate upon the air as you draw it into your lungs and then exhale.
Be aware of the whole atmosphere of the earth breathing.

In the House of Darkness

*The poets shut their doors and windows for a day's time, and lie
on their backs with a stone upon their belly, and plaids about their
heads, and their eyes being covered they pump their brains for
rhetorical encomium or panegyric.*

—Martin Martin, *Description of the Western Islands of Scotland,* in
Caitlín and John Matthews, *The Encyclopedia of Celtic Wisdom*

The seventeenth-century traveler Martin Martin toured the west coast
of Scotland and reported on the training used in the last of the bardic
schools, whose methods of composition had not varied from earliest
Celtic times. Students given subjects of composition would go to the
House of Darkness: a long, low hut divided into cubicles devoid of
light, in which the students lay upon couches alone and worked on
each poem in darkness. At nightfall, lights were brought in and the
students recited their compositions to their masters before going to
their evening meal. (See 31 August.)

What is the meaning of this desire for darkness? Inspiration was
able to spark more brightly, leading the poet's mind from metaphor to
metaphor with a greater assurance. For the one who lay upon the
"bed of reclining," there was no opportunity to make notes; words
were written first upon the memory. There is a more ancient reason
also: the early druidic and poetic method of incubating knowledge
out of sleep and darkness drew upon the fact that the ever-living otherworld is visitable in dream and in inspired soul-flight. This is not a
daytime experience, however, but one possible only when it is dark
(so that the subtle senses are able to work). Darkness, which so many
shun as synonymous with evil is actually an opportunity in which we
can respect our subtle senses and give rest to our physical ones. In the
darkness shines the greatest light of all: the three sparks of inspiration
that run like fire through charcoal and illuminate our own being.

Choose a subject to meditate upon without light this evening.

Scavengers

As I was walking all alane [alone],
I heard twa corbies making a mane [moan];
The tane unto the tither did say,
"Whar sall we gang and dine the day?"
— "The Twa Corbies," anon. Scots folk song

The two corbies in this song are ravens who are conferring about where they are going to dine. One tells the other that he knows where there is a newly slain knight and predicts that they will dine sweetly. Birds of prey, many kinds of insects, and other scavenging animals clean away the carcasses of the dead. Their very necessary way of life keeps our world free of decay and corruption. The work of the raven and other scavengers helps keep our world clean, as many of our pre-historic forebears realized: the practice of excarnation, whereby bodies are left in high places or on remote platforms to be stripped of flesh by the elements and the scavengers, was widely practiced throughout the northern hemisphere in early times.

We can learn from the action of the scavenger by applying its princi-ples to our own lives. If we think for one moment about what our world would look like without decay, we shudder. The same work of decay needs to be applied to ourselves. Without periodic clearing out and rooting up of old concepts, ideas, and burdens, our being would soon become as noisome as any bloated carcass by the highway. When we investigate what is hindering our spiritual path, we often find that it is something we have been holding onto, rather than any external circumstance.

What is hindering you? What needs to go away? Meditate upon this
and write down one major burden or worn-out notion that is obstruct-
ing your progress. Go outside and burn the paper on which you wrote,
letting go of your burden as the ashes fly free on the wind.

OCTOBER

Month of October—penetrable is the shelter;
Yellow the tops of the birch, solitary the summer dwelling;
Full of fat the birds and the fish.
                                        —anon. Welsh poem

October sees the last days of autumn and the presage of winter. The themes of this month are the ordinary and the extraordinary, conflict and consensus, adaptability and renewal, combat and competition, the work of women, the reality of joy.

Sacred Encounters

A sacred being cannot be anticipated; it must be encountered..
—W. H. AUDEN, *The Dyer's Hand*

Many people who are about to embark upon their spiritual quest come to consult me. They are curious about what they will find and who they will encounter. They have high expectations about the spiritual beings they are going to look up and "work with." As gently as I can, I try to explain that though they may be interested in encountering particular gods or goddesses, animals or heroic characters, they may not necessarily find the ones they hope to. Sometimes, it is true, there already exists a special relationship between a person and a spiritual being—a strong, enduring bond that takes no account whatever of the kind of spiritual discipline practiced or quest undergone. Whether that person treks into the realms of Christianity or the regions of Buddhism, this same being will turn up—sometimes bafflingly out of place, sometimes very much at home—in her meditations and dreams.

The most potent spiritual help may come from nameless and sometimes unknown figures who appear in meditation, soul-flights, dreams and visions. Occasionally, however, our helpers are well known—great figures of history, myth, or religion. At those times we may feel humbled or overwhelmed by the sacred encounter, as well as suspicious that we may have made up the encounter from an overactive imagination. Listen to the advice and wisdom that these figures give you, if they come to you; see if it works practically, if it is trustworthy. If everything checks out, you may well be privileged to be accompanied by a sacred being who is known and loved by many. But remember that our spiritual guides and teachers often take forms different from the ones we expect. Do not reject their teachings simply because their appearance does not accord with your expectations. If the help is good, then so is the teacher.

Who are your spiritual friends and teachers? Visit one today.

The Renewing Spiral of Life

It is one of their tenets that nothing perishes, but, as the Sun and the Year, is renewed and refreshed in its revolutions.
—Robert Kirk, *The Secret Commonwealth*

The Rev. Robert Kirk was a Scots clergyman with a great interest in faeries and the second sight. His research caused him to talk to many Gaelic people who had firsthand knowledge of these matters. He formed a whole philosophy of the faery world, including this understanding of the spiraling pilgrimage of life. The wisdom of any *turas* lies not in the arrival, but in the traveling. With our modern goal-centered, destination-seeking perspective, we have forgotten this concept of the renewal of the spiral of life. We pay attention to the end, to the certificate of achievement, to the self-congratulation of conclusion, when we should be more involved in our spiraling progress through life. Each year, on our own spiral path, things change and yet remain unchanging, freshly and eternally rediscovered, a delight to our senses, powerful enough to move our soul. This unchanging renewal is chanted by mystics all over the world who declare that "there is nothing new under heaven."

Yet these eternal things do not feel stale or repetitive to us when we experience them. They are rediscovered in moments when we have been exiled from or have neglected their savor and wonder: the unstained clarity of a new day, the urgent grasp of sexual need and its assuaging, the laughter of our child, which stays the same whatever age he reaches. All these things are ever new and always the same; time and perspective alone have renewed them for us.

What is old and always new, what is deep and always true for you this day?

Choosing a Soul-Friend

When is someone able to witness to the souls of others? When she is able to witness her own soul first. When is someone able to correct others? When he can first correct himself.

—COLMÁN MAC BÉOGNAE, *Apgitir Chábaid* (trans. CM)

The idea of the *anam-chara* (anum-KHAR'a), or soul-friend, arose in the early Celtic monastic tradition. Ideally, each monk or nun had his or her own spiritual adviser and companion, who was sometimes also the person's confessor. The task of a soul-friend was not to sit in judgment or to condemn, but to witness the person's soul and its journey through life. The role of soul-friend also included offering suggestions and setting tasks that would help correct the person's imbalances.

Each one of us needs our own special soul-friend, someone who can offer nonjudgmental attention as well as words of encouragement, someone in whom we can confide our secret fears and apprehensions as well as our joys and successes. Soul-friends offer us a very necessary reality check and bullshit detector when we delude ourselves or get into deeper waters than our abilities can support. A soul-friend, chosen from the ranks of our mature and discreet friends, is one who loves us sincerely and holds the good of our soul paramount.

A soul-friend must show resourceful perception and gentle strength, dismantle illusion and mirror reality clearly, encourage practice and cultivate trust, curb the tendency to be rash but not diminish the zeal that fuels it. The choice of a soul-friend to accompany us on our spiritual journey is determined by her unswerving dedication to our soul beyond considerations of emotional appeasement or polite restraint. Only the truth and a sensitive hand can bring polish to our soul.

Who is your soul-friend? What qualifications do you have to be a soul-friend to someone else?

The Illumination of Love

You are the star of each night,
You are the brightness of every morning,
You are the story of each guest,
You are the report of every land.

—Scots Gaelic blessing (trans. CM)

Celtic love-lyrics serenade the beloved by setting a particular love in the context of the universe, for the beloved is the one by whom the lover is connected to the wider world. Time, place, and dimension are utterly confounded in love, fused in one focused obsession. Being in love puts us in touch with the vital life-spark of every being: the commonplace becomes extraordinary and the daily round becomes a dance of joy. We greet and meet everything in a trance of deep enchantment.

But the real center of the universe turns around the beloved: whatever we turn our hands to do, wherever we look, the heart pulls the mind and other faculties back to the object of our love. The beloved becomes a lamp that illumines the dear world with its special ray. We find that the metaphors of poets leap readily to our lips, as in the blessing above, when we seek to express the immensity of our love. There are few lovers who have not at some time recorded their love in verse—however unskilled, however tentative.

As the floodgates of emotion are opened in us, a greater light is available to us, inundating the world in a fierce brightness. Though the sun grow weaker and the stars be overcast, though the dawn be misty, though the news be bad, the beloved shines over all and encloses us within an eternal story that the whole world is telling.

Make a blessing for the one you love, drawing on the metaphors that express your own feelings and perceptions.

Kindling the Hearth

Mother of our mothers,
Foremothers strong.
Guide our hands in yours,
Remind us how to kindle the hearth.

—Caitlín Matthews,
"A Blessing for the Hearth Keepers"

The hearth is a special shrine that is still ceremonially tended in some Gaelic households. Before retiring, the woman of the house "smoors" the fire—that is, covers any fresh fuel with ashes so that the fire is banked in and slowly burning. In the morning, the fire can then be easily woken without recourse to fresh kindling. Three blocks of peat (turf) are then placed in the grate, their ends touching so that they radiate out in the customary three-legged triskele symbol, and a prayer is made over the fire, normally invoking Brighid as saint or goddess, since she is the protectress of the hearth. Among traditional peoples, the tending of the hearth is one of the chief duties that fall to women, who also tend to be the repositories of practical spiritual traditions. These two tasks seem to be interlinked: keeping the hearth and maintaining spiritual practice are daily, habitual tasks that cannot be avoided without loss of integrity to the whole household. Today, we may no longer kindle the hearth, but this does not exempt us from kindling our spirit. Many people now incorporate small domestic rituals into their daily life: lighting a candle upon their hearth-shrine, acknowledging their guiding spirits and allies with flowers and offerings, spending time in meditation in a quiet room, making an earth-shrine in their gardens and window boxes. As each home becomes again the focus of dedicated spiritual practice, the hearth-light is rekindled and we remember our own part in the reverence of Spirit as ancestral hands guide our unremembering ones.

Create your own hearth-shrine and make it the kindling point of your
spiritual practice every day.

Burdens

God fits the back to the burden.

—Scots proverb

Whether great or small, burdens fall. We may feel that we do not deserve our particular fate, that some spiritual credit must be stored up somewhere that will remit our burden. If this Scots proverb were written the other way around—that God fits the burden to the back—perhaps we would feel better about the whole sorry business; but it is not. When burdens fall upon us, we cannot shift responsibility for them; they are indeed ours to carry. But our carrying power is something we cannot know until we try. Certainly there are many who have sunk under the strain into the distress of physical or nervous breakdown.

We can prepare our back for heavy responsibilities by bearing the strain with fortitude and human resourcefulness, by not giving up but seeking better and more effective ways. The most effective of those ways, the greatest help in fitting our back to carry whatever has befallen us, is simple beseeching: asking help of our most powerful spiritual sources to open the ways to possibility, to enable fresh perspectives that take the doggedness from our step, to bring the balm that will draw out our pain. Neither the good, the bad, nor the fortunate are spared from the burdens of life, but we can find ways of coping if we ask for help.

Whatever burdens you are carrying, leave them at the end of your bed before you sleep, entrusting them to your spiritual allies and asking for help to take them up with better heart on the morrow.

Measuring the Ages

Three stakes equal a hound's life; three hounds a steed; three steeds
a man; three men an eagle; three salmon a yew tree; three yew trees
a ridge; three ridges from the beginning to the end of the world.

—traditional Irish reckoning of time

Traditional measurements of time such as the one above do not trade
in numbered years but in lifetimes and generations—the chronological
criteria that predate numeration. The Irish peasants from whom this
saying was collected explained that stakes were hedges of woven hazel
twigs and that ridges, or *eitraí*, were the old wide furrows left from pre-
historic plowing, which have left their indelible mark on the earth. In
measurements such as this, the farming people connected themselves
through their own agricultural work with that of their ancestors, who
first began to farm. Throughout Celtic folk stories and legends, mythic
beings such as long-living animals and plants represent whole aeons of
time and reconnect us with our beginnings.

The memory of life is retained by animals, plants, and stones in a
true sense that in no way diminishes our ancestral Celtic wisdom. Each
cell of matter is encoded with memory in ways that are becoming clear
to science as we investigate the mysteries of DNA. The subtle changes in
life forms over millennia reveal new relationships and connections that
we never dreamed of. Time is relative to our personal experience. We
tend to think in terms of when we were in school, the year we moved
to the house on the corner, the day John F. Kennedy was assassinated,
the time our friend visited from France, and so on. We do not always
remember which year or month, although we can clearly visualize the
masses of cherry blossoms on the tree or the terrible heat on that occasion. The passage of time through our memory leaves its own landmarks, which serve to connect us to the *turas* of the ages.

What are the landmarks of your existence? How do you measure your
lifetime? How far does your living family memory extend?

The Land of Women

Do not fall on a bed of sloth,
Let not your intoxication overcome you,
Begin a voyage across the clear sea,
If you would reach the Land of Women.
—*Voyage of Bran mac Febal*, early Irish text (trans. CM)

These words are addressed to the Irish hero Bran mac Febal by an otherworldly woman who summons him to set forth on his quest to the Land of Women—a place that in early Celtic tradition was considered to be the abode of bliss, satisfaction, and achievement. She urges him to clear his sights, attend to the task in hand, conjure a vision of beauty and delight, and set off toward it. Regions of the Celtic otherworld can be reached by the voyage of the soul across the severing waters of the west, containing a series of island that must be encountered in sequence before the traveler comes to the innermost Land (or Island) of Women. The wisdom-keepers of the soul-voyage reveal themselves as a sisterhood of women who guard the mysteries of life. In Britain, there is the myth of Avalon being guarded by Morgen and her eight sisters; in Gaul, there are reports of sisterhoods dedicated to teaching, fostering, prophecy, healing, crafts, shape-shifting, and weather magic. (See 21 April.)

While we may not be summoned in so dramatic a way as Bran, we each have a quest to which we are called. This quest concerns the fulfillment of our life's purpose and is about using our innate gifts in the widest possible way. The inhabitants of the Land of Women have no patience with sloth. They are the energizers, keepers, and empowerers who maintain the dynamo of the world. To do this work, they need our assistance and application. If we make our voyage toward them, we will indeed find our way to the goal of desires.

What gifts have your faery godmothers given you? How are you using them to further your quest?

Culture

The purpose of culture is to enhance and intensify one's vision of that synthesis of truth and beauty which is the highest and deepest reality.

—John Cowper Powys, *The Meaning of Culture*

Culture is not only for the specialist, the expert, or the rich and powerful: it embraces everyone in its cloak. What are taken for the highest achievements of a civilization—the art, music, drama, poetry, film, and so on of a people—are not culture's only expressions. Culture also includes fashion, sport, science, gardening, and a mass of other areas that define a society's interest in itself and its environment.

How do we bring balance and harmony—the fruit of truth and beauty—to our culture? By honoring the wider vision of whatever branch of culture we are most involved with—not only guarding its boundaries from inappropriate incursions but also looking for ways through which we can expand our human vision to its fullest expression. By ensuring that commercial interest does not become the paramount thrust of our vision. By warranting that the vision does not become hidebound by custom.

This latter element is crucial. We cannot inhabit our romantic perception of past ages or keep culture in a traditional backwater. This is especially so of the Celtic traditions, which many people would like to have preserved as a time-warped romance. Such a vision may be fine in a museum, but it will not serve in daily life today. Taking only what is finest and fittest for our culture and submitting it to the tests of truth and beauty, we can find ways of living our culture with dynamism and delight.

How are you woven in the cloak of your culture? Reflect on the core principles that underlie your particular strand or interest.

The Triskele of Energy

Energy is eternal delight.

—William Blake, "Energy is eternal delight"

The Celtic peoples had a sacred symbol that embodied the energy of life. In the interlocking continuity of movement within the triskele—the three-legged cross—we see the spiraling movement of life. Its perpetual motion, turning its three legs ever sunwise, is the very *turas* of delight. The three-legged whirligig of the triskele appears in Celtic art from the fifth century B.C. on, adorning many articles as the central design feature. It is a sign of good fortune, all things moving sunwise in the centrifugal dance of life. The triskele preserves the wearer from scathe and gives him a long life.

The triskele spins like a whirlpool or a propeller blade, lending its threefold motion to the wheel of life. Stasis is not in its nature. The innate triplicity of the cosmos underscores the whole of Celtic culture, providing a sacred impetus for all action. Each leg of the triskele is one limb of the sacred spirit of all life; all three legs together imbue the universe with the energy to activate the body, heart, and mind of all beings with physical vitality, emotional responsiveness, and mental agility, unlocking the wealth of our potential from sheer inertia, emotional stasis, and mental laziness. The energy of the threefold triskele runs through every part of the universe and is available to us all. By drawing consciously upon its qualities, we can grace our lives with an ever-living energy that encompasses the beginning, middle, and end of everything we undertake.

If there is any leg of the triskele to which you are unresponsive, look to the appropriate areas in your own life to see what fear, doubt, or uncertainty is keeping you static and unmoving in your development.

Boasting

As blackbirds are to swans, as ounces to hundredweights,
As shapes of peasant-women are to noble queens . . .
As drones are to great music, as rushlights are to candles,
So is any sword to my own sword.

—Saying of *Colmán mac Léinín* (trans. CM)

Most accounts of the early Celts note that boastfulness was virtually an art form among them, often leading to factionalism and argumentative competitiveness. These factors were instrumental time after time in the downfall of sovereign Celtic nations, an inability to combine forces proving disastrous when organized foreign armies came against them.

When boasting is lighthearted and tongue-in-cheek, when everyone else is in on the joke, it can be a pleasant after-supper pastime. Such boasting was often the custom during and after feasts: heroes would boast of their deeds and possessions in a way that now reminds us of the bluster of world-class wrestlers. But when boasting becomes seriously competitive, there can be problems.

If we boast in the spirit of competition—whether we stretch the truth broadly or just embellish it—sooner or later we will be asked to run the race. One thoughtless boast can outrun our ability to perform it very easily; a lifetime habit of boasting can swathe the boaster in a garment of illusion that will eventually be seen through.

Check up on your own boast factor and ensure that it will not disturb the peace. Remember times when boasting caused you trouble.

Sleep and the Soul

In sleep what are you, in sleep,
in the ebb of the tide:
a body dormant, a thing breathing,
or a soul afloat?
What are you in sleep
in the small watch of the night
but a ray of life regathering forces,
the secret retreat of light.

—ROSS NICHOLS, *The Cosmic Shape*

While we may not have a strong sense of what our soul does in its mysterious circuit of the night, most of us value the coming of darkness as a time of quiet, of winding down from the day's activities, of restoring ourselves in the cavern of sleep. For those who remember some of their dreams, there is the added pleasure of sharing in the adventures of the soul. Sometimes these are only a recapitulation of the day's activities; other times they are strange revelations whose meanings we can only guess at. And very occasionally, we find a treasury of meaning so overwhelming as to make us conscious of the soul's capacity.

The circuits of the soul during sleep enter into a timelessness in which our past and future are inextricably mixed, in which we meet the dead, encounter the expected, and fly and dance and swim through elements that we normally do not move within. Whether or not the daytime consciousness has a spiritual framework or dedication, the night-wandering soul encounters spiritual allies and experiences inspirational truths. Within the compass of sleep and night, the soul explores the unseen universe with skillful knowledge, leaving the body as a secret retreat of the light that will emerge at dawning. But it is in the night that the light shines brightest and can be perceived.

Live the next twenty-four hours with awareness of the interconnectedness of night and day, soul and body.

Uninvited Guests

Three things that come without asking: fear, jealousy, love.
—Scots Gaelic triad

When fear grips us, our ability to act quickly or think clearly evaporates; we may become completely petrified and powerless. Fear often skims along just below the surface of perception, ready to appear when given opportunity. Its appeasing can lead to avoidance: we can be thrown out of the house of our soul by extreme fear. Fear cannot be evicted or overcome as such, though it can be transformed. Fear holds the key to lock away our abilities. To gain access to them again, we have to grasp the key and transform fear into power, recognizing that one becomes the other, just as water becomes ice.

Jealousy brings with it a fierce twisting of our perceptions so that everything concerning the object of our jealousy is distorted. When Cuchulainn fell in love with another woman, his wife, Emer, was consumed by a terrible jealousy that changed her perceptions utterly: "What's red is beautiful, what's new is bright, what's tall is fair, what's familiar is stale. The unknown is honored, the known is neglected." The only cure for Cuchulainn's enchantment and Emer's jealousy was for the God of the Otherworld, Manannan, to shake his cloak between them to bring them both forgetfulness. By all accounts, this is the only socially acceptable antidote to this particular guest.

Love is not altogether a welcome guest either. Its coming is often accompanied by disorientation and upheaval. It is frequently confounded with illness, as when King Ailell took to his bed with an unspecified disorder: his doctors finally proclaimed that he was suffering from "the two deadly pangs which no doctor can cure: love and jealousy." The only remedy for love is reciprocated love; this and nothing else can ease the pangs.

Which was the last of these uninvited guests to visit you? How did you cope? What did you learn from its visit?

Authority and Authenticity

Our deeds remain single till they wed perseverance.
—Welsh proverb (trans. CM)

Many people seek validation for their spiritual pathway. Because we may have garnered the components of our spiritual search from many different places and traditions, we often have a feeling of fraudulence or lack of authenticity. Our efforts to make sense of these components, to make a living habitation or pathway from them, are haunted by fear of authority. We feel that if we change the received pattern, if we deviate from the spiritual tradition into which we were born, we will be punished or shunned. This has certainly been the message given by organized religion to those on a spiritual search: authority is withheld from those who heretically deviate in our society; authenticity can derive only from the centrally authorized mandate.

No human being shares the exact same spiritual path as another. Each person constellates various elements of spirituality that speak to him, borrowing from old traditions and new perspectives. Finding authority for what we do, who we are, cannot come solely from the human world: authenticity arrives when we have begun to move from the known into the unknown through the unique thresholds that life opens to us. Perseverance is the key.

Answer these questions to get a sense of your own search for authority and authenticity:

- *Whose approval am I seeking?*
- *Who encourages me?*
- *How do I gain vitality? What drains my vitality?*
- *Who/what do I need to control?*
- *To whom/what do I consistently relinquish power?*
- *What do I need for self-nurture?*
- *Which old repeating patterns prevent me living in balance?*

Expectation and Remembrance

Still thou art blest, compar'd wi' me!
The present only toucheth thee:
But, och! I backward cast my ee [eye],
On prospects drear!
An' forward, tho' I canna see,
I guess an' fear!

—Robert Burns, "To a Mouse"

It is only humans who fetter themselves with the chains of past and future; animals experience a continual present. That they do not inhabit their memories or expectations is a blessed condition for them that we cannot share. We do not know at what point early hominids evolved from this blessed condition, although many of the world's creation myths speak about the fall from that state. Remembrance of the past and expectation of the future have proved a dangerous knowledge. The past has been used to dictate the false paradigms of history to terrible ends: the victim's justifications for terrorism; the bully's justifications for conquest, suppression, and genocide. The future has thrown back its shadow in no less startling ways: the utopian idealist's program of eugenics; the defensive group's overmilitarization. It would seem that when we call upon the past and future out of fear, we betray our animal origins again and again.

Expectation and remembrance can be balanced by the eternal now. By respecting the ancestors and the descendants equally, we can always find resourceful solutions to present difficulties, especially if we access the daring and courage within us without fear. A further evolution of human from animal origins will arrive when we can achieve the balance of remembrance and expectation with the now that is happening *now* . . . and *now* . . . and *now*.

Attend to the eternal present for an hour, an afternoon, or a whole day, without conscious recourse to remembrance or expectation.

Criticism

*To correct is good, for the mind accepts correction: not so is
reproach, against which the mind rebels.*

—COLMÁN MAC BÉOGNAE, *Apgitir Chábaid* (trans. CM)

Certain kinds of criticism stick in the mind like a thorn. The words of
the cleric Colmán are specifically addressed to teachers within his
monastery, but all who are in positions of authority and responsibility
should guard their words carefully, lest reproach rather than correction
come to their lips. This is especially true for parents, teachers, and all
who deal with the young, who are especially susceptible to reproach.
Continued criticism, offered in place of helpful suggestion, can overwhelm a child and leave her with little self-esteem. Correction shapes
technique and eliminates errors over the course of time, until the student himself becomes expert, able to guide and correct in his turn.
Reproach, on the other hand, is like lime: whatever it touches immediately shrinks away. Wherever reproach has spread its acid, nothing further grows. (See 15 August.)

Criticism springs from three desires: a desire to improve, a desire to
detract, and a desire to hide the same fault in oneself. The last of these
desires is the deadliest: by casting criticism on others, we throw a
convenient smoke screen over our own faults, which often perfectly
mirror the thing we have pointed at elsewhere. The only way to guard
against unwarranted criticism in daily life is to think first, keep silent
when possible, and speak only words that will be received without
undue offence.

*Consider a recent situation in which you were criticized or you criti-
cized others. Was correction or reproach used? What wisdom can you
learn from the situation?*

The Forger of the Elements

A shoemaker makes shoes without leather,
With all the four elements together,
Fire, Water, Earth, Air
And every customer takes two pair.

—ancient British riddle

This riddle refers to the work of the blacksmith, who heats the fire for the furnace by means of the bellows, who hammers the softened metal into shape with his hammer, and then plunges it into the water to cool and fix its shape. The blacksmith's customers are of course horses, who clop off with their two pair of shoes. The smith is a revered, almost magical figure among many traditional peoples worldwide because of the alchemy of his trade, which forges with the help of the elements. Those among the gods who are smiths play a prominent role in the defense of the land and the mysteries of the afterlife: the Welsh Gofannon and the Irish Goibniu (Go-VANN'on and GUB'noo), for example, both make weapons of extraordinary power. The power to curtail life or to prolong it is part of the smith-god's skill. Goibniu—when he was not smithing—presided over the otherworldly feasting of heroes, supplying the food and drink that preserved the lives of all who partook of them.

Whoever forges with the help of the elements is seen as a worthy guardian, one whose luck will embrace all in his household. The Celtic smith-god is one who stands between the worlds as a teacher and mediator of otherworldly skills and healing, and as one who can lead the dead from this world to the other. As we draw nearer to the festival of Samhain and toward the dark half of the year, we approach the time of introspection when the elements of our own life's forging can be refined and appreciated. When they no longer hold the life within our body, when our soul goes free of this life, they will become available for the smith to reforge another.

How are the elements part of your own life's forging?

Necessity

The art of our necessities is strange
That can make vile things precious.
—William Shakespeare, *King Lear*

A touch of necessity may remind us uncomfortably of our mortality and transience, but it can also bring us to greater resourcefulness and clarity. The human potential to overcome adversity has been proved in many extreme and hazardous circumstances. Those who can make do survive; those who are helpless without their conveniences do not. When life is pared to the bare bones, when stone soup is all there is to eat, the survivor will ensure that at least the soup is hot and reviving!

The clarity that necessity brings, that we feel when inessentials are stripped away, can be a great gift—one that helps put our life back on track. This is why many cultures have spiritual beggars and mendicants, men and women who forswear the luxuries of life in order to experience the space that necessity makes around them.

The ownership of good things by all is an ideal within our society. Though that ideal is complicated by the fact that one person's luxury is another person's necessity, by any standard we are far from it. Valuing the things that matter and not undervaluing our ability to be resourceful will help us to a more simple and less consumer-focused way of life, as well as setting a scale of necessity that brings us clarity.

Choose one convenient thing on which you depend in your life and contemplate the difference its lack would create. How would you manage without it; what would you use instead?

Transmigration of Souls

The same spirit has a body again elsewhere, and death is but the mid-point of a long life.

—Lucan, *Pharsalia*

The druidic belief in the transmigration of souls is evidenced in Celtic literature, as is a simultaneous belief in metamorphosis (a changing of one's shape), metempsychosis (a passing of the soul into another form), and reincarnation (a rebirth into a different human life). All three of these beliefs are evidenced in the story of Gwion (GWEE'on), who when chased by the goddess Ceridwen (Ker-RID'wen) assumes the shape of hare, fish, bird, and corn before being reborn as Taliesin (Tal-ee-ESS'in). (See 18 March.) In the story of the Irish heroine Etain (e-TAWN), we learn of her enchantment into a pool of water, a worm, and a fly—metamorphosis in action; but when the fly is consumed in a cup of wine by Queen Etar (e-TAR), a new Etain is reborn in a human shape (reincarnation).

Today many people are preoccupied with their past incarnations, more anxious to know the details of former lives than to get on and live the life they now inhabit. Such details rarely come to memory, however, and those that do are often very private and significant pointers to aspects of the current life that need attention. The Celtic belief in transmigration does not involve the past-dependency or life-sapping introversion that most modern reincarnational belief does.

The Celtic attitude toward transmigration rather draws upon the bodily and genetic knowledge of former lives that inform this life in active and positive ways. It does not linger in the past but lives attuned to the present, with a fearlessness toward death that reflects a healthy soul-spiral lived to the full. (See 11 June.)

What wisdom do you carry from the former habitations of your soul?

The Mantle of the Universe

You never enjoy the world aright, till the sea itself floweth in your veins, till you are clothed with the heavens, and crowned with the stars.

—THOMAS TRAHERNE, *Centuries*

To re-experience the integration of ourselves with nature, we have to take ourselves out of our four walls and set our life-story in the context of nature's terms. This means becoming especially aware of one area of the natural world—an area that is our listening place, an area where we tune out the old broadcasts of our separateness and retune to the original station of the universal belonging. In that place we enter into a new relationship with nature, conducting a dialogue of one with the other, in which both parties speak and both listen to the other.

In this communion, a further state of belonging may be experienced—initially just in brief glimpses, then sometimes for longer and longer periods. It is the condition that poet and mystic Thomas Traherne speaks of above: the temporary loss of our sense of identity, a softening of the hard boundaries that separate us from the tree and the animal, from the earth and the sunset. In this condition, we experience ourselves as no different from nature or anything within it. We come into true relationship with nature in such moments, which strip away our hubris, our control, and our feelings of separation and bring us once more under the mantle of the universe.

Sit in nature and just be with it, without judgment or mental comment. Let your attention be drawn to one feature around you. Be present to it as though it were another being: listen and speak; speak and listen. Finally, experience that feature and yourself occupying the same space, breathing the same air. Just be. Slowly reverse the steps above until you are fully restored to your own body and consciousness again.

The Language of Winter

We have all of us eaten the pomegranate seed of language, and we are its Persephones in its ways of structuring our experience of ourselves and the world.

—JOHN MORIARTY, *Turtle Was Gone a Long Time*

John Moriarty refers here to the Greek myth of Persephone, who went into the Underworld with the god Hades. When sought by her mother, Demeter, she was licensed by the gods to return to the middle world again, as long as she had not eaten anything while in the Underworld. But Persephone had partaken of six pomegranate seeds, and so it was judged that she could return to earth for only half of the year. During those six months that she remains in the Underworld, we have winter. Similarly, the ways in which we think and speak, the concepts that we use to frame experience, give their own limited seasonal coloration to our culture. Meaning is submerged in the very words we speak. We have little sophistication of expression in the West to speak about deeper, mythic states, which is probably why we have such a correspondingly rich folk-story tradition, which speaks of nothing else.

The revolt against the language of winter is everywhere around us as people attempt to explain their own subtle experiences. This revolt often expresses itself in extreme ways—as an unhealthy stretching out toward the bizarre, the unexplained, and the alien, when all the time the common but subtle experiences of life are so ordinary. When we begin to use the wisdom of the pomegranate seeds of language with the insight of those who have experienced the deep riches of the Underworld, we will be liberated Persephones, able to bring beautiful spring to our bare acres of expression.

Recall a subtle experience of your own. Write it down or speak it onto tape in a way that captures the mood and experience.

Ordinary Things

There are three slender things that support the world: the slender stream of cow's milk into a pail; the slender blade of green corn in the ground; the slender thread running over the hands of a skilled woman.

—ancient Irish triad

The comfort and nurture we derive from dairy products is the gift of the cow, that supremely important animal to the Celtic world. The cow, a unit of wealth, was so highly prized that it is remembered in the heavens among Gaelic speakers who know the Milky Way as "the Way of the White Cow." The fertility of the fields was always considered a measure of how committed a ruler or chieftain was to his land and people: poor crops were an indication of poor rulership. Along with the milk of the cow, the bannock (loaf) of bread made up the staple diet of most people before the advent of the New World potato, so grain was another measure of prosperity and well-being.

Before the coming of industrial looms, all clothing was made laboriously by hand. The woman of the house (with the help of her daughters) clothed her entire family; she would take the unwashed wool, comb and card it, and then time-consumingly spin it from the distaff until it could be labor-intensively woven on a hand-loom. That wool kept the cold out, but the greatest skill went into weaving fine linen garments for wear next to the skin. It is by the help of the ordinary things that much of our own living is supported. In different countries, there are different staple grains and foodstuffs, different materials. From their slender existence our own is sustained.

What three ordinary things are the supporters of your life? Make your own personal triad.

Conflict

On Tuesday they dressed in their finery,
On Wednesday their common desire was bitter,
On Thursday envoys were chosen,
On Friday carnage was assessed,
On Saturday action was forthright,
On Sunday bloody blades were distributed,
On Monday they were thigh-deep in blood.

—ANEIRIN, "Y Gododdin" (trans. CM)

The battle of Catreath in A.D. 600, fought between the northern Britons and the Angles, is commemorated in this epic Welsh poem. The resolution of conflict is never simple. We may long and pray for peace to come, but it cannot be built upon shaky foundations of wished-for pacification. We cannot tiptoe around areas of conflict forever. If we truly want to seek peaceful solutions, we have to be actively prepared to deal with conflict. Principles of arbitration and conflict resolution are traditionally part of the druid path: when conflicts, arguments, and differences arose in ancient times, a druid was consulted as an arbitrator.

Meditate upon some area of your life where you are in conflict with another person.

Visualize your opponent as an innocent child, an uncertain teenager, a mature adult, a wise elder. Cease to demonize your opponent. Consider how your conflict warps the world's web, the great net of life and consciousness that binds us all together. With your own issue of conflict in mind, repeat this prayer for peace, written by druid Cairistíona Worthington:

> *Deep within the still centre of my being may I find peace.*
> *Silently within the quiet of the Grove may we share peace.*
> *Gently within the greater circle of humankind may we radiate peace.*

Take a period of silence to allow solutions to arise.

Ancestral Dependence

The one whose solitary boast is his lineage, has no descendant of any virtue.

—Welsh proverb (trans. CM)

The Celtic peoples honored the keeping, remembrance, and repetition of genealogies and family lists. Such genealogies were "memory resident" in bards and poets, one of whose chief tasks was to recite these ancient lineages on important occasions. In our society, we generally leave such matters to the professional genealogist or herald, and so our own memory dwindles. As a result of this neglect, strange obsessions sometimes develop. People with no knowledge of their lineage sometimes invent family trees or make outrageously unsubstantiated claims regarding their descent. Such acts have a terrible pathos about them. At the other extreme, we find those who dine out on their ancestral achievements without any attempt to make their own mark. Both they and the people who invent their lineage fall into the trap of ancestral dependence. Whether actual or invented, our lineage is a path that moves through us to our own descendants. Our physical bloodline may have many great and good ancestors among its number, but their deeds do not flow through our veins or belong to us unless we make them ours by similar doing.

Dependence upon the ancestors is often just a manifestation of laziness, a way of absolving ourselves from total engagement in life; it is also a form of theft that robs our hard-working ancestors of their credit. We cannot live in the reflected glory of ancestral honors without absconding from own lives and missing the very real opportunities to become worthy ancestors in our turn.

Honor your ancestors, known or unknown, by a worthy act of your own.

The Passing of Arthur

Be brave, be impeccable!
Endure challenge, be cheerful!
I go to the summer world
Of Afallon, to recover.
But I'll come back to my land
Once more . . .

—THOMAS GWYNN JONES, "Arthur's Passing"

The prophecy that King Arthur will return has been often uttered and widely believed throughout Britain and beyond. It was so strong a belief centuries ago that twelfth-century cleric Alan of Insulis wrote, "Preach about the market places and villages that Arthur the Briton is dead as other men are dead, and . . . Hardly will you escape unscathed without being overwhelmed by curses or crushed by the stones of your hearers." Arthur the British war-leader—the King Arthur of the later medieval legends—derives from a potent Celtic archetype the function of which is to maintain the integrity of the land. His ending is seen as no death, but as a time of recovery for the healing of his wounds, after which he will come again. This legend fueled his Latin title *Rex Quondam Rexque Futurus:* the King Who Was and Who Shall Be. (See 21 May.)

There comes in every country's history a time of hardship and a corresponding time of shining deeds to overcome the hardship. When the land plummets into war or other difficulty, the inhabitants of the land need leaders who can reach into the very soul of the land and draw forth the necessary inspiration, courage, and resourcefulness to defend it and them. Every land has its own Arthur, called by a multitude of names, remembered in heroic stories that can be retold to encourage us in later times of trouble. And the same prophecy is uttered: that the hero or heroine is not dead, but shall come again.

What is the sacred trust of your own land? Which figures and emblems have been associated with it? How do they endure?

Surviving Marriage

The first year's a year of kisses,
The second year's a year of fists.

—Scots Gaelic proverb

The settling-down year of marriage needs to be handled with an understanding patience. And we may need to summon that same high level of patience again in another ten years, when long-term relationships often go into a place of stasis and stagnation. The chief method for surviving as a couple is to realize that two individuals brought into partnership have to find the point of balance and reciprocation. No longer separate, they keep developing as individuals even as the relationship itself is growing.

Behaviors, comments, and feelings that initially seem to be warning signs of fallout often are nothing more (and nothing less) than signs of growth. These little buds and shoots need space to spread, and a reciprocal understanding of personal needs. Such matters cannot be intuited by our partner, however; they have to be communicated. Petty domestic resentments and larger-scale problems can incubate at an alarming rate beneath the surface of married life, sometimes because both partners have grown together sufficiently to feel that they have one consciousness and that their wants and needs should be obvious to the other. They are not.

The second year of marriage does not have to be one of fists if we keep attuned to our own and our partner's needs, holding the communication channels open.

Take time to speak of your needs and concerns to your significant other and to inquire what his or her needs and concerns may be. If you are not in a relationship at present, consider a past relationship; ask yourself where and why the partnership worked.

Unleashing Joy

He who binds to himself a joy
Does a winged life destroy;
But he who kisses the joy as it flies
Lives in eternity's sun rise.

—William Blake, "Eternity"

Joy is not a creature of the cupboard; it is wild, free, and profligate, spending itself in one great burst of energy. The ability to enjoy and be part of something is a skill many of us lose; as we disengage from the immediacy of life, we are less able to sink ourselves deeply into things. This distancing of the self often arises from the need to protect ourselves from perceived dangers (physical and emotional). Whatever its cause, this form of separation from life clips the wings of joy very effectively.

Certain people want to restrain the freedoms of others; having hushed the ecstatic song of joy in their own lives as a thing too flighty or too dangerous to be allowed, they find it suspect in others as well. At the other extreme are people who, having tasted joy, want it all the time.

Whatever our condition, how do we make access to joy? It can come only when there are three conditions present: a state of lively engagement with life, a receptive and spacious heart, and a respect for other beings than ourselves. If we live in a closed-off bubble, forcing life to happen beyond us, joy cannot enter; but if we play ball with life, catching and throwing back the many experiences that come our way, we begin our true engagement. If we have a daily receptive space where we allow the universe to speak to us, joy will find its way. If we truly believe that the freedom of other beings is as important as our own, if we truly respect that freedom, joy will wing toward us.

Meditate upon the three conditions above and discover which ones will help you be hospitable to joy.

Finding Our Place in Nature

Did you hear what the fish said,
Floundering among the reeds?—
Nature's wiser than learning.
　　　　　　—fourteenth-century Welsh verse (CM)

In the Celtic and world folk traditions, reminders of this important fact emerge time and again in stories that tell of speaking animals. All young heroes and heroines who are sent out on the road of adventure eventually encounter animal allies who speak to them of deeper wisdoms than those they received at school. These encounters require that the young person treat the animal with respect, share her goods or food with the animal, and listen and act upon the animal's wisdom. The characters who do these things emerge unscathed; the ones who neglect to respect, share, or listen lose their way and fall prey to dangers. It is for this reason that so many spiritual traditions regard animals as their wisdom-keepers: animals are representatives of the oral, living world of nature—beings who know the implications and responsibilities of their belonging and guardianship.

All people now living have the responsibility of relearning the wisdom of nature, directly from nature: from the trees and hills, the birds and streams, the animals and fields, the fish and seas. Wherever we are, there is an older wisdom singing, which keeps the world in harmony. When we can join in that singing, we will begin to find our true place in nature and be at one with our brother and sister beings.

Be present with a being of nature; be present to it spirit to spirit. What is the wisdom of nature about the plan that is currently brooding in your heart? How does this differ from the received wisdom of your society, friends, advisers?

Living the Metaphor

Then as now the Cauldron of Ceridwen . . . was on the boil; and its
life-giving drops . . . were being scattered abroad, according to
what, by mere human computation, amount to nothing but the
accidents of pure chance.

—JOHN COWPER POWYS, *Obstinate Cymric*

From Ceridwen's vessel of inspiration three drops flew out and were caught by the child Gwion as he sat tending the cauldron. (See 18 March and 19 October.) When a spark of knowledge catches the tinder of our being, it runs through us like a forest fire. All the metaphors and images by which we have lived our lives become incandescent with immediacy and meaning. After the kiss of knowledge, Taliesin, who was once the boy Gwion, declares that he has been in many times and places, that he has been a drop in the air, a letter among words, a sword in the hand, a string in a harp, and many other conditions associated with the human state. It is the metaphor of himself in the immediacy of the realized present that sings.

To realize and truly live our metaphor, we need the random grace of the cauldron's drops to awaken us to our true potential. Suddenly, meaning explodes behind our eyes and thoughts run together and connect like the colors on an easel when it rains. This is the experience of the child Gwion when he puts his lips to his hand to cool the scalding drops. The incubation period of knowledge for Gwion is nine months in the womb of Ceridwen, where he brings together the many metaphors of himself and learns their truth. By the time he is born, they have become a part of him; he is living repository of his own knowledge.

What metaphors do you apply to your own life (e.g., a lone wolf, a
rolling stone, a busy beaver, a foolish clown)? What triggers knowledge
of these metaphors? What fixes their truth in you?

Flexibility

May we never be so straight that we cannot bend;
May we never be so unapproachable that children
Cannot climb up into our lower branches.

—CAITLÍN MATTHEWS, "Avebury Easter"

Wherever we have set our roots, there will we grow. The ability to be flexible and adaptable to different growing conditions determines the nature of our development. Learning to change and adapt with each new circumstance is a human gift that we share with all life. Evolution itself shows us that those species that cannot change die out. Opinions and attitudes can become like carapaces that harden about our shoulders, bringing rigidity to our life-flow. Rigidity of opinion causes us to become unapproachable, which may increase our sense of isolation or confirm us in our self-contented stasis. We begin to lose opportunities to exchange views, to receive love, to find other sources of nurture. It takes courage to allow children to swarm in our branches, to allow the questions and opinions of those younger than ourselves to bend our trunks in their fresh breeze. The beauty of the many-leveled generations alive at one time allows us great opportunities to practice our flexibility and share our wisdom.

Visualize what kind of tree you are. Check on how vital your root system is; assess the flexibility of your trunk, the reach of your branches. What opportunities for change and adaptability are available and needed by you at this time?

Samhain

Samhain night with its ancient lore
was occasion for new and merry custom;
it was learned in the wilderness, in oak-woods,
from spirits and fairies.

—*The Metrical Dindshenchas* (trans. CM)

The festival of Samhain (SOW'en) marked the start of Winter when beasts were brought in from the hills to the nearby fields for winter slaughter or for overwintering in barns. Samhain was a liminal time in which the world of the living and the ancestral realms overlapped. This was a time for the remembrance of the dead: candles were set in the window to welcome the loved ancestors and to shine upon the path of the unquiet dead to bless them on their way.

There was always an element of fear and trepidation about this night—the eve before Samhain—and also one of expectancy. When the dead were abroad, certain kinds of divination could be practiced, which asked questions of the ancestors. This night was one when young people disguised themselves and played pranks on the community. The modern custom of trick-or-treating is based upon the old tradition of "mischief night," where the guisers begged for food and drink from door to door. At inhospitable houses, the gate might be removed from its hinges, or other petty misdemeanors might be performed.

The great fear that many still have about this night is not aided by the commercialism of modern Hallowe'en, which emphasizes ghoulish fascination with ghosts rather than communal reverence for the beloved ancestors. As we enter the darkness of winter this evening, let us remember our own ancestors with love, with a prayer that all unquiet souls be led to blessedness and peace, with a hope that this sacred festival may be restored to its former respect as a time of communal honoring.

Light your own candle for the ancestors this evening and breathe your
blessing upon all who no longer walk in this world.

BIBLIOGRAPHY

Ahern, Nuala. *Network Magazine.* C/o R. Marshall, Ballydonahane, Bodyke, County Clare, Ireland.

A. E. (George Russell). *The Candle of Vision.* Dorset, England: Prism Press.

Auden, W. H. *The Dyer's Hand.* London: Faber, 1963.

Bergin, Osborn. *Irish Bardic Poetry.* Dublin: Dublin Institute for Advanced Studies, 1970.

Blake, William. *Poetry and Prose.* London: Nonsuch Press, 1975.

Boland, Eavan. *Object Lessons.* London: Vintage Press, 1993.

The Book of Irish Poetry. Edited by Alfred Perceval Graves. London: Gresham, n.d.

A Book of Scottish Verse. Edited by R. L. Mackie. London: Oxford University Press, 1967.

Carmina Gadelica (6 vols.). Edited by Alexander Carmichael. Edinburgh: Scottish American Press, 1972.

Carr-Gomm, Philip, ed. *The Druid Renaissance.* HarperCollins, 1996.

Carr-Gomm, Philip. *The Druid Tradition.* Shaftesbury, England: Element, 1991.

Carr-Gomm, Philip. *The Druid Way.* Shaftesbury, England: Element, 1995.

Carr-Gomm, Philip, and Stephanie Carr-Gomm. *The Druid Animal Oracle.* New York: Simon & Schuster, 1994.

Ceannas Nan Gàidheal. Armadale Castle, Sleat, Isle of Skye, Scotland: Clan Donald Lands Trust, 1985.

Clancy, T. O., and G. Markus. *Iona.* Edinburgh: Edinburgh University Press, 1995.

Conran, Tony. *Blodeuwedd.* Ogmore-by-Sea, Wales: Poetry Wales Press, 1988.

Conran, Tony, trans. *Welsh Verse.* Bridgend, Wales: Poetry Wales Press, 1986.

Cormac's Glossary. Edited by Kuno Meyer. Dublin: Halle A. S., 1913.

Devereux, Paul. *Revisioning the Earth.* New York: Fireside, 1996.

Dun, Aidan Andrew. *Vale Royal*. Uppingham: Goldmark, 1995.

Early Irish Literature. Edited by Eleanor Nott and Gerard Murphy. London: Routledge & Kegan Paul, 1966.

Earth Ascending. Edited by Jay Ramsay. Exeter, England: Stride, 1997.

Friel, Brian. *Translations*. London: Longmans, 1996.

Geoffrey of Monmouth. *Vita Merlini*. Edited by J. J. Parry. Illinois: University of Illinois Press, 1925.

Gerald of Wales. *Journey Through Wales*. Harmondsworth, England: Penguin, 1978.

Gregory, Lady Augusta. *Gods and Fighting Men*. Gerrard's Cross, England: Colin Smythe Ltd., 1970.

Gunn, Neil. *The Atom of Delight*. Edinburgh: Polygon Books, 1986.

Hawkes, Jacquetta. *A Land*. London: Cresset Press, 1951.

The Herbal Remedies of the Physicians of Myddfai. Edited by D. Bryce. Lampeter, Wales: Llanerch Press, 1987.

Hopkins, Gerard Manley. *Selected Poems*. London: Heinemann, 1953.

Humphreys, Emyr. *The Taliesin Tradition*. London: Black Raven Press, 1983.

Joyce, James. *Portrait of an Artist as a Young Man*. London: Jonathan Cape, 1998.

Julius Caesar. *The Conquest of Gaul*. Translated by S. A. Handsford. Harmondsworth, England: Penguin, 1982.

Keating, Geoffrey. *Forus Feasa ar Eirinn*. Dublin: Irish Texts Society, 1987.

Kirk, Rev. Robert. *The Secret Commonwealth*. Edited by Stewart Sanderson. Cambridge, England: D. S. Brewer, 1976.

Laws of Hywel Dda. Translated by Melville Richards. Liverpool, England: University Press, 1954.

Leade, Jane. *A Fountain of Gardens*. London: n.p., 1697.

Lebor Gabala Erenn. Edited by R. A. S. MacAlister. Dublin: Irish Texts Society, 1956.

Levy, Peter. *The Flutes of Autumn*. London: Harvill Press, 1983.

Llewellyn-Williams, Hilary. *The Tree Calendar*. Bridgend: Poetry Wales Press, 1987.

Lucan. *Pharsalia*. Translated by J. W. Joyce. Ithaca: Cornell University Press, 1993.

Lyra Celtica. Edited by Elizabeth A. Sharp. Edinburgh: Patrick Geddes, 1896.

The Mabinogion. Translated by Lady Charlotte Guest. London: Ballantine Press, 1917.

MacLean, Alistair. *Hebridean Altars*. Moray Press, 1937.

MacLeod, Fiona. *Iona*. London: Heinemann, 1927.

Macy, Joanna. *World as Lover, World as Self*. London: Rider, 1993.

The Martyrology of Oengus. Edited by W. Stokes. Dublin: Dublin Institute for Advanced Studies, 1984.

McNeil, Marion. *The Silver Bough*. Glasgow, Scotland: William McClennan, 1961.

Matthews, Caitlín. *Arthur and the Sovereignty of Britain*. London: Arkana, 1989.

Matthews, Caitlín. *The Celtic Book of the Dead*. New York: St Martin's Press, 1992.

Matthews, Caitlín. *Celtic Devotional*. New Alresford, Hants: Godsfield Press, 1996.

Matthews, Caitlín. "Dancing with Daimons." Unpublished poetry.

Matthews, Caitlín. *In Search of Woman's Passionate Soul: Revealing the Daimon Lover Within*. Rockport: Element, 1997.

Matthews, Caitlín. *The Little Book of Celtic Blessings*. Rockport: Element, 1994.

Matthews, Caitlín. *Mabon and the Mysteries of Britain*. London: Arkana, 1987.

Matthews, Caitlín. *Singing the Soul Back Home*. Rockport: Element, 1995.

Matthews, Caitlín, and John Matthews. *Encyclopedia of Celtic Wisdom*. Rockport: Element, 1995.

Matthews, Caitlín, and John Matthews. *Ladies of the Lake*. London: Harper-Collins, 1996.

Matthews, Caitlín, and John Matthews. *The Little Book of Celtic Wisdom*. Rockport: Element, 1993.

Matthews, John. *The Druid Source Book*. London: Cassell, 1996.

Matthews, John. *Healing the Wounded King*. Shaftesbury, England: Element, 1997.

Matthews, John, ed. *Paths to Peace*. London: Random Century, 1992.

Matthews, John, ed. *Sources of the Grail*. Hudson, New York: Lindisfarne Press, 1996.

Matthews, John. *Taliesin, Bardic, and Shamanic Mysteries in Britain and Ireland*. London: HarperCollins, 1991.

May, Jo. *Fogou*. Glastonbury, England: Gothic Image Press, 1997.

The Metrical Dindshenchas. 5 vols. Edited by Edward Gwynn. Dublin: School of Celtic Studies, 1991.

Minehane, John. *The Christian Druids*. Dublin: Sanas Press, 1993.

Moncrieffe, Sir Iain. *The Highland Clans*. London: Barrie & Jenkins, 1967.

Moriarty, John. *Turtle Was Gone a Long Time*. Vol. 1: *Crossing the Kedron*. Dublin: Lilliput Press, 1996.

Moriarty, John. *Turtle Was Gone a Long Time*. Vol. 2: *Horsehead Nebula Neighing*. Dublin: Lilliput Press, 1997.

Nichols, Ross. *The Book of Druidry*. Shaftesbury, England: Element, 1990.

Nichols, Ross, and James Kirkup. *The Cosmic Shape*. London: Forge Press, 1946.

Nott, Eleanor, and Gerard Murphy. *Early Irish Literature*. London: Routledge & Kegan Paul, 1966.

Pennick, Nigel. *Celtic Sacred Landscapes*. London: Thames & Hudson, 1996.

Popular Tales of the West Highlands. 4 vols. edited by J. F. Campbell. Hounslow, England: Wildwood House, 1984.

Powys, John Cowper. *The Meaning of Culture*. London: Village Press, 1971.

Powys, John Cowper. *Morwyn*. London: Villiers Publications Ltd., 1980.

Powys, John Cowper. *Obstinate Cymric*. Carmarthen, Wales: Druid Press, 1947.

Powys, Llewelyn. *Earth Memories*. Radfield Press, n.d.

Raine, Kathleen. *The Lion's Mouth*. London: Hamish Hamilton, 1977.

Raine, Kathleen. *The Oracle in the Heart*. Portlaoise, Ireland: Dolmen Press, 1980.

Rees, Alwyn and Brinley. *Celtic Heritage*. London: Thames and Hudson, 1961.

Rudkin, David. *Penda's Fen*. London: Davis Poynter, 1975.

Ryan, Mark, and Chesca Potter. *The Greenwood Tarot*. London: HarperCollins, 1996.

Scottish Love Poetry. Edited by Antonia Fraser. Harmondsworth, England: Penguin, 1975.

Senchus Mor. Dublin: Alexander Thom, 1985.

Shaw, Margaret Fay. *Folksongs and Folklore of South Uist*. London: Routledge & Kegan Paul, 1955.

Skelton, Robin, and Margaret Blackwood. *Earth, Air, Fire, Water*. London: Arkana, 1990.

Stewart, R. J. *Power Within the Land*. Shaftesbury, England: Element, 1991.

Stewart, R. J. *Psychology and the Spiritual Traditions*. Shaftesbury, England: Element, 1990.

Sutherland, Elizabeth. *Ravens and Black Rain*. London: Constable, 1985.

Táin Bó Cuailgne. Edited by Cecile O'Rahilly. Dublin: Dublin Institute for Advanced Studies, 1976.

Traherne, Thomas. *Centuries*. London: Faith Press, 1960.

Traherne, Thomas. *Poetical Works*. London: Dobell, 1932.

Welsh Proverbs. Edited by Henry H. Vaughan. Felinfach: Llanerch Press, 1993.

Yeats, W. B. *Collected Poems*. London: Macmillan, 1933.

INDEX

To find out more about Caitlín and John Matthews' work, courses, books etc. you can subscribe to their quarterly publication, the *Hallowquest Newsletter.* Please send $20 in notes (not checks) or £12 in *sterling* international money order payable to Graal Publications, Caitlín Matthews, BCM Hallowquest, London WC1N 3XX, U.K. The author regrets that she cannot enter into personal correspondence.

Our Web Site address is http://www.hallowquest.org.uk